AFRICAN ETHNOGRAPHIC STUDIES
OF THE 20TH CENTURY

Volume 18

WITCHCRAFT AND SORCERY
IN RHODESIA

WITCHCRAFT AND SORCERY IN RHODESIA

J. R. CRAWFORD

LONDON AND NEW YORK

First published in 1967 by Oxford University Press for the International African Institute

This edition first published in 2018
by Routledge
2 Park Square, Milton Park, Abingdon, Oxon OX14 4RN

and by Routledge
711 Third Avenue, New York, NY 10017

Routledge is an imprint of the Taylor & Francis Group, an informa business

© 1967 International African Institute

All rights reserved. No part of this book may be reprinted or reproduced or utilised in any form or by any electronic, mechanical, or other means, now known or hereafter invented, including photocopying and recording, or in any information storage or retrieval system, without permission in writing from the publishers.

Trademark notice: Product or corporate names may be trademarks or registered trademarks, and are used only for identification and explanation without intent to infringe.

British Library Cataloguing in Publication Data
A catalogue record for this book is available from the British Library

ISBN: 978-0-8153-8713-8 (Set)
ISBN: 978-0-429-48813-9 (Set) (ebk)
ISBN: 978-1-138-50049-5 (Volume 18) (hbk)
ISBN: 978-1-351-00924-9 (Volume 18) (ebk)

Publisher's Note
The publisher has gone to great lengths to ensure the quality of this reprint but points out that some imperfections in the original copies may be apparent.

Disclaimer
The publisher has made every effort to trace copyright holders and would welcome correspondence from those they have been unable to trace.

Due to modern production methods, it has not been possible to reproduce the fold-out maps within the book. Please visit www.routledge.com to view them.

A carved model of a human head with bead decoration,
part of a diviner's equipment

WITCHCRAFT AND SORCERY IN RHODESIA

by

J. R. CRAWFORD

Published for the
INTERNATIONAL AFRICAN INSTITUTE
by the
OXFORD UNIVERSITY PRESS
1967

Oxford University Press, Ely House, London W.1

GLASGOW NEW YORK TORONTO MELBOURNE WELLINGTON
CAPE TOWN SALISBURY IBADAN NAIROBI LUSAKA ADDIS ABABA
BOMBAY CALCUTTA MADRAS KARACHI LAHORE DACCA
KUALA LUMPUR HONG KONG

© International African Institute 1967

*Printed in Great Britain
by Ebenezer Baylis & Son, Ltd.
The Trinity Press, Worcester, and London*

PREFACE

I HAVE attempted in this book to give an account of my researches into witchcraft and sorcery beliefs and accusations in Rhodesia. Although I have relied extensively on informants, the principal source of information has been the records of the Attorney-General of Rhodesia. I am greatly in debt for the assistance of the Attorney-General and the staff of his office, both for affording facilities to undertake the research and in drawing attention to what I might, otherwise, have overlooked.

I am greatly indebted also to my various informants for the long-suffering way they put up with my many questions and, in particular, to Thomas and Arthur, the High Court Interpreters, to Mr. Roger Wright, M. S. Ndoro, Mr. B. Vambe and Mr. W. Mkwesha. Arthur is, I am sorry to say, now dead, victim, so his friends say, of his own belief in sorcery.

To Mr. A. Sommerfelt I am particularly indebted both for the advice he has given me and for reading and advising me on the manuscript in its various stages.

Thanks are also owing to Mrs. C. Cramb, who typed much of the previous draft of the manuscript, and to the University of Basutoland, Bechuanaland Protectorate and Swaziland for a grant in aid of the final preparation of the manuscript for publication.

J.R.C.

CONTENTS

Preface	v
Introduction	1
Sources of material	1
The Shona in the context of Rhodesian society	8

Part I: Evidence and Confessions of Wizardry — 40

I. *Evidence of wizardry beliefs in criminal cases*	42
II. *The problem of the confession of witchcraft*	44

Part II: The Nature of Wizardry Beliefs (with particular reference to the Shona) — 66

III. *The basis of wizardry beliefs*	66
IV. *Witchcraft and religion*	73
The *vadzimu*	77
The *mashave*	82
The *mhondoro*	86
The *ngozi*	88
Shona beliefs today	90
V. *Witchcraft and misfortune*	93
Witchcraft	94
The Spirit world	94
Sorcery	95
Breaking a taboo or other prohibition	99
Medicines	103
Summary	106
VI. *The making of a Shona witch*	107
Spirit possession	108
The making of a witch by another witch	111
VII. *Beliefs in the manifestations of witchcraft*	111
Cannibalism and the use of human flesh	112
The witch's familiars	115
The nocturnal travels of witches	121
The control by witches over the forces of nature	122
The sending of the *ngozi* by a Shona witch	124
The witch's medicines	125
VIII. *Protection against wizardry*	127

Part III: The Allegation of Wizardry — 130

IX. *The pattern of accusations* — 130
X. *Wizardry allegations where no diviner was present* — 161
XI. *Divination in general* — 179
XII. *Traditional diviners and divination methods* — 183
    The Ndebele and Kalanga — 183
    The Shona — 190
    Foreign diviners — 197
    The effect of modern social conditions on the traditional diviner — 202
XIII. *The supernatural indication of a wizard* — 208
XIV. *Shona names* — 212
XV. *The ordeal* — 214
    The poison ordeal — 215
    The boiling water ordeal — 218
    The *muchapi* ordeal — 220
XVI. *Divination in the Pentecostal Churches* — 221
    Divination during the course of a religious service: baptism — 230
    The prophet on the mountain of God — 233
    The prophet at the gate of heaven — 234
    Divination during the course of a service for the sick — 236
    Divinations on request — 238

Part IV: The Consequences of the Allegation of Wizardry — 244

XVII. *Behaviour of persons involved* — 244
    The attitude of the wizard — 224
    Attitudes of other persons to the person accused of wizardry — 248
    Attitude of the husband of the witch — 255
    Legal action by the person defamed — 257
XVIII. *Magical vengeance against a wizard* — 259
XIX. *The cure of the wizard's victim* — 265
    Removing oneself from the area of the witch's activities — 265
    Getting a wizard to withdraw her wizardry — 267
    Calling in the doctor — 268
XX. *The cure of the witch* — 271
XXI. Conclusion — 276

Appendixes
>   I. Table of cases involving accusations of
>   wizardry   *between pages* 296 & 297
>   II. The Witchcraft Suppression Act (*Chapter* 50)   297
>   III. African Nganga Association of Southern Rhodesia
>   Constitution   300

Bibliography   303

Index   307

ILLUSTRATIONS

PLATES

A carved model of a human head with bead decoration, part of a diviner's equipment *frontispiece*

facing page

I. Diviner's equipment: horns, gourd rattle, wooden elephant and head 198

II. Diviner's equipment: animal with skin covering and horns inserted in holes running along the back 199

FIGURE

A Zezuru lineage 30

TABLES

I. Pattern of allegations of wizardry: the Eastern Shona 133
II. Pattern of allegations of wizardry: Ndebele and Kalanga 135
III. Patterns of allegations by percentages 140
IV. Treatment of a wizard 250

INTRODUCTION

SOURCES OF MATERIAL

IN this book I have attempted to study beliefs in wizardry and also the part played in African society in Rhodesia by the allegation of wizardry during the years 1956 to 1962. By wizardry I mean witchcraft and sorcery. The difference between witchcraft and sorcery is important and will be discussed later.

While informants have been used to amplify and explain the material, the primary source of data has been the judicial records in the custody of the Attorney-General of Rhodesia. The reason why, with few exceptions, records prior to 1956 have not been used is because they were not readily available to me. This, however, means that this is a study of a more or less contemporary society.

In some ways the use of judicial records enables a broader picture to be obtained of Rhodesian society as a whole than is possible with conventional anthropological or sociological methods, which must generally, for financial or other reasons, be of limited scope. At the same time the picture obtained must lack some of the detail obtainable from the close study of a particular group. Records relating to a large group such as the Shona peoples are commoner than records relating to the smaller groups; and this is so, not only because of population figures, but also because many of the smaller groups are not in such close contact with the administration as the more closely administered central groups. Of necessity, then, information is more complete about the Eastern Shona and, to a lesser degree, the Ndebele and Kalanga, than about other groups. For this reason this study has been limited to the areas of the country occupied by the Shona, Ndebele and Kalanga. This is not quite the same thing as limiting the study to these tribal groups because there are many multitribal and multiracial communities within these areas and to present a true picture of contemporary society it would be wrong to exclude alien elements. Again, the activities of the prophets of the Pentecostal churches cut across tribal barriers. These prophets are important because of the large role they play in witchcraft allegations. The material from the Ndebele-Kalanga area is less satisfactory than that from the Eastern Shona areas, partly because there is less of it, and partly because of the difficulty of distinguishing the Ndebele from the Kalanga in the case material available to me. I freely admit that this difficulty has caused defects in this book; but the material from this area contains much that is valuable and I have considered it necessary to include it. I have also included the occasional case from other cultural areas where it illustrates a point not clearly illustrated by the other material. All wizardry allegations, the records of which are available to me, whether included within the ambit of this study or coming from areas excluded from it, are listed in the Table in Appendix I.

To explain the nature of the material used some description of the structure and nature of the criminal court procedure of Rhodesa is necessary, since the records used relate mainly to criminal proceedings.

No tribal court has criminal jurisdiction. All criminal prosecutions during the period under examination commenced in the magistrates' courts. All presiding officers were, and are, Europeans; and although non-Europeans are now eligible for appointment, none have so far been appointed, nor is it likely that an African will be appointed in the next few years.[1] All larger towns have stipendiary magistrates; but in country districts native commissioners were, until October 1962, *ex officio* assistant magistrates. Petty matters are tried summarily by magistrates under their ordinary jurisdiction which was, in 1963, six months' imprisonment with hard labour or a fine of £50 or whipping not exceeding ten strokes. Magistrates could try all crimes other than murder, treason and, until recently, rape. Should the case be of some seriousness, and always in the case of treason, murder and rape, a preparatory examination was held. In such an examination the

[1] The judicial system is described as it was in 1963.

Introduction 3

Crown prosecutor leads the evidence incriminating the accused, who is thereafter, charged. If he replies to the charge, the accused may give evidence on oath, in which case he can be cross-examined, or he may give an unsworn statement, which precludes cross-examination. Quite commonly the defence is reserved. The record of the examination is then forwarded to the Attorney-General who may, unless he declines to prosecute or decides to remit for further evidence, either indict the case for trial before the High Court or remit it under ordinary or increased jurisdiction to the magistrate from whom the case originated. Only comparatively few wizardry cases are indicted, most of those taken as preparatory examinations being remitted. If a case is remitted on increased jurisdiction, as usually happens, the magistrate may impose a sentence of imprisonment for a year, a fine of £100 or a whipping of twelve strokes. A special magistrate's jurisdiction is greater. The High Court's jurisdiction in indicted cases is unlimited and it has exclusive jurisdiction in cases of murder. Appeal lies to it from the magistrates' courts and lay from it until the dissolution of Federation to the Federal Supreme Court. The High Court may review all proceedings of inferior courts and automatically reviews all cases in which the accused is sentenced to more than three months' imprisonment or is fined more than £25 or receives lashes or strokes.

The records used by me consist chiefly of preparatory examination records. Duplicates of the records in preparatory examinations in cases indicted for trial have in recent years been retained by the High Court but in cases not so indicted copies of recent examinations (other than those in the Attorney-General's office) can be found only in their court of origin. Shorthand writers are not available outside Salisbury and Bulawayo and the evidence must therefore be recorded in longhand by the presiding officer. The clerks of the court in country districts are seldom skilled typists and errors in transcription in the records used by me were not uncommon but seldom affected the general sense of the record. Errors in interpretation of witnesses' statements no doubt occur; but many judicial officers, particularly those of the former

Native Department, have some knowledge of the vernacular. The evidence recorded is thus usually a reasonably accurate statement of what was said although a person recording evidence in longhand inevitably condenses this to a greater or less degree. Most of the passages of evidence quoted or referred to by me were taken from the evidence in chief of the witness and were elicited by means of the prosecutor's questions. Leading questions are, or should be, avoided except in undisputed matters. It is otherwise in cross-examination. Frequently prosecutors lead the evidence relating to a person's place of abode and the date of an event. Questions are seldom recorded in the case of records originally recorded in longhand.

On a number of occasions I have used 'warned and cautioned' statements of the accused which were produced in evidence at the examination. These are statements made to the police by a suspect and admissible in evidence only if proved to have been made freely and voluntarily and without the police having brought any 'undue influence' to bear on the suspect. Such statements ought not to be elicited by means of questions.

It is, of course, true that a witness may lie; but the motive for perjured evidence is usually apparent. For example, accused persons often lie to escape conviction and women may lie to protect lovers. Most of the cases examined led to convictions and most of the statements used are made by witnesses attempting to tell the truth. However, in those cases where a witness's veracity is suspect he will normally lie in accordance with the social norms of the community he belongs to and, for the purposes of this book, the fact that a few statements may be suspect is not, I think, of any great moment.

In addition to preparatory examination records a few records sent to the High Court for automatic review or on appeal have been used. Except that these are trial records the nature of the record resembles that of preparatory examinations. Some use also has been made of High Court trial records but, although evidence is recorded in shorthand, no transcript is made unless an appeal is lodged or in capital cases. In some High Court prosecutions,

Introduction

therefore, reliance had to be placed on the memory of the prosecutor. Records of inquests and inquiries into sudden death are examined by the Attorney-General and some use has been made of these. All documents used are, of course, public documents.

For the present purposes the principal drawback of judicial records is that an effort is generally made by the court to confine a witness's evidence to evidence relevant to the decision in the case. However, concepts of relevance differ and, again, the court may make a deliberate attempt to elicit some of the 'background' to the case; so, while all records suffer to some extent from this drawback, in many cases quite considerable information is given.

Most of the cases used by me were examinations of persons accused under the Witchcraft Suppression Act (*Chapter* 50) although relevant material was also found in examinations into common law offences such as murder, assault and rape. The common law referred to is the Roman-Dutch common law which, in the sphere of criminal law, has been strongly influenced by English law. The Witchcraft Suppression Act dates from 1899 and replaced the Witchcraft Regulations, 1895, promulgated only five years after the occupation of Rhodesia and at the time when the first real attempt was being made to administer the indigenous population. Because of the Act's importance in providing the material upon which this work is based I have included a copy of it in the Appendices. While the wording of the Act reveals confusion in the mind of the draftsman between witchcraft and witch finding (a confusion common in similar legislation throughout Africa) the general purpose of the Act is clear and is to prevent the imputation of witchcraft and the activities in general of the doctor diviner. Most cases examined were prosecutions under section 3. Prosecutions under paragraph (a) of subsection 5 are rare, since persons do not employ diviners to name a witch but to indicate the cause of misfortune. Prosecutions under paragraphs (b) and (c) of section 5 are also rare, as are prosecutions under section 6; but there is an occasional prosecution under section 7. The balance of the cases examined which were prosecuted under the Act fall thus under sections 8 and 9.

A question of some importance is the relationship the number of cases prosecuted under the Act, and examined by me, bears to the total number of cases reported to the police. Unfortunately, satisfactory recent statistics are not available to me; but the earlier reports of the Secretary for Justice and Internal Affairs afford some guidance. The figures in the following Table have been extracted from these reports. Figures in brackets show the total number of all offences, and the other figures the prosecutions under the Act:

Year	Total of all cases prosecuted	Cases taken as preparatory examinations
1942	101 (72,573)	64 (3,344)
1945	135 (88,538)	114 (2,478)
1949	118 (91,945)	103 (2,736)
1956	—	32 (2,655)
1957	—	27 (2,609)
1958	—	63 (3,211)
1959	—	27 (3,102)
1960	—	11 (3,622)
1961	—	24 (3,414)
1962	—	47 (3,440)

The number of offences taken on preparatory examination has remained fairly constant during a period when the work of the criminal courts has greatly increased and this would indicate that an increasing percentage of petty cases are tried summarily. The decrease in the number of examinations under the Act in recent years is thus probably not entirely due to a decrease in the frequency of offences reported to the authorities. Nevertheless it would seem that the majority of the more serious cases under the Act are taken as preparatory examinations. The High Court ruled, in the case of *R v Chiangwa* 1945 S.R. 2, that cases where an imputation of 'witchcraft' has had serious consequences to the person indicated as a 'witch', should not be tried summarily. Although offences under the Act may be reported to the authorities

Introduction

by the person indicated as a witch, if force is used against her, there is, undoubtedly, reluctance to report such offences and the cases which come before the courts are frequently the result of police investigation into reports of suicide, assault and arson. Not all offences under the Witchcraft Suppression Act are relevant to the present study. For example, the fairly common crime of selling medicine to multiply money is usually prosecuted as fraud, in contravention of section 9 of the Act.

I have altered the original text of records quoted by me as little as possible. Abbreviations have been avoided and obvious mistakes rectified. For the sake of clarity I have, on occasion, substituted pronouns for nouns and vice-versa and, for the sake of euphony, amended the punctuation. I have not gone further than this. It is better for the English of a text to be clumsy and to convey the meaning it was intended to convey than to attempt to improve the text and, thereby, lose its meaning. I have spelt Shona words according to the standard orthography; for example, by reading *'chitukwani'* for *'stukwaan'*; but I have corrected only obvious mistakes in the case of Sindebele words.

I have made use of the services of a number of informants. These have been mainly either Zezuru, or Manyika-speaking. It has been curiously difficult to obtain information concerning the Ndebele in Salisbury and Sindebele is, indeed, a rare language in the courts of Salisbury, few court interpreters even knowing the language. One advantage of conducting an inquiry such as the present in an urban area has been the ease with which it has been possible to obtain informants who were both educated and knowledgeable. There are few Shona-speaking persons in Salisbury who were not brought up in country districts, and so information is not difficult to obtain. An advantage of using relatively well educated informants is that it is possible to discuss ideas with them in a manner which is not easy in the case of the unsophisticated witness. They also lack the reluctance of the less educated informant to discuss a subject such as witchcraft, where a display of too much knowledge might lead to a suggestion that the person imparting that knowledge was himself a witch. In making use of such informants, I have, however, endeavoured to keep in mind the possibility that they might have attempted to rationalize their beliefs in a manner which the less sophisticated informant would not. Undoubtedly the best informants as far as the realm of belief is concerned are the ritual specialists, the doctor diviners and the members of their families. However most of my informants did not belong to this class.

I have tried throughout to make it clear to which tribal group I am referring but if it is not clear from the context which group is intended then it can be taken that reference is to the Shona of Mashonaland. The word 'Shona' refers again primarily to the Eastern Shona, the Kalanga or Western Shona being referred to here as Kalanga.

Because witchcraft allegations are predominantly against women I have treated the noun 'witch' as feminine; but this usage is not to be understood as meaning that the word applies only to women, for the people of Rhodesia recognize both male and female witches. Witchcraft and sorcery are distinguished wherever possible; where this is not possible or where an all-embracing term is required the word 'wizardry' is used. The distinction between witchcraft and sorcery will be discussed at greater length later (p. 73ff.). The Witchcraft Suppression Act uses the word 'witch' to refer to both a witch and a sorcerer. This is the normal usage of the courts. Except in extracts from court records where the words 'witch' and 'witchcraft' have been allowed to stand, the fact that these words are used, not in the strict sense, but in the manner in which they are used in the Act will be indicated by the use of inverted commas. 'Witchcraft' and 'witch' are thus similar in meaning to wizardry and wizard. It is hoped that confusion will not result from this.

THE SHONA IN THE CONTEXT OF RHODESIAN SOCIETY

Wizardry beliefs and their manifestation in the form of accusations of witchcraft or in other ways can only be properly studied in the context of the society from which they originate. Others have shown on numerous occasions. both how the structure and nature of the society concerned throws light upon the nature and function of wizardry beliefs and accusations and also how wizardry beliefs and accusations can be used in the analysis of the structure of that society, or certain aspects thereof, and to understand better the nature of the social forces working in the society.

In this book we are concerned mainly with the nature of Shona society, since most of the material upon which it is based relates to this group. The Shona are, however, merely an element, albeit an important one, in the structure of Rhodesian society as a whole and it is, therefore, necessary to know something of the nature of this larger society.

Rhodesia differs from most other countries in tropical Africa in the possession of a large settler population of European origin. According to the Central Statistical Office, Europeans numbered 223,000 in 1962 and they constitute the politically dominant group. European administration has incorporated the various tribal units of the past into the structure of a modern state and Europeans have had a strong cultural influence, particularly on the peoples of central Mashonaland and Matabeleland. As in South Africa, the social structure of the country resembles, or resembled, a combination of Colony and Metropolitan State combined into one. This feature was perhaps rather more obvious during much of the period studied than it is at the date of writing. Although technically a Colony, Rhodesia was originally settled under the auspices of the British South Africa Company and has never been ruled directly from London as a Crown Colony. The European population has, since 1923, governed the country and has developed most of the institutions of central and local government with which one is familiar in a European state. The African, on the other hand, was, until recently, administered almost entirely by the erstwhile Native Department. Few aspects of African life were not the concern of this Department which treated their affairs in a manner which was authoritarian, albeit paternal. In the country districts the Native Commissioner performed, in relation to the African population, most of the functions, both administrative and judicial, which the District Commissioner performed in the territories of British Colonial Africa. The Parliamentary franchise was, and is, based on property and educational qualifications and, until recently, few Africans were enrolled as voters and Africans had little opportunity to influence Government policies directly. The position has been altered to some extent by the 1961 Constitution; but the effect of this Constitution need not here concern us. African townships, usually known as 'locations', are generally excluded from the areas of local authorities and thus few Africans qualify for the franchise in local government areas. African townships are usually administered by the municipality or other local authority concerned. The colour bar still pervades many aspects of life in the country but is based more on convention than on law, although the Land Apportionment Act (*Chapter* 257), as read with the provisions relating to Tribal Trust Land in the Constitution, ensures residential segregation, with some exceptions, and except on a master and servant basis. A very real attempt has, however, been made by the Legislature to break the industrial colour bar by means of the Industrial Conciliation Act (*Chapter* 246) and the Apprenticeship Act (*Chapter* 245), although the effect of this legislation is not yet fully apparent. Sexual relations between African and European have not, since 1961, constituted a criminal offence but are strongly disapproved. Intermarriage is practically unheard of. There is little social mingling, except on a master and servant basis, and few Europeans speak an African language, English or 'kitchen kaffir' being the principal media of communication.

Apart from the politically dominant Europeans, who are mainly of British and South African origin, and the numerically insignificant Bushmen of the Wankie and Nyamandhlou districts, the people of Rhodesia speak languages which belong to the Bantu group and, although of diverse racial origins, have all been negritized to a greater or lesser degree. The total African population was 3,618,000 (unless otherwise stated statistics are taken from the Final Report of the April/May 1962 Census of Africans in Southern Rhodesia) in 1962 of whom 406,000 were migrant workers living either on European-owned farms, in mining locations or in urban areas.

All Bantu-speaking tribes in Rhodesia were in the past hoe cultivators. Now the plough is largely used. Outside the Zambesi Valley this form of cultivation involved the usual moves when land became exhausted. Cattle keeping depended, and depends, on the presence or absence of the tsetse fly and formerly on the propinquity of the cattle-raiding Ndebele and other predatory groups. Goats were, and are, widely kept. While farming methods are improving most Africans are still subsistence farmers, the cash economy of the country depending largely on the products of the European-owned farms, the mines and growing, but still relatively small, secondary industry. Africans live in the Tribal Trust Lands, which are composed of the former Reserves and Special Native Areas, where they are subject to their traditional authorities; the Native Purchase Areas where they may, if they possess the necessary qualifications, own farms of some hundreds of acres; on European-owned farms where they may live in 'compounds' or be left very much to their own devices; in mine compounds or in the towns, where they live either in segregated townships or on their employer's property. The country is dominated politically, socially and economically by the capital, Salisbury.

The Bantu-speaking groups of Rhodesia belong mainly to the Southern Bantu, the Central and Eastern Bantu being confined to comparatively small groups in the North, although many migrant labourers belong to these groups. The Western Bantu are practically absent except as migrants, mainly from Barotseland, at Wankie and in other parts of Matabeleland.

The Shona are by far the most important indigenous group in Southern Rhodesia. They are composed of a number of tribes speaking allied languages and inhabit the major part of the country as well as large areas in Portuguese East Africa. In the past they were incorporated into the empire of the Shona-speaking Monomotapa and, in the 18th century, into the Rozwi empire. Memories of Rozwi rule persist in certain accession ceremonies; but otherwise the political unions of the past are hardly even a legend, although the Shona have a definite feeling of unity as a group. The name Shona is probably modern.

The Shona are divisible into two main groups, the Eastern Shona and the Western Shona. The most important dialects recognized amongst the Eastern Shona are Karanga, Zezuru, Korekore, Manyika and Ndau. The main Western Shona groups consist of the Kalanga of the Plumtree area and the Manbyzya of the Wankie district. The Kalanga were politically subject to the Ndebele in the last century and have come under considerable Ndebele influence. Persons of Kalanga origin form the lowest caste, the *amahole* or *lozwi*, of the Ndebele nation. The Rozwi spoke a Western Shona dialect within living memory; but the groups scattered throughout Mashonaland now speak mainly the dialects of the areas they inhabit.

Fortune (1959, p. 6) estimated the Shona in Southern Rhodesia to total 1,712,280 out of a total indigenous population of 2,221,000. To obtain the figures for 1962, Fortune's figures must be multiplied by at least 45%. Fortune, who would appear to base his figures largely upon Doke (1931), making allowance for population growth, gives the following figures for the speakers of the principal Shona dialects in Southern Rhodesia—

Kalanga	50,000
Ndau	60,000
Zezuru	429,000
Karanga	615,750
Manyika	212,650
Korekore	334,880

Both the Manyika and Ndau groups are considerably larger than the above figures indicate as many of both groups live in Portuguese East Africa. There are many Kalanga in Botswana.

The 1962 census results contain much of interest concerning the African population of Rhodesia; but unfortunately the census did not distinguish between the Shona and others. However, in view of the numerical predominance of the Shona, census figures are largely reflective of conditions among the Shona and it is fortunate, in this respect, that a distinction is usually made between the indigenous population and migrants, and that separate figures are supplied for each.

As far as the distribution of population is concerned, the census shows that in 1962 51.1% of all Africans lived on Tribal Trust land. This group is composed almost entirely of indigenous Africans. The figure given rises to 65.5% of the African population if migrant labourers are ignored. 19.2% of the indigenous population and 23.1% of the total population lived in the European farming areas; and 15.3% of the indigenous population and 18.1% of the total African population lived in urban areas. The balance of the African population lived mainly in the African Purchase Area. On Tribal Trust land the average density was about 23 per square mile but the population of the country is unevenly distributed and varies from 100 per square mile amongst the Zezuru of the Goromonzi district to 8 per square mile amongst the Valley Tonga and Korekore of the Binga and Gokwe Areas. On the whole, the area inhabited by the Central Shona has a fairly high population density by African standards. A demographic factor of considerable importance is that there is a surplus of men in urban areas and of women in rural areas. In Salisbury in 1962 there were 111,490 African males born before 1946 and 36,060 females. Of this number 62,790 males and 29,130 females were born in Rhodesia and would have been mainly Shona-speaking. While the surplus of men over women was marked in the case of indigenous Africans, it is smaller than is the case with non-indigenous migrants and it is clear that in the towns relatively more indigenous Africans are living in conditions of normal family life than is the case with the migrants. As far as country districts are concerned Kingsley Garbett (1960, p. 43) found that in the area studied by him, a Zezuru-speaking area in the Mrewa district, 49.6% of married males were absent in 1958 and 83.4% of single males between 15 and 20 years. Although the tendency has long been for able-bodied men to leave Tribal Trust Land, it would appear that the process became accelerated in the 1950's, a period of general economic expansion. In the early 1960's the economic growth of the country became somewhat retarded and it became less easy to find employment outside the Tribal Trust Areas.

The imbalance between the sexes in town and country has given rise to, or contributed to, the familiar social evils that occur in similar situations elsewhere. Apart from its effect on family life the absence of men from the tribal areas renders attempts to improve the standard of husbandry in these areas difficult. The ordinary Shona is strongly attached emotionally to the land and is unwilling to surrender his land rights when he leaves to work in town—it is at any event probable that he will leave his wife and children when he goes. Nevertheless he is, increasingly, looking upon his land-holding as merely an additional or supplementary source of income and as an insurance against old age or unemployment.

The Shona man, when not cultivating his own land as a subsistence farmer, is normally to be found as an employee of a non-African. In urban and European farming areas only 1.3% of African males are self-employed. Most of the Africans listed as self-employed are probably engaged in such occupations as hawking and manufacturing goods to be hawked, small-scale building contracting and small-scale trading of various sorts. Much of the road transport services of the country districts is in African hands.

Wages for Africans throughout Southern Rhodesia are, on the whole, low and the maintenance of standards difficult. In his study of a Shona ward, Kingsley Garbett found that the mean wage for males originating from the area studied was, during the period of their first employment, 62.26 shillings a month in 1958, and that the wage of married men accompanied by their wives was 120.9 shillings. In occupations covered by regulations or agreements made under the Industrial Conciliation Act (*Chapter* 246) the minimum wage for labourers is normally in excess of eight pounds a month. The Act, however, does not extend to domestic servants or to the farming industry.

Today the primary differences between the various Shona groups is occasioned not so much by differences in the traditional background as by the degree to which European culture and techniques have permeated the traditional structure of society and to the extent to which the group in question has entered the money economy. No group is, of course, entirely outside the money economy as money is necessary if only to pay the taxes imposed by the Government or to buy those manufactured articles which are now regarded as necessities, including such things as soap and matches. Near the larger urban centres the material culture of the Shona has been largely Westernized. An indication of the extent to which the traditional material culture of the Shona has disappeared is to be found in the nature of houses built, a brick building being normally a safe indication that its inmates are attempting to live, in so far as is possible, in the European manner. Census figures show that 35% of houses in African rural areas were brick built. However, distribution was unequal and among the central Shona in the province of Mashonaland South 60% of the houses were built of brick. It is true that in the villages of an area such as the Chinamora Reserve one still finds that each married woman expects to have a cooking and sleeping hut and somewhere to store her grain; but the huts themselves are usually made of burned brick and the more important buildings are usually built square with windows in the normal European manner. The principal sleeping hut becomes a unit, often consisting of a living room, complete with dining room table, sideboard and Chesterfield suite, with the main bedroom leading off it. The only objects not of European origin which can be seen in the houses of the area are items of kitchen equipment, including a mortar and winnowing basket, and possibly some clay pots. Even in the kitchen most of the utensils are shop bought. There is normally, as often as not, at least one car kept in the village although this was not as common at the beginning of the period studied as it is now. In the Chinamora Reserve the process of Westernization has, of course, gone further than in the more remote areas. If one takes a more remote area, for example, Kadzi kraal, a Korekore village below the Sipolilo escarpment, one will find that while dress is European in manner and many European objects are in evidence, much of the traditional material culture remains.

One of the greatest agents of acculturation is the schools. By the standards of Africa an extraordinarily high proportion of African children attend school. Attendance, however, often lasts for only a few years and few children proceed further than Standard Three. Nevertheless, although children often leave school barely literate and with no more than a smattering of English, education has had a profound influence upon them. These children cannot be regarded wholly as the products of a society of traditional type, for which, indeed, they often express contempt, but are also, in part, the products of an educational system which is national in character and which is designed to suit the needs of Rhodesia as a whole. Most schools are run by missionary bodies and the religious and other teachings of these bodies not only run counter to, but may also be deliberately designed to modify, traditional beliefs and attitudes.

Apart from speeding the process of acculturation, education has important economic effects. It is seldom that school is free and moneys for school fees have, somehow, to be found. Not only is the need to obtain the money for school fees an added inducement for the adult to seek work in the European areas but also the schools remove children for much of the day from what they would otherwise be doing. In the past children played an important part in the economy of the tribe. This was particularly the case with boys who were the cattle herds and who, thereby, relieved adults of this time-consuming task. In areas where most of the children go to school cattle have to be herded by women and adults who would otherwise be engaged in more productive tasks about the fields and home and there is a tendency to keep cattle kraaled for longer than is necessary. A frequently voiced complaint is that 'there is now no one to herd the cattle'.

Shona who are old or middle-aged are less likely to have been to school than persons of a younger generation. 34.6% of adult males born in Rhodesia and 48.1% of all females have never been to school and these figures include many in the older age groups.

Introduction

At the present somewhat over 60% of all male children in the country and somewhat under 60% of all female children are at school; but the figures given are lower than they would otherwise be by reason of the inclusion of the children of migrants and of figures relating to the less well developed areas of the country. Amongst the central Shona a child will normally receive some schooling. A child who has attended school is, of course, not necessarily literate, in the sense of being able to read and write, when he leaves school. In the country as a whole, 36% of all males and 32% of all females left school, at or below, Standard Three and can at best be regarded as barely literate. Standards of literacy are lower in the European farming area than in Tribal Trust Land or the towns.

Outside Tribal Trust Land the Shona are in continuous contact, and must compete economically, with the large numbers of immigrant labourers who come from Zambia, Malawi and Mozambique to work in the country. Only 47.6% of the labour force in European farming areas was born in Rhodesia, while in the towns the corresponding figure was 58.9%. From the economic point of view there can be little doubt that the presence of a large number of migrant workers prepared to work for low wages has the effect of depressing wage rates in the country. For this reason restrictions have been placed upon the employment of migrant workers in certain areas. E. M. Bell's study of a Salisbury factory (1961, p. 37) showed that, in the factory studied, the percentage of indigenous Shona in employment increased the higher the status of the post. Thus in a group of 437 unskilled labourers, only 199 were Shona but in a group of 74 skilled workers, 55 were Shona. My impression is that the factory studied by Bell is not atypical. In the courts, in criminal cases concerning members of the labouring classes, the persons concerned are, in Salisbury, as often as not Nyasa-speaking but the African upper and middle class is, in my experience, almost entirely Shona-speaking. My wife has taught in schools both on the borders of the Chinamora Reserve and in the Highfields township of Salisbury and she found that Shona-speaking children came from homes that were quite definitely superior to those of migrant labourers and, by and large, formed *vis à vis* these migrants a distinct middle class.

The African in the towns is probably economically better off than those remaining in the Tribal Trust Lands, although his income is generally low and his expenses high. Townships such as Salisbury's Harari township are close to town, but the usual practice is to site the 'location' well away from town and away from European residential areas. As a result, transport expenses play a large part in most family budgets. Transport may be subsidized by means of a levy on employers under the Services Levy Act (*Chapter* 78). Employers in urban areas are compelled by law to provide accommodation for their servants under the Africans (Urban Areas) Accommodation and Registration Act (*Chapter* 110). If employees are not housed on the employer's property, they must be accommodated in the townships at the employer's expense. The employer bears the whole cost of what is termed 'ordinary accommodation'. Housing of a higher standard is called 'special accommodation' and the employee pays the difference between the amount charged for ordinary accommodation and the rental of the premises. In order to avoid throwing the burden of increasing costs on employers, there has been a tendency to increase the amount of special accommodation supplied, at the expense of ordinary accommodation. Single men are normally housed in large barrack-style buildings in rooms which have to be shared with a number of others. Married persons obtain, if available, small cottage-style houses. Industrial regulations frequently provide for the payment of a housing allowance to employees.

Of the African population 66% lives in the African Purchase Areas which were 4,220,000 acres in extent in 1963 (Internal Affairs, 1964, p. 7). In these areas a holding may be some hundreds of acres in extent as compared with perhaps some eight acres of arable land, which, together with grazing rights, make up the usual holding in Tribal Trust Land. Land in the Purchase Areas may be purchased on the basis of individual tenure by the farmer. If an applicant is to obtain a holding the Administration must be

Introduction

satisfied with his farming capabilities. Individual farmers in the Purchase Area are progressive and prosperous; but the usual difficulties created by lack of capital and experience mean that the experiment in individual land-holding has not been an unqualified success. An attempt is being made by means of loans and technical assistance to overcome these difficulties.

Tribal Trust Land is the category of land to which more land in the country is assigned to than any other. In 1963 (Internal Affairs, 1964, p. 7) Tribal Trust Land was 40,020,000 acres in area as compared with the 35,950,000 acres of the European Area. National Land forests, game reserves and so forth accounted for 10,540,000 acres. It is often claimed by Africans that the European Area contains all the 'best' land in the country. This is almost certainly incorrect, although the amount of land held by Europeans is disproportionate to their numbers. It is, however, true that land in the European Area is, on the whole, economically more valuable than Tribal Trust Land, not only because of the greater amount of development, but also because of better communications and better access to markets.

An important social development since the Second World War and, more particularly, since the late 1950's, has been the growth of African nationalism. Although a number of the leaders of the nationalist movement are not of Shona origin, including persons such as Joshua Nkomo and Ndabaningi Sithole, the primary strength of the various African political parties has been derived from the Shona. The growth of nationalism is a world-wide phenomenon and in Rhodesia was, in part at least, a consequence of the attainment of independence by Ghana and, subsequently, by other African states. It is difficult to estimate the real strength of the nationalist movements. Their leaders claim almost universal membership. The official Government view is that real support for the nationalist parties is very limited and that such successes as have been obtained by them, for example, the boycotting of the electoral rolls and of the schools, has been due to intimidation. The truth probably lies somewhere in between. My impression is that most educated and semi-educated Africans of the younger generation sympathize with the nationalists and that they have a considerable following in the towns. In the country areas the support for nationalist politicians comes largely from those areas which are disaffected for one reason or another. The nature of the nationalist movement as a grievance party in rural areas was particularly noticeable in areas where opposition to the implementation of the African Land Husbandry Act (*Chapter* 103) was strongest as in the Mrewa district amongst the Zezuru-speaking Vanowe, where the Administration had found it necessary to depose the then chief, Mangwende, and install another in his place. The rise of nationalism has been accompanied by much violence and other crimes of a political nature. The nationalist leader who commands the greatest support is Mr. Joshua Nkomo who, since 1957, has formed a number of parties which have all, in turn, been suppressed by the Government. In each case the formation of a new party, whether it was the African National Congress, the Zimbabwe African Peoples' Union or the Peoples' Caretaker Council was followed by a period of intense political activity and a concomitant rise in the number of politically inspired crimes which eventually led the Government to take action. Thereafter followed a brief period of political calm lasting until the formation of a new party. After the suppression of the Zimbabwe African Peoples' Union the nationalist movement split, to some extent apparently on class lines, and in the earlier part of 1964 there was considerable faction fighting between the supporters of the two groups. The politically inspired crime of the last few years has undoubtedly been one of the factors which has led to a hardening of racial attitudes among Europeans in Southern Rhodesia.

The large majority of the cases from the courts which have contributed the basic material for this study originated from the Tribal Trust Land and it is, therefore, necessary to examine the political and social structure in this area in more detail.

The various tribal groups are, of course, incorporated into the political structure of Rhodesian society and are not the independent political entities of pre-occupation days. The central Government is represented in Tribal Trust Land primarily by the district commissioner (formerly known as the native commissioner). The district commissioner forms the principal channel of communication between the Government and the tribesmen and collects tax and other moneys owing to the Government. He hears such civil cases as are not heard in the chief's court, including all actions for divorce and, until recently, he also had the jurisdiction of an Assistant Magistrate in criminal cases. The day-to-day administration of the Tribal Trust Lands, in so far as it is not carried out by the tribesmen themselves, is almost entirely in his hands. The central Government is further represented by the British South Africa Police and various agricultural and other experts, including land development officers and community development agents. Apart from the organs and representatives of the central Government, the other, non-traditional, element in the political hierarchy of the Tribal Trust Lands is the African councils, established under the African Councils Act (*Chapter* 95). These are elected bodies of the usual local government type with power to raise money by taxation, including the power to impose a poll tax and a dog tax. Some now own bottle stores as an additional way of raising revenue. The interest in these councils has varied from area to area and, in some areas, councils have had to be abolished. The chairman of the council is usually the district commissioner. Failure may be due in part to the fact that these councils have, in consequence, become regarded as agents of the central Government. A further factor in some areas may be that the local chief fears transfer of his powers to the council. These councils are important in the implementation of the Government's policy of 'community development'.

In many areas community development agents have met with considerable success; but the Secretary for Internal Affairs (1963, p. 84) records at least one district where such agents have been completely rejected as 'the chiefs adopt the line that they are the leaders of the people, know their wants, and can quite easily convey this information without the *mubatsiri's* (agents) help'.

Beneath the structure of government imposed from above lies

the traditional political order of the Shona. Of course, now that political independence has been lost, the nature and functions of the tribal authorities have changed in some ways. Chieftaincies among the Shona are, on the whole, fairly small and, compared with the old Ndebele kingdom or that of the modern Swazi or Basuto, are weak and fragmented. The weakness and fragmentation of Shona chieftaincies should not, however, be overstressed as many chiefs still wield considerable power, on occasion, over fairly large areas of territory. Considerable resilience has been shown in the face of change. The chief himself is normally the senior member of the dominant agnatic lineage in the tribal area and the political hierarchy of the tribe is based largely on the chief's group of agnatic kinsmen (see Holleman 1952, p. 3ff and 26ff), the tribe being in some ways an extension of the structure of the lineage. In my view, the exogamous clan structure is also, at least in the Salisbury district, an important political force behind the power of the chief. This aspect has not been sufficiently stressed by recent writers about the Shona. In theory, of course, the clan is an extension of the lineage, clan members believing that they are all agnatically related, but in practice descent cannot be traced back to a common ancestor. While much fragmentation of clans has taken place most of the persons, other than persons who have married into the tribe, in some chieftaincies and many persons in all chieftaincies will be found to have the same clan names (*mutupo* and *chidawo*) as that of the chief. Thus the Shawasha of the Salisbury district are of the *soko* (monkey) clan, and the Gova of the Concession Area are of the *shava* (eland) clan. The importance of this is illustrated by the following examples. The father of one of my informants is a headman under Chief Chinamora and is thus part of the political hierarchy of the Shawasha tribe. Nevertheless his *mutupo* is *shawa* (and his *chidawo*, if I remember rightly, *mufakose*) and, as a result, he regards himself, and is regarded by others, not as a Shawasha but as a Gova whose 'real' chief is Chiweshe and not Chinamora. On the other hand my former gardener came from the Mrewa district and belonged to a group which does not owe political allegiance to chief Chinamora and which split off from the Shawasha tribe a long time ago. Nevertheless his *mutupo* is *soko* (*chidawo* is *murewa*) and when he visits the Chinamora Reserve he is regarded by those who live there as a Shawasha. It is not incorrect to call him *Chinamora* after the chief, because he is regarded as a member of the Shawasha tribe. Clans are not political or social entities but they strengthen the political structure. Political fragmentation of the tribe has often been, historically, accompanied by changes in the sub-clan name, a change which has the advantage that persons of the fragmenting groups can intermarry with one another.

In strict law in Rhodesia a chief does not hold office by hereditary right, being the nominee of the Governor. In fact regard is had to customary laws of succession when appointing a chief. A chief is in a somewhat ambiguous position in that his people see him as representing the tribe in its relations with the Government, while the Government sees him as representing it in its relations with the people. There is clearly, on occasion, a conflict of interests and this became particularly obvious in those areas where there was opposition to the introduction of the Land Husbandry Act (*Chapter* 103). The obvious way of resolving the conflict of interest, at least outside the relatively non-controversial judicial field, is for chiefs to take little or no action except where pressure from the one side or the other becomes so intense that action is clearly necessary. This tendency is accentuated by the relatively high average age of Shona chiefs brought about by the law of succession. In the words of the Secretary for Internal Affairs (1963, p. 5):—

'So often the successors to chieftainship in Mashonaland, because of the custom of collateral succession, are very old and unable to carry out the onerous duties of chieftainship in this modern age. Not only does this system invariably mean that a chief can only expect a few more years of life, but it also precludes any possibility of training his successor in the role of chief because the likely choice, besides being too old to train, might well die before the chief.'

The ordinary principles of succession are described by Holleman (1952, p. 21) and are in essence that the chieftaincy descends collaterally from the eldest brother to his junior brothers in succession until the generation of brothers is exhausted and the eldest grandson succeeds to the name and position of the grandfather. The above must, however, be usually read with the qualification that a man cannot be chief unless his father was, at some time, chief. The customary law as to the succession of the chief varies to some extent in the various chieftaincies and it would appear that the rules of succession seldom point unequivocably to a particular individual and that there are normally a number of potential candidates for the chieftaincy. Sometimes disputes over succession used to result in civil war. In the Mangwende chieftaincy of the Nowe tribe in the Mrewa area disputes over the chieftaincy have frequently occurred. The chieftaincy alternates between two 'houses'—the older the chieftaincy, usually the fewer the 'houses'—and recently the Administration found it necessary to depose the then chief, Munhuwepasi. The question that arose and which had led to much trouble in the area was whether the deposition of a chief was analogous to his death and the chieftaincy should, therefore, pass to the other house or whether, as the chieftaincy had not run its full term, the new chief should be appointed from the same house. A third group held that there could not be another chief while the deposed chief was still alive and that his successor could have, at most, an acting appointment. The conflict was resolved, but not to everyone's satisfaction, by the appointment of a chief by the Government. In this case, of course, a new and unprecedented thing happened, the deposition of a chief, but somewhat similar disputes have arisen in the past in the history of the tribe and have been resolved by force. In the Mutasa chieftaincy of the Manyika, succession was, so it is said, almost succession by assassination, the murderer succeeding to his victim's position. On the whole, however, the Shona prefer to avoid conflict over succession by letting the spirit medium of the tribe, the tribal *mhondoro* (see below p. 86), indicate the successor, no chief being appointed until the spirit has indicated its choice. Even today the Government usually does not appoint a chief until the *mhondoro* has indicated its wishes although it may take years to do so. The delay in the appointment of a new chief results in an *interregnum,* often of many years' duration, during which the tribe has no chief. To avoid the difficulties occasioned, an acting appointment is now usually made and there are usually a number of tribes at any one time ruled by acting chiefs.

The chief is at the apex of the judicial hierarchy of the tribe. From the judicial decisions of the chief, appeal lies to the district commissioner and, ultimately, to the African Appeal Court and the High Court. A chief may lawfully adjudicate only in civil cases and may not, strictly speaking, preside in actions for divorce or for the return of the marriage consideration consequent to the dissolution of a marriage. In fact, actions for the return of marriage consideration would appear to take up much of the time of the chief's court. There is considerable pressure from the chiefs to have criminal jurisdiction granted to them or, at least, to regularize the levying of *ropa,* or blood fine, in cases which have a criminal aspect. As chiefs have no criminal jurisdiction it is not now lawful for chiefs to levy *ropa.* Beneath the court of the chiefs are the courts of the ward and village heads. The Shona word *'dare'* is perhaps a better word to use than 'court' in this connection as it can be used in the case of both formal and informal gatherings and lacks the rather formal and institutionalized associations of the English word. It is only the *dare* of certain of the ward heads that are recognized as 'courts' under the African Law and Courts Act (*Chapter* 104) and which have, in law, the power to enforce their judgements but, in practice, it probably makes very little difference whether the *dare* is recognized by the Administration as a court or not. Usually the village head or heads concerned try initially to settle any dispute which arises. If the case is a serious one by reason of its subject matter or the status of the parties, the village head will normally refer the matter to his chief or ward head, as he will also do if it is clear that the parties to the dispute will not accept his arbitration. The manner in which the tribal courts resolve disputes is similar to that of customary tribunals throughout Africa and has been described by various writers. Basically the aim of the *dare* is not so much to determine the legal rights of the persons involved but to reconcile the parties to the dispute and to restore the social equilibrium. The rules of customary law are, of course, of importance in the process as they determine whether a litigant has acted in the way an upright man would have been expected to act. The *dare* is made up both of experienced counsellors of the chief or headman and of casual bystanders, all of whom may take an active part in the proceedings. The matter will ordinarily be determined by the chief or headman after assessing the general opinion of those present after all issues have been thoroughly canvassed. Recourse to the tribal courts can, therefore, be regarded as coming close to an appeal to public opinion.

The ease with which it is possible to appeal against the decision of the chief must inevitably affect his status in the eyes of the community; but chiefs are still greatly respected and even the nationalist politicians are, or were, at least ostensibly in favour of restoring to chiefs at least some of their former rights and privileges. This is, however, in part because no chief is powerful enough to be a serious danger to the nationalist movement. The sentiment that the chief ought to be respected is strong.

The chief is, or was, not only the political but also to some extent the religious leader of the tribe. He does not seem to have possessed anything analogous to the 'coil of power' of the Nguni chiefs, but his duties included the propitiation of the ancestral spirits of his own clan. Because of the dominance of the clan of the chief in the affairs of the tribe this function had the effect of making him the dominant ritual elder of the tribe. Many tribes possessed their own tribal spirit or *mhondoro* and the chief normally had various functions in respect of this spirit. Many chiefs are now Christians.

An attempt has recently been made to educate the chiefs despite the difficulties mentioned above. This has included a world tour at Government expense in which many chiefs took part. The recent creation of a Council of Chiefs appears to be fostering a feeling of common purpose between the various chiefs and gives them an institutionalized method of expressing their wishes and desires.

The chief is assisted in his duties by tribal officials. These can be divided into two classes: firstly the ward heads and village heads; secondly, a number of people, normally related to the chief, who have been selected by him to be his personal advisers and henchmen (Holleman 1952, p. 20). Under the Native Law and Courts Regulations, 1938, chiefs may, and do, appoint a clerk to make the necessary entries in the civil record book which his court is obliged to keep, and also persons to act as messengers of the court.

Below the chiefs in the hierarchy of the tribal structure are the ward heads (*sadunhu*). The ward has well defined territorial boundaries. Its size differs from area to area. According to Holleman (1952, p. 12) its headman is often, but need not necessarily be, a member of the chief's lineage. The population of the ward is normally composed of a nuclear body of the agnatic kinsmen of the ward head. Holleman found that the primary function of the ward was as a land unit and that the ward held the communal right over all the territory within its boundries. This right is, of course, largely suspended where land is occupied by a village. The ward head is expected to take action to protect the interest of the community against unlawful use of the territory and he arbitrates in land disputes. Because of the importance of the ward head in land matters the implementation of the African Land Husbandry Act (*Chapter* 103), which provides for the survey and allocation of land, must presumably, if continued with, affect the status of the ward head who, unless he can achieve recognition by the Government as a 'sub-chief' must tend to be reduced to the status of a village head.

A ward is divided into a number of villages. The nature and structure of the village is of considerable importance in this study because it is the intimate contacts of village life which result in those frictions which are so often expressed in the form of an allegation of witchcraft. Villages are not usually very large. Larger villages existed in the past, mainly because of the unsettled state of the country, but these were deliberately broken up by the Government after the 1896 rebellion and have not re-formed. In some areas villages have been formed into 'lines' for the better management of the veld, the line of huts serving to demarcate and separate the arable from the grazing land. Each 'line' is normally composed of a number of villages each under its own head. Usually, however, villages are scattered haphazardly through the Tribal Trust Land, if possible, being sited in a place where the granaries can be built upon rock so as to prevent insect attack. The bigger villages may be split into a number of geographically separated subsections. The head of the village is know as the *samusha* or *sabuku*. The latter name is derived from the tax register kept by the village head. The possession of this register means that the village head is recognized by the Government. A village is normally composed of men related agnatically to the village head, their wives, probably some maternal kin and, perhaps, a few affines as well as a number of unrelated strangers (see Holleman 1952, p. 5ff and Kingsley Garbett 1960, p. 3). The power of the headman is normally derived from the fact that he is the head of the dominant lineage in the village. An important function of the village head is in the allocation of land. Land is normally allocated to the adult men, usually the family heads who, thereafter, allot individual portions to each of their wives. Once land has been allocated it belongs to the individual to whom it has been allotted for so long as he remains a member of the village. Unmarried men and women may also obtain rights to land. The village head settles disputes, in so far as he is able, which arise in the village. His *dare* has something of the nature of an arbitration proceeding or, as Holleman (1952, p. 8) puts it 'the character of a family circle'. As a chief is assisted in his duties by the tribal elders, so a headman is assisted by the elders of his village.

The political importance of the Shona lineage structure has been touched upon in the preceding paragraphs, the position of the chief, ward head and village head being all based on the fact that each of them is head of the dominant lineage of the tribe, ward or village concerned. It is not only from the political point of view that the Shona lineage is important. Social relationships generally, among the Shona, are expressed either as relationships between

Introduction

members of the lineage or as relationships between members of one lineage and members of another.

The Shona lineage[1] is arranged on seniority principles, particularly in so far as persons of the same sex are concerned. A person distinguishes at his own generation level between those who are older than he (or she) and of the same sex and whom he will call *mukoma,* and those who are younger than himself and whom he calls *mununguna* or *muninyina.* The attitude to a *mukuma* is one of respect, while one's *mununguna* is in a position of subordination. Brothers and sisters including classificatory brothers and sisters call one another *hanzvadzi,* irrespective of their relative ages. A person will call his father, and other persons of the lineage of the same generation level *baba,* father, distinguishing between those older than his own father who are termed *mukuru* (elder) and those who are younger, *whom* he will call *mudiki* (younger). A father's sister is called *vatete* or *samukadzi.* The difference in position of the father (*baba*) or father's sister (*vatete*) and that of the 'son' or 'daughter' (*mwana,* i.e. child) is one marked by superordination on the one hand and by respect and deference on the other. The relationship between grandfather (*sekuru*) and grandson (*muzukuru*) is, however, one of relative equality and is often, emotionally, one of the closest ties in the Shona family. One's grandmother (*ambuya*) is not, of course, of the same lineage as oneself, but here again the relationship between grandparent and grandchild is usually intimate.

It would appear that witchcraft allegations are, on occasion, associated with the segmentation of the lineage and, perhaps, attempts to prevent it from segmenting. Holleman (1952, p. 324ff) has given an account of the manner in which a Shona lineage segments, in so far as it is relevant for the understanding of the law of succession; but for present purposes it is probably simpler to approach the matter from the point of view of the right and duty to propitiate the ancestral spirits (*vadzimu*). I am concerned here with the lineage of a commoner and not that of a chief, which would appear to have a somewhat greater depth in time. It is only

[1] This description of the Shona lineage inevitably relies heavily on Holleman (1952)

the grandparents of the senior living generation who are remembered by name when the *vadzimu* are propitiated. The agnatic descendants of such a grandparent may be regarded as forming the group which I shall term the major lineage. However this major lineage is ordinarily divided into segments, the heads of which are usually village heads in their own right and it is the heads of these segments who propitiate the *vadzimu* on behalf of their own groups. Such a segment I shall term the minor lineage. The diagram below represents, in simplified form, the structure of a typical Zezuru lineage—

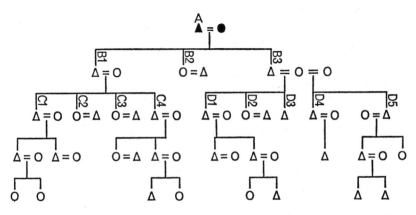

Suppose that initially B1 is the senior living member of the oldest living generation. During his lifetime B1 will propitiate the *vadzimu* on behalf of the whole lineage. His sister, B2, is a member of the lineage but her children belong to the lineage of her husband, although these children can still be affected by their maternal *vadzimu* and B1 may be required to sacrifice on their behalf. The same is true of the descendants of any other women of the lineage. On B1's death his brother, B3, will propitiate the *vadzimu* on behalf of the whole lineage; but on the death of B3 and all A's other sons, C1 will propitiate the *vadzimu* on behalf of his own minor lineage, and D1 on behalf of his. This segmentation may not always take place but it is regarded as a natural occurrence. If, however, a member of D1's minor lineage becomes ill, a diviner may state that C1 is the proper person to propitiate the *vadzimu*

Introduction

and the existence of the major lineage may, for the purpose of the ceremony, become of importance; but ordinarily D1's segment will not have much to do with C1's. Should C1 quarrel with his uterine brother, C4, or live very far from him, C4's dependants may recognize his right to propitiate the *vadzimu* but, as likely as not, if a diviner is consulted because of some illness, he will insist that C1 is the proper person to propitiate the *vadzimu* and C4's attempt to create a segment of his own is, during C1's lifetime and the lifetime of any other brother senior to C4, likely to fail. The links between the children of co-wives tend, however, to disappear after the death of their father and D4's right to propitiate the *vadzimu* should he quarrel or otherwise be separated from D1 is far more likely to be recognized by his family group than is C4's right during C1's life. Such recognition will mean that the segmentation of the lineage has now become an accomplished fact.

A lineage enters into a relationship with another lineage by marriage. As a lineage is an exogamous group it must seek its wives from another group. A person should not, indeed, marry anyone with the same *mutupo* and *chidawo* as his own, although where the relationship is remote, a ceremony may be performed (*kucheka uhama*) whereby the relationship is severed and marriage can take place. Although various forms of marriage, including marriage by service, existed in the past, and may persist in some areas, the only form of marriage of any real importance today is where payment of a consideration known as *rovoro* or *pfuma* is made by the husband or his lineage to the father of the bride. Whether or not the marriage is by Christian or civil rights under the Marriage Act (*Chapter* 177), under the African Marriages Act (*Chapter* 105) or not registered at all, *rovoro* is, in the eyes of most Shona, the essential feature which gives a marriage the quality of a marriage. Marriage negotiations may be started formally, through an intermediary, in the traditional manner or the parties concerned may commence proceedings by an elopement—*kutizisa makumbo*—in which case, however, matters must be regularized by the payment of *rovoro* if the father-in-law is prepared to recognize the suitor as son-in-law. *Rovoro* consists basically of a cash portion, known as *rutsambo* (a bracelet) and a payment expressed as a predetermined number of cattle. There are a large number of other customary gifts payable during the various stages of the marriage negotiations but these are of less significance and are not repayable, for example, on divorce. Although the amount of *rovoro* may be expressed in cattle there is an increasing tendency to settle the debt in money. In the Salisbury district the total value of the marriage consideration paid may well exceed £100. The function of the marriage consideration is not so much to confer on the husband sexual rights in respect of his wife, but to transfer rights in the children born to the wife from the lineage of the wife or (as the courts would regard it), from the guardian of the woman, usually her father, to the lineage of the husband or (at least in the view of the courts) to their father, that is to say, their legal father or *pater*. The legal or social father of the children may be, but is not always, their natural father or *genitor*. A *genitor* has the right to claim a child from the *pater* on payment of consideration, although the *pater* is not obliged to surrender it, the child being his until and unless he chooses to relinquish his rights. The function of the marriage consideration in transferring rights to the children from one lineage to another is illustrated in a number of ways. Notwithstanding that the parties to the marriage have lived together as husband and wife for many years, if the *rovoro* has not been paid and the parties are divorced, rights to the children, including the right of receiving *rovoro* on the marriage of a daughter, remain with the woman's lineage until and unless *rovoro* is paid. Again, on divorce, the amount of *rovoro* returned by the father-in-law depends on the number of children which have been born to the marriage. If a woman is barren the return of *rovoro* can be demanded and the marriage dissolved. Otherwise a sister can be married for the payment of no, or a reduced, *rovoro*. The service marriage, largely a thing of the past, also illustrates the function of *rovoro*. In such a marriage the children, usually with certain exceptions, 'belonged' to the father of the wife and could only be claimed by their *genitor* on the payment of proper marriage consideration, the services rendered by him not being accounted as such. It should be pointed out that although the guardianship of children vests in the father (i.e. the *pater*) once sufficient *rovoro* has been paid, the custody of very small children naturally belongs to the mother in the event of a divorce. The father can claim such children only if he pays a beast (*mombe yo kurera*) in consideration of the expenses to which the mother's lineage have been put in maintaining the children.

I should here point out that my account of the Shona lineage structure and of Shona marriage has been deliberately generalized. It is primarily an account of the Shona of the Salisbury district although I have drawn considerably on Holleman (1952) whose studies relate to the Sabi, Wedza and Narira Reserves in central Mashonaland. Minor variations occur between the various groups and there is considerable variation in kinship terminology. The account given here is, however, broadly true of the majority of Shona-speaking groups in Mashonaland.

In Shona customary law the link forged by the payment of *rovoro* is primarily one between lineages and not one between husband and wife only. Although considerable affection between husband and wife often exists, the relationship is one of superordination on the part of the husband and respect and subordination on the part of the wife which renders difficult the intimacy which ought to characterize marriage in our own society. Shona society is, however, in a state of change and the ideal of romantic love and marriage has had its effect, at least on the younger generation. Marriage negotiations were, in the past, conducted between the senior representatives of the lineages of the parties concerned or, at least, by their parents, and by means of an intermediary. Even if men now largely arrange their own marriages as, in the past, would normally have been the case with a chief or in the event of a second or subsequent wife—the position of the father of the bride (*tezvara*) in the marriage negotiations appears to be largely unaffected, and perhaps even strengthened by changes in the structure of Shona society. For in the past, senior members of the lineage would appear to have been more directly concerned with the marriage than is the case now. It is the *tezvara* who determines the amount of *rovoro* which his son-in-law (*mukuwasha*) must pay. The marriage relationship is not terminated by the death of the parties concerned. If a wife dies young the position is very much the same as if she were barren. That is to say, either a 'divorce' will be effected and a refund made of part or all of the *rovoro,* the amount depending on the number of children of the marriage, or else the husband may take another wife from the lineage of his deceased wife as in the case of barrenness. No obligation rests on the lineage of the wife if the woman has borne a satisfactory number of children. If the husband dies, the widow may be inherited by a brother or other member of her husband's lineage. In such a case she would become normally the wife of the person by whom she is inherited although traces of the levirate (Crawford, 1963, p. 27) are found amongst the Shona. If she is unwilling to be inherited, a 'divorce' takes place, unless she is old and past childbearing, and all or part of the marriage consideration must be returned by the *tezvara*. The creation of a marriage brings into being the relationship of *tezvara* and *mukuwasha,* not only between the parties to the marriage but between other members of the respective lineage also.

Shona marriage is, at least potentially, polygamous whether or not it is registered under the African Marriages Act (*Chapter* 105). Strickly speaking, if the marriage is not registered it is not a marriage at all; but the tribal courts apparently overlook this and, in any event, an unregistered marriage even if it is not, as far as the courts of the land are concerned, technically a marriage, is regarded as valid in law as far as the rights of the children are concerned. A marriage under the Marriage Act (*Chapter* 177) is, of course, monogamous.

The link between lineages forged by marriage can be looked upon from a number of different aspects, depending upon the point of view of the observer and his position in the lineage structure. The primary link is the relationship between the husband's lineage and the wife's lineage and is marked by a position of inferiority on the side of the *mukuwasha's* lineage and a position of superiority on the part of that of the *tezvara*. The *tezvara's* lineage, or rather the men thereof, are regarded as being in the same relative position as far as members of the *mukuwasha's* lineage are concerned, whatever their position in their own lineage, and are all styled *tezvara*. The effect of this is to treat male members of the wife's lineage as being in a genealogical category equivalent to that of the first ascending generation. All women of the wife's lineage are similarly placed in a single category. This time, however, they are regarded as being of the same generation as the wife and are called by the husband and those of his generation *muramu*, a term indicating potential connubium. The mother of the wife is, of course, a member of yet another lineage. This lineage, being the *tezvara* of the *tezvara*, is regarded as being two generations senior to the husband's lineage and all male members of this lineage are, accordingly, called *sekuru* or grandfather, and female members are called *mbuya washa* or grandmother in law.

While the husband will regard his wife's lineage as a unity, his relationship to members of that lineage depending on their sex, regardless of their position in the hierarchy of their own lineage, the wife is in a rather different position *vis à vis* the members of her husband's lineage. To her all the males of her husband's generation are *murume* (husband). Males of all generations senior to her husband are called *tezvara* and are, therefore, treated as being members of the first ascending generation. Notwithstanding the fact that males of the wife's lineage are regarded as genealogically senior to those of her husband's, the position is reversed as far as the wife's position in the home of her husband is concerned. This is perhaps best brought out by the term with which she addresses her husband's sister, that is, *vanwene* or 'owner'. A sister will call her brother's wife *murovora*.

The above description of the relationship between one lineage and another which are linked by marriage holds good so far as the generation of the persons marrying and the ascending generations are concerned. Holleman (1952, p. 40), to whom any description of the Shona kinship structure must owe much, points out that one of the objects of the classification of relatives amongst the Shona is to prevent males on a different generation level, in the same lineage, from marrying females from the same lineage, as this would disrupt the rank situation within the lineage. The relationship between the males of a lineage and the males of another linked to it by marriage is the same whatever the generation level of those who marry; but this cannot be the case as far as the females of the wife-providing lineage are concerned. It is necessary to distinguish between those whom the husband's generation can marry and those whom, being children of their daughter's generation, it cannot because they are the potential wives of their son's generation. The latter class of females are known to members of the husband's generation as *varovora* and are known by them as *tezvara*.

The relationship between lineages is, for obvious reasons, normally one-sided in that a lineage cannot normally be in the position of both wife-giving and wife-receiving lineage in relation to another. A form of exchange marriage does exist amongst the Shona where a female in one lineage is exchanged as a wife for a female in another, the main advantage of which is that *rovoro* payments are avoided. This, however, complicates the kinship pattern and, for this reason, is disapproved of.

Apart from relationships of affinity, marriage creates, with time, relationships by cognation between the lineages concerned. While the relationship of members of the wife-receiving lineage to members of the wife-giving lineage, where this is based on affinity, is one of social inequality, the cognatic relationship between maternal classificatory grandparents and their 'grandchildren' is intimate. The principle of lineage unity is here again apparent. A person will call all the females of his mother's generation and of his mother's lineage 'mother' (*mai*) and all the females of his paternal grandmother's generation and lineage 'grandmother' (*mbuya*). The men of both the mother's and the paternal grandmother's generation are called 'grandfather' (*sekuru*). The relationship between a mother's brother and his *muzukuru* is the most intimate relationship in the Shona kinship pattern. Although not a member of his mother's lineage, he shares its blood and cannot be treated as a stranger. The relationship of *muzukuru and* mother's brother is such that the *muzukuru* can even help himself to his *sekuru's* property.

A man treats the lineage of the *tezvara* of his *tezvara* as belonging to the second ascending generation. Marriage with this lineage is, therefore, excluded. The position is, however, otherwise, as far as the children of that man are concerned; for the son of a female agnate can marry the *varamu* (potential wives) of his mother's brother (his *sekuru*) because these women are classified as his *varamu* also. The converse is, however, not the case and the *sekuru* calls his sister's son's wives *murovora*, a term which excludes connubium.

So much for the traditional structure of Shona kinship. In the towns the traditional family structure is breaking down and the extended family tends more and more to be replaced by the simple family of husband, wife and minor children. However, few families are so cut off from their rural relations that the traditional lineage structure has lost all significance. In some ways the pattern of kinship has obtained a new significance in assisting a man to adapt to an urban environment by ensuring that he is never entirely socially isolated.

Comparatively little of the material used in this book comes from the Ndebele groups. However, a little needs to be said about them. They are, in origin, a Zulu offshoot and entered the country in the first half of the last century under the leadership of Mzilikazi. The western Shona or Kalanga bore the initial brunt of their invasion and many Kalanga groups were incorporated into the Ndebele nation where they formed the lower caste, the *amahole,* of the caste society which eventually developed, the other castes being the *zanzi*, those of Zulu or Swazi stock, and the *enhla*, those who were incorporated into the Ndebele nation during its stay in the Transvaal. Informants still recognize these castes but it is difficult to say to what extent they are of importance today. The Ndebele number about a sixth of the total indigenous population of the country.

The Ndebele chieftaincies originated in a manner rather different from that in which the Shona chieftaincies did. Chiefs do not hold office as being the descendants of the Ndebele kings, Mzilikazi and his successor Lobengula, but are the descendants of the former regimental chiefs, the *izinduna zamabuto*. The Ndebele were organized into regiments in much the same way as the Zulu, although Ndebele regiments did not, apparently, have the character of age sets (see Kuper *et al.*, 1955, p. 64ff). Under the chief there are usually a number of ward heads (*abalisa*) who are derived historically from the ward heads of the old regimental towns. Beneath these ward heads comes the village headman, the *upwate webuku* or *usobuku* whose position is the same as his Shona equivalent. The formal hierarchy of authority is very similar to that of the Shona, but while the Shona chief is of the same stock as the people he rules, the Ndebele chief is, or was, a member of the ruling aristocracy.

The Ndebele language is virtually a dialect of Zulu, the Ndebele being one of the few Zulu offshoots in Central Africa which have retained their language. Many groups which formerly spoke Kalanga or Venda now speak Ndebele.

The structure of the Ndebele family and village groups would appear to resemble very closely that of the Shona. (Hughes, 1956, Chap. IV) describes the process of lineage segmentation and homestead division among the Ndebele. This process would appear to take place on lines very much like similar segmentations among the Shona. While both Ndebele and Shona are patrilineal peoples and marriage in both groups is usually virilocal and exogamous, certain differences in family law exist. Thus, while both people regard marriage with one's wife's sister as desirable, among the Ndebele this develops into a form of marriage where the younger sister bears children for her sister's house where the elder sister is barren (Whitfield, 1948, p. 309). The levirate is found among the Ndebele but not usually among the Shona. Among the Shona widows are inherited and the children belong to their new husbands. The concept of house property is more strongly developed among the Ndebele and the ranking of wives more complex than is the case with the Shona where they rank simply in order of marriage.

It is very difficult to obtain reliable modern information about the Ndebele. There is some reason to believe that the social structure is becoming increasingly similar to that of the Shona but field work has been inadequate to say definitely that this is so. The African Appeal Court has given very little recognition to Ndebele law as being a system of law separate and distinct from that of the Shona. There ought to be a number of important differences if Ndebele law still resembles Zulu law, but far too lax standards in regard to the proof of law have been permitted and the approach of the courts may not, therefore, correctly reflect Ndebele custom. Customary law, being mainly family law, is largely a reflection of family structure.

PART I

EVIDENCE AND CONFESSIONS OF WIZARDRY

I SHALL here discuss briefly the nature of the evidence concerning wizardry beliefs which may be adduced before a court of law and which has formed the main source of information used in this book and will then give a fairly full account of certain cases where people confessed to being witches, on occasion, in lengthy and detailed statements. The mythological and other matters referred to in these cases will serve to introduce Shona witchcraft beliefs. These cases also raise the interesting problem as to why people should make a confession of witchcraft which, from its nature, cannot be objectively valid and which can attract only odium upon the person concerned. Some of the texts are strikingly reminiscent of analogous confessions in mediaeval and post-mediaeval Europe. It was these cases which first led me to take an interest in Shona witchcraft.

The Shona make a distinction between sorcery and witchcraft although they use the same word for both (*uroyi*). It will suffice at this stage to say that witchcraft is essentially a psychic act and is, objectively speaking, impossible, while sorcery, which involves the use of spells, medicines and ritual to harm others, while no doubt ineffective in achieving its object, can be attempted by anyone.

Shona witchcraft and sorcery beliefs will be described more fully in Part II. An effort will be made to show the function of these beliefs, whether as a theory of causation or otherwise, and also to show why these beliefs are socially relevant. The distinction between sorcery and witchcraft will be considered and the reason why the Shona have two very similar types of belief to account for misfortune where, on the face of it, one is adequate. Witchcraft beliefs form part of the cosmological ideas of the Shona and, because of this, it is necessary to see such beliefs against the background of religious and other ideas of the Shona. Religious beliefs are relevant not only because witchcraft beliefs are, in some aspects, an inversion of Shona religious beliefs, but also because Shona religious beliefs provide alternative explanations for the cause of misfortune. Attention will then be focused on the mythology of witchcraft, on how a person is believed to acquire the powers of a witch and on how it is believed such persons act and the perversions which characterize them. Thereafter follows a brief description of the manner in which one can seek to avoid the attentions of wizards.

The allegation of wizardry forms the subject of Part III. Althought this part is concerned mainly with the Eastern Shona, use is made for comparative purposes of material from the Ndebele, Kalanga and other groups. I have attempted, so far as the data allow, to show the part that wizardry allegations play in the functioning of Shona society and to seek an explanation in the structure of that society for the fact that wizardry allegations are more frequent against certain persons, and certain categories of persons, than against others. A large number of allegations of wizardry that become the concern of the courts follow upon the divination of a professional diviner and an account is, accordingly, given of their methods and techniques. Wizardry can be revealed not only by a diviner but by supernatural intervention in dreams and in other ways. Although the poison ordeal is, among the Shona, largely a thing of the past, some material has been gathered from court records on this and other forms of the ordeal. The cases studied show that, increasingly, the prophets of the Pentecostal Churches are taking the place of the traditional diviners and of the ordeal and, therefore, the nature of these churches will be discussed in some detail and texts will be quoted in which various persons describe the manner in which prophets divine wizardry. Reasons will be sought for the increasingly important role which the Pentecostal Churches play in the life of the Shona.

In Part IV which is, admittedly, somewhat inadequate because of the difficulty in obtaining information, an attempt will be made to describe the consequences of allegations of wizardry and of the attitudes of both the person accused and of other persons towards him. If action is taken against a wizard it need not be physical action, for the Shona believe in the efficacy of various forms of vengeance magic. Where the relatives of a person accused of witchcraft accept that she is a witch, and often they do not, it may be possible, if she is willing to be cured, to cure her of witchcraft.

CHAPTER I

EVIDENCE OF WIZARDRY BELIEFS IN CRIMINAL CASES

BELIEFS in wizardry may be relevant in a criminal prosecution in a number of ways. It may be the beliefs of the person accused which are on trial, as where a person is prosecuted for indicating a 'witch' in contravention of section 3 of the Witchcraft Suppression Act (*Chapter* 50). Where a person is prosecuted for fraud, in contravention of section 9 of the Act, it is the beliefs of the complainant which are relevant for it was those beliefs which enabled the accused to obtain money or some other advantage from the complainant. The same may be true of rape cases in which a doctor-diviner makes use of his patients' gullibility to ensure acquiescence. A trial of a diviner may be a trial of the beliefs of both the diviner and of his clients, and may include the beliefs of the person indicated as a 'witch', as a charge may be brought both under section 3 of the Act, because a 'witch' was indicated, and under section 9 of the Act, because the diviner accepted payment for his services. Both counts would, however, usually be treated as one when it comes to sentence.

Beliefs in wizardry and magic are also relevant to the case where the beliefs serve to explain the actions of the person accused or of other persons whose conduct is at issue. Thus, such beliefs may be adduced as a mitigating factor as they were in the case of *R v Kani* (p. 166) which was a murder trial where a man was accused of killing a relative because he thought that she was a 'witch'; or they may be adduced as an aggravating circumstance as in the case of *R v Garayi* (p. 210) where evidence was led that a chief assaulted the complainant because he thought he was a 'witch', it being the duty of the chief to prevent such assaults.

The traditional concepts of morality and the attitude of the courts diverge most strongly in cases brought under the Witchcraft Suppression Act. For example, a person accused under section 3 of the Act imputing to another person the use of non-natural means in causing harm, normally regards himself in the light of a person who has done a service to the community. The person deserving of punishment is, in his eyes, the person indicated as a 'witch'. The Act aims at suppressing the activities of diviners, a class of person which the Rhodesian African regards as beneficial to the welfare of the community; the Act leaves unpunished the 'witch' who, in his opinion, belongs to a class which should be treated with the utmost rigour of the law.

In cases of violence and other common law offences the attitude of the African public and of the courts does not usually differ as greatly as it does where cases are brought under this Act. A court will here usually regard an intent to practise sorcery as being the worst of motives for committing a crime, and a genuinely held belief that a person has been bewitched, as a mitigating factor. Thus in the case of *R v William* the accused, who committed a murder in order to obtain human flesh as medicine for gambling, was sentenced to death by the High Court sitting at Umtali (2/10/57). It is unlikely that any court would hold there were any mitigating circumstances in a case such as this which would justify the imposition of a sentence less than death and none were found here. William would have been regarded as a sorcerer by the African population. On the other hand in *R v Dawu* (p. 45) where the accused was charged with killing the child of a person whom she thought was a witch and had killed her own child, the belief in witchcraft was regarded by the court as a mitigating factor and Dawu was sentenced by the High Court sitting at Fort Victoria to only two years' imprisonment (2/8/60). Belief in witchcraft cannot, however, constitute a defence to the charge. Thus a person charged with murdering another whom he thought to be a witch cannot plead his belief as a defence. Under customary law if the person was 'known' to be a witch the killing would, presumably, not have been unlawful.

It is not only where wizardry beliefs are strictly relevant to the case in hand that they may come before the courts. Sometimes the evidence given may be, on the face of it, very much against the interests of the person giving it. In such cases the motive in leading the evidence is usually one personal to the person concerned. The evidence is, in fact, not given for the benefit of the court but for the gallery. These cases are, perhaps, the most interesting of all, although they form a small minority of the cases examined. If the evidence were entirely irrelevant it would be excluded by the court, so this sort of evidence is usually of doubtful relevance rather than entirely irrelevant. An example of such a case is *Mazwita's case* (p. 49). Here the accused could merely have admitted to poisoning the deceased, if they had wanted to admit to the crime. There was no necessity for them to give an account of the manner in which they flew through the air and of the familiars they possessed. This type of case, and the problem of the confession of witchcraft to the court, will be discussed in greater detail in the following pages.

CHAPTER II

THE PROBLEM OF THE CONFESSION OF
WITCHCRAFT

I SHALL, now and then, have occasion to make use of confessions of witchcraft made by persons either in court or during the course of investigations into the commission of criminal offences. Of cases containing records of such confessions three are so important that it is necessary to give a full account of them. They are cases in which a certain amount of repetition of evidence is unavoidable

The Problem of the Confession of Witchcraft

since the nature and extent of the corroboration of one witness's account by another is of the very greatest importance. It must not be assumed that such cases come often before the courts; they do not, but they are of value not only for the study of witchcraft beliefs in Rhodesia but also for the understanding of the records of those cases in Europe during the Middle Ages and elsewhere where similar confessions of witchcraft have been made. In the cases of *R v Dawu, R v Mazwita and Others* and *R v Rosi*, which are of this type, there is no need to reproduce the purely formal evidence, that of the investigating officer that he arrested the accused, saw the body and drew a plan; the evidence of the Government Medical Officer that he conducted a post-mortem, etc; but otherwise I have endeavoured to give a fairly full account of the evidence.

R v Dawu. The accused in this case, an African woman, was found guilty by the High Court sitting at Fort Victoria on the 2nd of August, 1960. The following extracts are, however, taken from the record of the preparatory examination held at Nuanetsi on the 25th of March, 1960 for, as so often happens, the High Court record was not transcribed. Dawu was charged with the murder of Shani, the child of a woman called Muhlava. Dawu had had a child whom she believed had been killed by Muhlava, although when the body of the child was examined at post-mortem no sign of any injury was found. The motive for the crime was apparently revenge. The 'warned and cautioned' statement of the accused explained how the murder came about. Dawu told the police:

'I was pregnant by my husband and had a baby which died recently. When I gave birth to the child she was unable to suck and I brought her to the kraal of my parents. The child was still not able to suck at my parent's kraal and I was made to state the name of my boy friends with whom I had had sexual intercourse. This took place in the kraal of my husband's parents and I voluntarily told native woman Maswirira —the mother of my husband—about this child because I wanted my child to be well. Native female Muhlava told me that I should not mention out the names of all my lovers because this was my first born and it was better for the first born to die. Muhlava then took a razor blade and cut me on my right breast and put *muti* (medicine) into the cuts (indicates several small healed marks on the bottom of the right breast). She then told me not to mention her name to other people as she had done this for me. I came to Muhlava's shelter in the lands and I slept there. On the following morning Muhlava said she was going to report the death of my child to chief Neshuro. Muhlava went to chief Neshuro before the sun rose and left me asleep with my young sister Wami. When I remained asleep . . . I woke up Wami and told her to go and get some fire. She went and got up. Before Wami returned from the place where she got the fire I got up and took that stick (a pole for stamping maize) and struck Shani twice with it. Shani was sleeping at the time when I hit her on the back of her neck. I saw that my child was dead and my heart was sore. I struck Shani that she might also be dead. I killed Shani because it was Muhlava the mother of Shani who had killed my child also. Because I killed Shani we can all cry together. Muhlava told me it was better for the first born to die. She tried to take the child from me but I refused. She conquered me and took the child from my arms. She held it by the legs and struck its head once against the ground. The child was alive when she did this and this caused it to die. She then handed it back to me. In addition to this Muhlava told me that she did not have her first born, meaning that her first born had died and mine should also die. This happened when Muhlava and I were being two alone on Sunday at the kraal of my husband's parents . . . After I had killed Muhlava's child I told her I had done it and it was all finished and no one could say that either of us should pay something to the other.'

Muhlava's evidence was as follows:

'I reside at Chidava kraal under chief Neshuro. I am the third wife of the dead kraal head Chidava. I am the third wife and I have six children by my husband but only three are still living. The last one to die was the deceased Shani, the other two died from natural causes. I have no belief that the first child should die or be put to death. I know the accused, she is the daughter of my husband's second wife.

Before my menstrual periods began I visited a certain woman whose name was Tsatsawani in order that she might instruct me in midwifery and sex matters in general. This lasted for about a month. At the end of the course some beer was brewed to mark the end of the course. On that day Tsatsawani took me down to the river and there cooked some porridge and put into it little things which looked like small black stones. It was all to do with witchcraft. I slept in Tsatsawani's room and later that night I saw a light in the doorway. There was a fire outside the door and I went outside. There I saw two things but I do not know what they were. On the following day I was sick. Tsatsawani said that this was a sign that we should do witchcraft together. This is all at the end of my course. I then went home to my kraal. I was at this time a member of the Zionist church. I was also sick. I went to the church and asked about my sickness. I testified as to what I had seen on the night at the end of the course with Tsatsawani. I was told that I was a witch. I believed this. Some months after this I married Chidava. My first born was Machanja. At about six months he became ill, he cried, and eventually the boy passed away. I went with my husband to find out the cause of this death to Tsumele, a witch doctor. Tsumele said that the child had been bewitched by the people of the country.

I know a native woman by the name of Chirunga (i.e. Tsatsawani), she is a witch. We go about at night bewitching people. We have gone out five times. The accused came to my huts one day and said she wanted to be friendly with me. Later she came again and we went to the fields and there I made certain incisions on the accused on the hips. I applied some magic to these cuts, some white medicine. This is the same stuff that Tsatsawani had given me some years previously. The accused was at this time quite a young girl, she was not married and was still living with her parents. I explained to Dawu, the accused, that this meant she was now a witch. I explained that we should go about at night bewitching people. Once I went out with Chirunga and the accused to see my husband. They both came to my hut, that is the accused and Chirunga. They came riding hyenas at night. We all went to my husband's hut. They came with me in order to bewitch my husband Chidava. This was also to teach the accused. I cannot explain the reason for this, it only comes to us in a dream. We poured some *maheo* or sweet beer into Chidava's mouth, there was bewitching medicine in it. We then sprinkled some more medicine on his body. We then left and went to bed. The accused and Chirunga then took their hyenas and rode away into the night. Three days later my husband died. A little later my two friends, the accused and Chirunga, came at night on hyenas and we all went to the place where the body was buried. We exhumed the body of my husband, we skinned the body, we cut a piece of meat and took it to my hut. We reinterred the body in the grave. At the hut we cooked the meat and ate it, it was good. We departed then. Some time later we three went to visit Meke, the brother of Chidava. We all rode hyenas. Near the kraal we talked amongst ourselves and decided to kill Meke. We went into the village and we found him sleeping. We each of us laid hands on him. The next morning Meke was ill. The kraal head then came to us and said that we should not bewitch the man Meke so we relented and Meke lived. After this the accused married and went to live in Maranda's area. Quite recently myself and the mother of the accused were attending a beer drink. A report was made to us by Maswirira. Two days later I went to visit the accused in chief Maranda's area. I went at night on a hyena's back. I stood outside the hut where the accused was sleeping. The infant was in the accused's arms. I got hold of the legs of the infant and the accused the arms. We pulled the baby and later I rode off on my hyena. I wanted the child to bewitch the child. We wanted to bewitch the child—I cannot tell the reason because it only came to us as if we were dreaming. We fought over the child. We wanted to bewitch the child so it would die. We wanted to eat it. The child was never dropped during the struggle. I then returned to my kraal.

At this time I was living in the lands in the shelter protecting the crops. I was alone with my three children, Wani, Shani, Musiwo. Shani is the deceased in this case. I remained at this shelter for three days after seeing the accused. At night on the fourth day after the visit the accused and her Mother came to see me. Kayasi, the Mother of the accused, brought the child and put it down in front of the doorway and left without saying anything. Dawu remained. I asked why she had come. She indicated that the child was sick and was not sucking. It was her intention to stay at the shelter. I reported to my brother Dana that there was a person with a sick child in the hut. He came to the hut and later left. On the next day I went to the kraal head Zwidzai Chidawa. Dawu, her mother, Meke, Zwidzai and myself were there. The purpose of this meeting was to decide about Dawu bringing the child to my hut. This meeting decided that I should stay with the accused. On the night of the following day the accused's infant died. At the time the infant died the accused was sitting at the door of the shelter nursing the child. The child actually died in my presence. I sent the accused with Wani to report to the headman. They returned to the hut but the Headman did not come. We spent the whole day with the dead child and on the next day I went to report to chief Neshuro. I went before sunrise with Musiwa leaving Dawu, Wani and Shani in the shelter. They were all sleeping outside the hut when I left. My two children were together but Dawu was apart from them, there was a fire between them. Dawu was awake when I left but the two children were asleep. I told Dawu where I was going. He sent his son to report to the manager at the Neshuro sub-office. I returned to the hut in the lands. I met Msesenyani on the way. He made a report. On my arrival I found that my child was dead, Shani was dead. Dana was present, also Meke and in a little while accused arrived with her mother. Wani was in the garden crying. I did not examine Shani, I could not bring myself to examine the body. I was upset. The policeman for the chief was also present. In due course, after the arrival of the

The Problem of the Confession of Witchcraft

accused and her mother, the chief, Neshuro, and the messenger from the sub office arrived . . . The accused could have bewitched my child instead of hitting it on the head like a beast.'

Another of the self-styled witches who gave evidence in this case was Chirunga Tsatsawani whose evidence largely corroborates Muhlava's:

'I am Chirunga Tsatsawani. I live in Chidava kraal under chief Neshuro. I know the accused, her sister is married to my husband. I have known her for a long time. We, that is, myself, the accused and Muhlava are all witches. After I had five children I began to practise witchcraft. I was invited by Muhlava to go to Chidava's kraal one night. We rode hyenas. Arriving at the kraal we tied the hyenas to the trees and we entered the kraal. We took some white magic (i.e. white in colour). We entered Chidava's house and made some marks with the mixture on his body joints. We were bewitching him. Dawu and myself untied the hyenas and rode home. A few days later Chidava died. On the night of the burial of Chidava we went to the grave, that is myself, Muhlava and Dawu. We exhumed the body and cut off a piece of meat and the remainder we returned to the grave. We took the piece of meat to Muhlava's hut and cooked and ate it. Dawu and myself returned home after this. A few days later Meke was sick. We had gone to his kraal and bewitched him. We had gone to his kraal leaving our hyenas hitched outside the kraal. We entered Meke's hut and found him asleep. We applied some white magic to his legs and later took our hyenas and returned to our kraal. The purpose of the bewitching was to kill Meke. Meke became sick. Later Chavani spoke to us and said that we had bewitched Meke and that we must stop it. We went back to his kraal at night and decided to draw off the spell—"we" being myself, the accused and Muhlava. We did not go out again in this way. I know of no difference of opinion between Muhlava and the accused. I know there is a practice of witches killing their first born but it is not universally followed.'

R v Mazwita and Others. Mazwita, Puna and Netsayi, three Karanga women, were committed for trial at Bikita on the 10th of February, 1959, and were subsequently indicted before the High Court sitting at Fort Victoria on a charge of attempted murder, alternatively of contravening section 7 of the Witchcraft Suppression Act. They were acquitted on the 17th March, 1959. The following extracts are taken from the record of the preparatory examination. The deceased in this case was named Mukozho and the evidence of Revandi, otherwise known as Dendere, explains how it was that he died:

'I am kraal head of Dendere kraal. All three accuseds are resident at my kraal. As far as I know all are friendly to one another. Mukozho was the husband of Mazwita. Netsayi is married and Puna is a widow. I know of no trouble between Mazwita and her husband Mukozho. Mukozho first became sick about the beginning of October. I saw him, his stomach was swollen as well as his legs. He made complaints about his sickness. I saw him regularly after this. He appeared to get worse. He was at that time resident at the kraal. He moved to a different hut in the kraal. His condition did not improve. I do not know if he went elsewhere. In native belief if a person moves from his own hut to another it means that he hopes to recover there. By this time I inferred that Mukozho thought that he had been bewitched and moved there to get out of the influence of the person bewitching him (note by court; witness very reluctant to give the meaning of *kusengudza*). Mukozho then returned to his son's hut, Jim alias Sangurayi. He did not return to his wife's hut. I infer from this that Mukozho thought that the cause of illness originated in his hut. I remember the 4th of December, 1958. Mukozho was still alive but very sick. His legs, stomach and face were swollen. He had open sores on his lips. He could not walk and was able to sit up for a short while only. I was called by Zivinayi. I went to Mukozho who was outside the hut. Present was Mazwita amongst others. Mazwita asked me to call a *dare* (formal gathering) and that she wanted Puna and Netsayi to be present. I called a *dare* as requested. The three accuseds were present and various elders including Sangurayi alias Jim. The *dare* was held outside the hut where the deceased was lying. The door of the hut was open. It is likely that the deceased Mukozho would have heard what was said. Mazwita spoke at the *dare* saying that Puna and Netsayi should make thin porridge to give to her husband Mukozho as they had bewitched him. Puna and Netsayi denied this (that they were witches) but later admitted. Mazwita said that she had given Mukozho *muti* (medicine). She did not say what. Puna said that she had given Mukozho the skin of a snake and Netsayi said she had given the heart of a crocodile, which she said had been given her by Puna. Mazwita said that this medicine had been ground, mixed with beer and poured into the mouth of the sleeping Mukozho. The other two agreed to this. Each of the three accuseds then went to make thin porridge. I saw each of the accuseds go to the hut of Mukozho with the thin porridge. Puna went first, then Mazwita and then Netsayi. The giving of thin porridge in native belief means that the giver has bewitched the person and that person is now unbewitching him. It is a well known belief. I reported what had occurred to Chief Mkanganwe on Saturday the 6th of December and he gave me certain instructions. Mukozho, on my return, was taken to the clinic—two days later. I was at the clinic on the 8th of December, 1958 and found that Mukozho had died and was present at his burial on the 9th of December.'

The death of Mukozho was reported to the police, who considered it possible that Mukozho had been poisoned, and the three accused were arrested. All of them made long statements of an extraordinary character to the police. It is, I think, fair to say that they boasted of their nefarious activities. Mazwita's statement reads as follows:

'We discussed together being three of us, Puna, Netsayi and myself. Puna suggested that we give my husband, the deceased, some beer containing medicine. The medicine was to bewitch him that he should die. It was arranged between us that we would all give certain portions of our own medicine and that this should be mixed together and given to my husband in beer. We each produced our medicine, I produced pounded roots of a bush which has no proper name but is known locally as *mushonga* (medicine) for bewitching by night. Puna produced powder which she stated was the ground skin of a snake and Netsayi produced a powder which she alleged was the heart of a crocodile. I had not seen the actual snake or the actual heart of the crocodile. These three portions were mixed and placed in an open calabash. We took a little beer in a lid of a billy can and poured this on the roots and powders —that is not correct—we poured a little beer into the billy can lid and then mixed the roots and powders in this beer. The three of us went to the hut where my husband was sleeping. He was on his left side and we turned him so that he lay on his back with his head slightly on one side. Puna held my husband's mouth open and I made him drink. After he had drunk we laid him in the position in which we had found him. We covered him with a blanket and then left him. I remained with my husband, nothing more we did. I then later found the deceased was ill—after four days. I felt pain in my heart when my husband was being ill. I realized that he was being ill because of what we had given him that night. I then told the other two that we should unbewitch my husband and I brought the other two women before the *dare*, before Dendere. I told the elders at the *dare* how we had bewitched my husband and pointed to Puna and Netsayi and told them that we should now unbewitch my husband. Puna went away first. She made a thin porridge and brought it, giving it to my husband. Netsayi also did the same. I also made thin porridge and gave it to my husband. The persons then attending the *dare* left. In front of the members of the *dare* before they left I told Puna and Netsayi that their porridge did not contain the medicine to unbewitch my husband. This was on the next day. They both refused to make the thin porridge a second time and left to their own huts. Later Puna agreed to make this second lot of porridge and gave it to my husband. I gave him a lot more. Netsayi did not make a second lot of thin porridge. The kraal head then suggested that he take the matter to the chief as he could settle the matter. He told me he was going to see chief Mkanganwe. The following day the chief's police boy arrived who instructed us to report to the chief's *dare* the next day together with the kraal head Dendere. The headman Dendere related the story to chief Mkanganwe in the way that I had told him. The chief asked if what the headman had told him was correct. I agreed that it was. Puna was also asked by chief Mkanganwe whether the story was correct and she also agreed. Netsayi would not admit to chief Mkanganwe in my presence.'

Netsayi's statement to the police is, if anything, even more extraordinary than Mazwita's. Puna's is very similar to Mazwita's. The following is Netsayi's statement:

'I live in the same kraal as Mazwita and Puna. I have been very friendly with these two women for the last two years. Early this year, 1958, Puna approached me and asked whether she could give me *mushonga* (medicine) to enable me to "travel by night", that is, to be able to bewitch people. I agreed to this and was instructed to meet her and Mazwita at a certain place in the bush near the kraal in the vicinity of three trees. Mazwita was present at the time when I received these instructions. That same night after dark I went to the area of the three trees and there I met Puna and Mazwita. I had previously been given instructions to appear at that place naked. This I did and found that both Puna and Mazwita were in the same condition. I was instructed to sit down with my back to one of the trees with my knees bent. Puna then approached me. I could see her rubbing something in her hands and this appeared to be a white ointment. She rubbed this ointment all over my face and as she did so she said that she wanted me to accompany them in their night excursions so that we should be three. I felt things going very dark and felt as if I wanted to vomit. We all

The Problem of the Confession of Witchcraft

three then left the area and I returned to my hut and washed my face. I was never called again until a few days before the inauguration of chief Mkanganwe. This was carried out on October the 4th, making it about September the 28th. I remember it was Sunday evening. I was in the hut after dark. My husband was in the hut with me but was sleeping. I heard Mazwita call me from outside the hut. I went out and saw Mazwita and Puna. They were naked. I was also naked as I had taken off my clothes before retiring to bed. I had walked to the door with a blanket around me but I was told by Puna that I was to leave the blanket as we were all three going out to bewitch. I followed the two other women to the area of the trees previously mentioned. I sat with my back to the original tree and the other two women sat with their backs to their respective trees. Puna then came to me and handed me powder from her hands. I took it in my hand. Puna then told me that this was powdered crocodile heart and it was used for killing people. The three of us then came together and I saw Mazwita was holding the billycan. I could not see sufficiently well to observe what it was. Puna did the same and then I placed the powder which had been given me by Puna into the lid. Mazwita carried the lid and then the can and we all returned to the kraal. The three of us entered the hut of Mazwita. Mukozho, the deceased, was lying on the floor asleep on his side. I assisted Puna in holding the deceased's body upright. It was then that I saw Mazwita with the billycan lid which I now saw contained what appeared to be beer. She held this to the deceased's mouth and forced him to drink the contents. He appeared to be asleep. He drank all the contents. I had seen the deceased the day before when he complained of feeling cold. He said this to his wife in my presence. It had been a hot day. Prior to this, however, he had given no sign that he was ill. After the beer had been given to the deceased, Puna and I returned to our respective huts. After this night the deceased became ill. I had received a report to this effect and about a week later I went to see him. His arms, face and legs were swollen and his stomach was distended. He spoke to me and complained that he had a "snake in his stomach" and pains in his legs. I had gone to see him because he was sick. In native custom if I had not done so other people would begin to ask why I had not gone and to suggest that I was causing the sickness. I did not tell other people that he had been bewitched because his wife Mazwita had told me not to. I know that the deceased *sengudza'd* himself (moved to escape influence of witchcraft) from the kraal. This again is native belief, that is, that a person who is ill and who thinks that he is being bewitched will remove himself or cause himself to be removed from the kraal and close confines of the witchcraft to another kraal. I cannot remember what kraal but his wife would. I was present when after two weeks deceased returned to the kraal. He was still sick and if anything was worse. The health of the deceased deteriorated until Thursday the 4th of December when Mazwita called Puna and myself before the kraal head Dendere. At this *dare* which was held Mazwita told everyone present that we three had bewitched the deceased and were causing his illness. She asked Puna and myself to prepare thin porridge. By native custom this is done to unbewitch a person and would contain medicine to make the sick person better. I made the porridge but did not put in it medicine as I was not given any and did not know what it consisted of or where it was obtained. I did not see Puna making the porridge but later saw her giving some to the deceased. I did not see Mazwita giving the porridge. When I gave the deceased some porridge he appeared to know what was going on. He spoke to me and said that if this was medicine and I was giving it to him for unbewitching him it was a good thing. The deceased was not present at the *dare* itself. He was then lying in a hut close by. I think he could have heard what was being said had he been able to. At this *dare* Puna at first denied that we had bewitched the deceased. Puna then admitted and I admitted later at chief Mkanganwe's *dare*. I later heard that the deceased had died. I believe the medicine that we had given him caused his death. I wish to rectify a certain fact that I have previously mentioned in this statement. I had, in fact, been "travelling by night" with Puna and Mazwita six times. On each occasion we travelled about naked and we appeared to travel through the air. I remember three kraals we visited—Mukobvu, Makota and Dendere, where we live. We were looking for someone to bewitch but on each occasion could not find anyone. I was never given any charms or other medicines by Puna and Mazwita. I used to accompany them when they took food to this cave with which to feed their evil spirits. The food was usually *sadza* (maize porridge). I saw these evil spirits on three occasions. If the spirits were not present when we arrived then Puna and Mazwita would call them by their names—Jack, Robayi and Majika etc. There were no charms or such things in this cave. I indicated the cave and the three trees to the police at the kraal on the 12th of December. I know that the deceased had refused to buy or give new clothes to his wife Mazwita. I have never seen her dressed in new clothes. Deceased's other wife is about the same age as Mazwita. I do not know whether the first wife has clothes. I saw the root that Mazwita indicated to the police on the 12th of December. I have never seen it before.'

Netsayi in the last portion of her statement mentions the indica-

The Problem of the Confession of Witchcraft

tions she and the others made on the 12th of December, 1958. On this occasion Constable M. Farrow and his African assistant Sergeant Willis were present and their statements are of interest as the accused seem to have been eager to impart information. Constable M. Farrow told the court:

'On the afternoon of Friday the 12th of December, 1958 I went to Dendere kraal together with the three accused. There Mazwita freely and voluntarily took me to a place in the bush close to the kraal on the side of a kopje. She made certain indications and indicated a plant growing at that place. African Constable Smart who was with me interpreted and took possession of this plant. I returned with it to the kraal. Mazwita and Puna argued about this root at the kraal. As a result of a report made to me by African Sergeant Willis I accompanied Mazwita to another place in the bush close to the kraal in the opposite direction to that previously taken where Mazwita indicated to me another bush of the vine type. Constable Smart took possession of this bush. With the three accused I went to the top of a small kopje close to the kraal. There they indicated to me a certain small hole in the ground in the form of a small cave. An adult human would not fit into it. Mazwita and Puna made certain indications to me freely and voluntarily. Mazwita with her hand to her mouth shouted "Jacko, Jacko, Jacko" and another name which I cannot recall. Puna at another hole nearby with her hands to her mouth called another name which I took to be "Rovesayi". She called several times. I gained the impression they were calling somebody. There was no one there. We returned and went towards a stream. There the accuseds indicated to me three trees. The trees were close together in a group in an open place. They were not large. Each accused went and leant against a tree . . . I carried out a search of the accused's huts. I found no impedimenta to suggest they practised witchcraft. On the top of the kopje I found in one of the "holes" a wicker fish trap. There was nothing inside it.'

African Sergeant Willis's account of the proceedings is as follows:

'Puna indicated a hole where she alleged she had put a snake skin. I did not find any such skin. Mazwita said that she wished to show me the root medicines with which she had killed her husband. African Constable Smart and Constable Farrow then left with Mazwita. They returned after a short time. Smart was carrying a small bush with root attached. Puna then said, on seeing the bush, that that was not the medicine which had been used to bewitch the deceased. Puna's outburst was spontaneous. Mazwita agreed that the bush was not the one. Constable Farrow, African Constable Smart and Mazwita then left again and later returned. Smart then was carrying a small bush with roots attached quite different from the first. Puna then agreed that that bush was the one. The three accuseds then took us to the top of a small kopje where a small hole was indicated by Puna and Netsayi. As far as I can remember there was only one hole with stones on top. Mazwita said that this was the place where they came to give food to their *zwidoma* (familiars). Puna agreed and Netsayi said that she had come to this place but that she had not yet been given any familiars. Mazwita called out three names—firstly "Jack" and two others I have forgotten —in a loud voice. She advised me that they were her *zwidoma*. Puna also called out in the same manner calling "Rorayi". She alleged that this was one of her *zwidoma*. We then came down from the kopje and three trees were indicated in an opening by each of the accused. Each indicated her tree and stood near the tree. Each stated that this was where they met before going on their "pursuit of witchcraft". They said that these excursions took place at night. Netsayi said that when she joined the other two accused in their witchcraft excursions she was initiated by having ointment rubbed in her face. She also indicated the position she was in when this ointment was rubbed on her face. Netsayi said that this ointment was so that she would not fear when "travelling at night".'

The root indicated by Mazwita as the substance she had used to kill Mukozho was identified as *Teramnus Labialis* (L.f.) Spring. Mazwita alleged that the medicine was prepared by taking off the outer skin of the main root, waiting until it became dry and grinding it into powder form. This powder would then be mixed with any fluid for the purpose of administering it. It was found not to be poisonous. Mazwita also indicated a small plant as an antidote and said it was administered in the same way as the previous medicines. It was this antidote that was given to deceased. The antidote was identified as *Acalpha Alenii* Hutch., and was also quite innocuous. The plant indicated by Puna when she challenged Mazwita's identification was, apparently, of the *Dolichos* species and, again, quite harmless. Nothing suspicious was revealed by the post-mortem on Mukozho although, of course, many organic poisons are hard to detect.

R v Rosi. The accused in this case was committed for trial at Nuanetsi, on the charge of contravening section 3 of the Witchcraft Suppression Act, on the 16th of March, 1962. The Attorney-General declined to prosecute since she had been charged with imputing to a certain Ngurirayi that she was a 'witch' and had harmed her by non-natural means and there was no evidence on the latter point. It is essential in the case of a prosecution under section 3 of the Act to prove that the imputation of 'witchcraft' includes the allegation that non-natural means have been used to harm another. To call a person a 'witch' is not, in itself, sufficient. The principal Crown witness was Rabson whose evidence reads:

'I live in Munhudagwa kraal, Chief Mawarire. Accused is my half sister. She lives in the same kraal as I do. Her husband has his own kraal. Accused actually lives in her husband's kraal. I recall about a month ago when accused gave birth to her baby. She was staying at my kraal. I was called to the hut during the birth. There were difficulties and she was still in labour and in pain. Birth had not actually taken place. In our custom if a woman has difficulty in labour she is asked to confess a secret she has in her heart. When I went into the hut I asked the accused to confess the secret she had as she was dying in childbirth. Accused replied that she had been bewitched. She said "I was bewitched by Ngurirayi. I was told by Ngurirayi that my first-born should not be alive but should be killed. I will become a proper witch and walk at night bewitching people." She said Ngurirayi had told her this. Soon after she had told me this the child was born without any more difficulties. In our custom a new born child must excrete to show that it is all right and will not be ill or in bad health. When the accused's child was born it excreted and passed urine and it appeared all right. A few days later it did not excrete properly so I asked the accused again what her secret was. She replied "Ngurirayi told me that I should kill my baby but I refused. Then Ngurirayi told me that I must kill my husband. I again refused. Ngurirayi then said she would kill me." Accused told me that Ngurirayi had given her a *chitukwani* (see p. 118), a crocodile, two snakes, a pole cat and a hyena. By saying this, accused implied that Ngurirayi was herself a witch. Only a witch can make another person a witch. Some days after the birth of this baby I called people to hear the accusation of the accused.'

The story is then continued by Hinani who was Ngurirayi's husband:

'I recall going to a meeting at the accused's huts. I was called by Rabson. Present was Fambi, Rabson, Chimbudzi and my wife Ngurirayi and the accused. At this meeting I heard accused say "I was given medicine by Ngurirayi. I was given red medicine. I was also given a hyena by Ngurirayi, also a pole cat and a *chitukwani*, also a crocodile." She then said Ngurirayi had given her these things so she could become a witch and work as a witch together with my wife Ngurirayi. Accused then said "Ngurirayi has told me to kill my baby and she and I will eat it together." She then said that Ngurirayi and she had eaten three of my children. She had done this with my wife. Four of my children have actually died. Only three of my children have survived. These children are mine by my wife Ngurirayi. Accused's baby was ill on that day and she wanted it to get better. My wife Ngurirayi denied that she meddled in witchcraft. Fambi then stood up and kicked my wife under the chin and she fell on her back. I did nothing to Fambi because my wife had been accused of bewitching the accused. I could not dispute the allegations. Accused had witnessed my wife's witchcraft, I accepted this testimony as being the truth. After the meeting, as a result of the accused's evidence, I took my wife to her parents and left her there. I have rejected her completely as I cannot live with a witch. I can never live with her again. In our custom a person who eats human flesh is a witch. I have never known my wife to have anything to do with witchcraft.'

The matter was investigated by the police and the following statement by the accused was recorded by the European investigating detail:

'The first day I was made a witch by Ngurirayi she told me that I should kill three of my babies before I could become a proper witch because she, Ngurirayi, had had to kill three of hers. This was before I had any babies of my own and before I was even married. During the time I was being made a witch by Ngurirayi I helped her to eat her three dead children. The son that I have now born is my first child and I am unwilling to kill him. That is why I have revealed my secret. I now want to give the *muti* (medicine), the snake, the crocodile, the hyena and the pole cat that Ngurirayi gave me when she made me a witch back to her.'

Although Rosi made no statement at the preparatory examination she persisted in alleging that Ngurirayi was a witch and cross-examined Ngurirayi, putting to her that she had brought a crocodile into Rosi's hut and made it walk and told Rosi to give her the new-born child so that she could hit it on the ground and kill it. Needless to say Ngurirayi denied these allegations.

One of the most interesting features of these three cases is that the persons who claimed to be witches, far from being reticent and ashamed of their calling, seem almost to be boasting of their activities. Accused persons are seldom particularly verbose when called upon to make a statement to the police, yet, in the case of *R v Mazwita and Others* all accused made lengthy statements and were, I believe, equally talkative at the trial. After the trial, the interpreter tells me, they invited him home with them so they could teach him to be a witch. He politely declined the invitation. These lengthy confessions of witchcraft are by no means confined to Africa. One is reminded of the confessions of European witches, such as that of Agnes Sampson before James I where similar psychic events were testified to (Wilson, 1944). Any explanation for these confessions must be such that it will account for similar confessions in communities widely separated in space and time.

The Shona and, apparently, also the Ndebele regard doctor-diviners as partaking of the nature of a witch. In the case of *R v Zalepi* (p. 114) there was evidence that the witness who admitted being a witch and eating part of the body of a child used some of the child's blood for a love potion. This, combined with other rather unusual features in the case, makes it extremely probable that the witness was in the process of building up a reputation as a particularly powerful *inyanga*. Such an explanation does not, however, account for the confessions in *Dawu's* and *Mazwita's cases*. Apart from the fact that there is not the slightest indication in the records of these cases to suggest such a motive, it is in the highest degree improbable that anyone should try to set up a community of doctor-diviners. A person wanting to become a *nganga* does not deliberately encourage competition, although he may take apprentices for a fee.

Any suggestion that the alleged witches were forced to confess is, I think, belied by the very nature of the confessions themselves. Forced confessions are generally grudgingly made and retracted as soon as the threat is removed. The confessions in *Dawu's* and *Mazwita's cases* were not of this nature and were first made in front of a definitely sceptical European policeman and then repeated or admitted in front of a European magistrate and later a European judge. As far as one can tell there is no reason to suppose that the police brought any pressure to bear on these people. There would, in any event, be no reason to bring pressure to bear on such talkative persons. Again, there seem to be no reasons one can suggest why the community in which these people were living should demand confessions of the sort which were made, for—even if a confession were demanded—a mere confession of witchcraft lacking in circumstantial detail would suffice.

While, no doubt, no normal, well-adjusted person would give the evidence these alleged witches gave, there is no reason to suppose that any of them was insane. Certainly they were considered sane enough to give evidence or to stand trial and, in any event, it is hardly possible that a group of women in one village should be similarly attacked by identical forms of the same mental disorder.

When I asked an intelligent Zezuru informant why it was that women confessed to being witches he stated without hesitation that this was done to enhance the status of the alleged witch. To be feared has, after all, many advantages. He stated that it was only the old who would confess to being a witch and this confession would become a family secret as it is not the sort of thing that a family likes to admit. For a young woman, on the other hand, the confession of witchcraft could only bring odium. He thought a woman would, of course, only confess to witchcraft if she were a witch.

In *Puna's* and *Mazwita's cases* the women concerned were not, however, all elderly women. In *Puna's case* the persons seem, indeed, to have been relatively young married women. In *Mazwita's case,* Mazwita was aged about forty years and Puna, who was a married woman, a little older. Netsayi was a widow and aged about twenty five. Mazwita and Puna were, therefore, by the standards of a rural African community, fairly old. The reason why it would seem that, ordinarily, it is the old who may confess to witchcraft and not the young lies in the nature of the Shona family structure. I shall discuss the position of a young married woman in her husband's village later (p. 151). Very often she is a virtual stranger living in a potentially hostile environment. If she confessed to witchcraft she would, almost certainly, be driven away. An elderly woman, on the other hand, may be very much in the position of mother or grandmother to most of the people about her and, her position being secure, she could afford to make such a confession. The reason why in the cases under discussion comparatively young women made confessions of witchcraft must surely be because several women were prepared to confess to being witches and, accordingly, no one was likely to take action against one witch for fear that the others might exact vengeance. Because the European authorities were present and could intervene if the matter were reported to them, which would be almost inevitable were concerted action taken against all three witches, it was relatively safe for a person to confess to witchcraft.

The reasons which might motivate a woman to attempt to enhance her status by making a confession of witchcraft are doubtless many; but in the cases of Dawu and Muhlava it would appear they had both lost children, and, therefore, in the eyes of their husbands and their groups would probably have been women of little account, for a very high value is placed on the bearing of children and their successful upbringing. It should be appreciated that although Shona women are by no means chattels their legal status is basically one of minority. Status must not be understood as meaning quite the same thing when dealing with customary law as when the word is used when referring to the common law; but on the whole it is probably fair to say that, with certain exceptions, women retain the status of minors throughout their lives being either under the tutelage of their husbands or members of their husband's lineage, or of their fathers or a senior agnate of their father's group. To what extent the legal status under customary law coincides with the actual status of a woman living in a village depends on a number of factors and, in particular, on the personalities of the persons concerned. In approaching the problem of the witchcraft confession it must be remembered that it is very difficult for a woman to enhance her political or social position in the community. It is true that the political importance of elderly women should not be underestimated but, on the whole, all political office is closed to women; although there were certain exceptions in the past such as the women who were sub-chiefs under the Manyika chief, Mutasa. If there is a doctor-diviner willing to teach her she might become a *nyahana* (female doctor) and, in the towns, there are a number of women who, through their trading activities, have acquired a considerable measure of independence, as have also the urban prostitutes.

However, for a woman in a country district, there are few avenues open through which she can increase her status and the temptation to enhance it by calling herself a witch and earning the respect that fear brings must exist.

I do not wish to suggest from the above that the status of all women is the same, for the social position of a woman in the community is enhanced by marriage and the bearing of children, but their position is in no way analogous to that of men. Men can increase their status by creating their own homesteads and becoming village heads in their own right; by marrying many women and having many children and by binding others to them through the web of kinship and so become powerful, even though they may not be eligible to become chiefs. For a woman these avenues to power are largely closed. Presumably a woman who is happily married and allowed reasonable freedom of action by her husband is unlikely to make a confession of witchcraft; but if she is not, then the frustrations aroused by her subordinate position may lead her to do something dramatic. In addition to persons who deliberately seek to enhance their status by confessions of witchcraft there are probably persons who confess who are emotionally unstable and vent their feelings of frustration by seeking to cause a sensation. A parallel in our own society would be those who confess to committing sensational murders that they did not commit.

Rosi's confessions are, perhaps, of a somewhat different nature. Her first confession was made on an occasion when a confession was expected, that is, during the course of a difficult labour. Holleman (1952, p. 216) has discussed the nature of Shona beliefs in this regard. The usual confession expected is one of marital infidelity and failure to make the confession is believed to prolong the confinement and imperil the life of the baby. Considerable pressure is often brought to bear by the midwives to force the expectant mother to confess. This practice is quite frequently mentioned in criminal trials since the confession often provokes violence.

It is clear that Rosi disliked Ngurirayi. For Rosi to confess to being a witch and to indicate Ngurirayi as being a witch also would have had the advantages of avoiding a confession of adultery, which she may have been reluctant to make, either because she wished to protect herself or a lover or because she had been faithful to her husband and could not make a true confession, and of settling an old score with Ngurirayi. Whether these reasons, in fact, motivated her is difficult to say. The odium attaching to a witch is greater than the odium attaching to an adulteress. If Rosi's intention was to get rid of Ngurirayi she certainly succeeded in her object.

The three cases recorded here illustrate the difficulty of deciding where the shadowy boundary between truth and fantasy lies. The general impression of the prosecutors in both *Dawu's case* and *Mazwita's case* was that the women were not deliberately lying. In *Dawu's case* there can be no doubt that Dawu hit the child Shani with a stamping pole, but in *Mazwita's case* one cannot be certain whether Mukozho was poisoned or not. Certainly the police seem to have thought he was poisoned and to have discounted the supernatural aspects of the case, but the High Court acquitted, and in my view the administering of the medicine was as psychic an act as the ride through the air.

The next striking feature of the evidence is the degree of coroboration between the various witnesses. Muhlava (p. 47) stated in her evidence 'I cannot explain the reason for this (the bewitching of Chidava) it only comes to us in a dream.' Again (p. 48) she said 'We wanted to bewitch the child—I cannot tell the reason because it only came to us as if we were dreaming.' However, one can hardly postulate a communal dream to account for the similarity between various witnesses' evidence. There had undoubtedly been an exchange of ideas between the women involved in *Dawu's* and *Mazwita's cases* and this exchange took place in all probability prior to their arrest or detention for questioning as statements were recorded from them at an early stage of investigation by the police. The problem is what form the association took. In Part II I shall discuss witchcraft beliefs and will show that the Shona believe that a witch is a witch because she is possessed by certain spirits, often *shave* (wandering) spirits. Informants do not treat as ridiculous the idea that some sort of ritual is performed by witches to placate the spirits, such ritual being, of course, performed secretly. However, there is not a scrap of evidence in these cases, nor in any other cases which I have examined, to indicate that such a ritual takes place and one would certainly have expected witnesses as voluble as Netsayi and the others to have mentioned it. It would seem to form no part of Shona belief that the spirits of a witch can be placated in any other way than by conducting oneself as a witch and by killing if told to do so. Such association as there was seems, thus, to have been purely one of friendship. The women concerned were certainly friends.

An interesting feature of *Dawu's case* is the breakdown of witchcraft and the use of physical force by Muhlava and Dawu to accomplish their ends. Because of this the evidence of witchcraft is largely irrelevant for the purposes of the case. Muhlava's reply, probably to the question, 'Could not Dawu have killed your child by witchcraft?' is of interest; for by saying 'The accused could have bewitched my child instead of hitting it on the head like a beast' (p. 49), she would seem to imply that her feelings would have been less outraged if the child had been killed by witchcraft than they were as a result of the child having been killed by brute force. While I have not been able to establish whether the Shona regard killing by witchcraft as a crime somewhat less serious than murder as known to the law, for any informant would deny that there is a difference in moral guilt, there is little doubt that no killing by witchcraft could have originated feuds as bitter as that which runs through the history of, say, the Mangwende chieftaincy. Killings by witchcraft are usually soon forgotten, it is the killings by violence that become part of tribal or family history. On the other hand the emotional reaction to an accusation of witchcraft is often greater than that which results from a knifing. It is probably correct to say that witchcraft, being uncanny, is feared more than physical force and the immediate emotional reaction when a witch is discovered is accordingly frequently greater than when a murderer is found, but there is a certain lack of conviction that the person accused is, in fact, the witch. The reaction to a witch resembles, in other words, the ordinary man's reaction to a snake which one kills without any too close inquiry as to whether it is poisonous or not.

The problem of the confession of witchcraft calls for explanation not only in sociological but also in psychological terms. I am not competent to express views on the latter, but there may be some sort of linkage on the occasion between such confessions and nutrition. Smartt (1964, p. 9) found that confusional states were extremely common in Rhodesia and were related to malnutrition. Such states were usually accompanied by the idea of bewitchment or punishment by the ancestors. In Ghana confessions of witchcraft are common at the various spirit shrines. Field (1960, p. 149ff) would ascribe the majority of such confessions to the mental state of 'depression', although they can occur also as an accompaniment of a variety of mental disorders.

PART II

THE NATURE OF WIZARDRY BELIEFS
(with particular reference to the Shona)

CHAPTER III

THE BASIS OF WIZARDRY BELIEFS

BELIEF in wizardry provides a solution to the problem of causation. It is not, of course, the only solution. Wizardry is regarded by the Shona as a cause of death, illness or misfortune. They believe that these things can be caused by other agencies as well. Their belief in wizardry must be understood in the context of their other beliefs. The basic assumption of the believer in wizardry, which is also one of the basic assumptions of the believers in most religions, is that misfortune and death do not occur fortuitously but are caused by some external agency. Whether people believe in a God or gods or in the ancestral spirits or the forces of nature these entities are usually regarded as being essentially good. While most gods or spirits may become angry if provoked it is thought that they do not punish wantonly or capriciously. So, at least, is the approach of the Shona. It is easier to see in misfortunes the machinations of one's fellow men than the work of those beings or forces upon whom one's religion centres. One lives in close contact with other people and to suppose that some of them wish to harm you is not unreasonable and, indeed, may be fully justified. If he may attempt to harm you by physical means may he not also attempt to harm you by non-natural means? It is only in the last hundred years or so in our own society that we have been able to draw fairly clearly the line between what is scientifically possible and what is not. Certainly no person without some knowledge of modern science is likely to appreciate fully the difference between the mysterious action of a poison, such as arsenic, and the mysterious action of a medicine used for sorcery. If the one can kill why should not the other?

I do not wish it to be understood that the African cannot think 'scientifically' but only that many of his fundamental hypotheses are, objectively speaking, erroneous.

Increasing scientific knowledge does not necessarily destroy beliefs in wizardry. The African knows perfectly well that lightning strikes during a thunderstorm or that snakes are poisonous, and that if lightning strikes a man or a snake bites him he is likely to die; but this knowledge does not solve the problem as to why the lightning or snake should have killed the particular person in question. The knowledge that disease is caused by bacteria still does not solve the problem as to why the disease was 'sent'.

Sceptics are found in all societies and African society is no exception. However strong beliefs in wizardry, these beliefs would be unlikely to persist if no 'proof' were offered as to their truth. In our society many people believe in ghosts because of the considerable number of allegedly authentic stories of haunting that are told and retold, usually at second hand. Similarly, African beliefs are strengthened by stories that are told to 'prove' that witchcraft exists. Some of these stories will serve to illustrate aspects of belief. An example is the story told of a man who lived in the Mhondoro Tribal Trust Land. This man was a school teacher and contrary to advice he married into a family which was reputed to contain witches. After marriage he wasted away. The palms of his hands became hard and horny. A *nganga* was consulted. He revealed that the teacher's wife was a witch. The reason for the man's condition was that he was ridden at night by his wife when she was engaged in her nocturnal travels. The teacher thereafter divorced his wife. As soon as the woman had departed his hands healed and he began to put on weight. There are few Shona who cannot relate some such story allegedly obtained from a reliable source and perhaps told of some relation. In addition we have seen how persons sometimes confess to witchcraft, often with considerable circumstantial detail. Knowledge of such a confession becomes, of course, widespread and again convinces the doubter.

To name a person as a wizard and treat him as an outcast is essentially an act which damages the unity of the community and this is particularly the case where an allegation is made against a person closely related to the accuser or victim. Beliefs in wizardry are, however, not wholly destructive. It is believed that wizards are motivated by malice and, hence, wizardry allegations are made against persons who are believed to harbour malice, in other words against the social misfit and, again, the diviner in divining the cause of illness seeks usually to discover the nature of conflicts within a community and to divine in terms of these conflicts thereby, to some extent, resolving them.

It is believed that even if a person is a witch, she is unlikely to harm people if she lacks malice and, indeed, the Shona think it is not entirely a bad thing to have a 'good witch' in the family since she will protect it against other witches. More will be said on this subject later. But allegations also tend to result from envy and jealousy and therefore tend to be made against the exceptionally successful or talented member of the community. Belief in wizardry thus tends both to maintain the cohesion of the community and to discourage change. While belief in wizardry is both constructive and destructive in its effects, usually the constructive and destructive aspects are fairly evenly balanced.

Belief in wizardry provides not only a theory of causation as far as misfortune, death and illness are concerned but also explains why animals and things do not always behave in the manner in which they are expected to behave. Witchcraft amongst the Shona explains, at least when social tensions render witchcraft beliefs relevant, why the owl comes to the village at night, the appearance of an antbear, which is normally a shy animal, the reason why a buck turns on a hunter, a will-o-the-wisp, lightning striking near the village, and banshee wailing at night. Ndebele also explain drought and the eclipse of the moon in these terms. By providing a reason for unexpected behaviour and events, beliefs in wizardry makes that which is difficult to understand, comprehensible. Man

The Basis of Wizardry Beliefs

feels less helpless in the face of adverse natural conditions and can take necessary remedial measures whether by way of countermagic or by finding and destroying the wizard. The countermeasures may, in themselves, be useless but the feelings of confidence inspired by them at the best enables other, more effective, measures to be successfully undertaken or, at worst, improves morale. Beliefs in wizardry may thus have a definite social and psychological value in enabling man to act purposefully in the face of adversity. The cathartic effect of the wizardry allegation in 'clearing the air' when the tensions of community life become unbearable has been noted by several writers.

It is not only unusual behaviour in the natural world that is ascribed to wizardry. Wizardry may be adduced as an explanation of the irrational behaviour of persons. Diseases involving delirium are, quite naturally, ascribed to wizardry and it may be also adduced as an explanation of sleep walking. Thus an informant of mine narrated how he had attended a boys' boarding school as a child. One night one of the boys was found to be missing from the dormitory and, as all his clothes were left behind, it was clear he had gone out stark naked. The alarm was sounded and the boy eventually found. When asked for an explanation he was unable to remember what had happened but ascribed his wanderings to a charm his father had given him. He produced the charm which everyone saw. It was immediately assumed he was a witch. Although, I am told, the African headmaster adopted a definitely sceptical attitude, the belief that the boy was a witch was so strong that he was eventually ordered to leave the school. The same informant told me of an occasion when a man was found dancing on the roof of a hut where the body of a man killed in a mine accident lay. As one would expect, the dancer was accused of being the wizard who had killed the mineworker.

It must not be supposed that the cause of all misfortunes or unusual behaviour is thought to be wizardry. It is only on occasion that wizardry beliefs are socially relevant. I shall later discuss beliefs in regard to the cause of disease and misfortune and it will be observed that wizardry is one of a variety of beliefs which supply reasons for the occurrence of events. As far as untoward behaviour in the natural world is concerned alternative explanations to wizardry are also offered. For example, the lion or snake that does not bite may, amongst the Shona, be accounted for by explaining that it was the embodiment of an ancestral spirit. Rain may not fall because the tribal *mhondoro* (lion spirit) is annoyed. The goblins of the veld, the *madzimudzangara,* are responsible for many of the queer noises one hears at night and play all sorts of peculiar tricks on people as may also the *nzuzu* or water spirits. It cannot be too strongly stressed that the living mythology of a people such as the Shona, with which is included the mythology of wizardry, is no mere collection of folk tales of antiquarian interest, but has an immediate social importance in the life of the community. In a study of this nature it is necessary to isolate wizardry beliefs to some extent but it should be realized that such beliefs must always be seen against the background of the totality of the beliefs of the people concerned.

To regard witchcraft beliefs as providing a theory of causation offers only a partial explanation of the role of such beliefs in a society such as that of the Shona. Such an explanation does not account for the rich mythology of witchcraft throughout the world nor does it adequately account for the emotional reactions of people when a person is 'proved' to be a witch. As a theory of causation a belief in sorcery is quite as satisfactory as a belief in witchcraft. People can believe in many things which have little relevance to their everyday conduct. To believe that the sun revolves round the earth or vice-versa in no way affects one's everyday actions. In our own society many people believe devoutly in God, yet no longer are there spontaneous outbreaks of violence against heretics such as there are today amongst the Shona against persons accused of witchcraft. To regard witchcraft as a theory of causation does not fully account for the social relevance of such beliefs and the emotions raised by an accusation of witchcraft.

The Shona attach great importance to the maintenance of the social values of their society and, in particular, to the maintenance of proper standards of conduct between persons. Where a society is structured primarily on the basis of kinship, those standards of conduct are intended mainly to preserve and maintain the pattern of kinship. Radcliffe-Brown (1952, p. 151) has suggested that the primary basis of ritual is the 'attribution of ritual value to objects and occasions which are either themselves objects of important common interests linking together persons of a community or are symbolically representative of such objects'. Kinship and social obligations are one of those matters which, because of their importance to the existence of the community, evoke ritual values. This is seen clearly in the ritual of the cult of the *vadzimu* amongst the Shona community which serves both as an expression of the social values attached to the kin group and as a method of keeping that group intact. There is a similar ritual value attached to the forces that tend to disrupt the life of the community, envy, jealousy, failure to perform one's obligations and so forth. Among the Shona a witch is a personification of the disruptive forces in community life. For that reason the reactions to a person accused of witchcraft have a ritual aspect—the community as a whole participates in the divination and also participates in the action taken against a witch. Further, the fact that a witch is a personification of moral evil probably accounts for the mythology of witchcraft, for as a personification she becomes the image of all that is evil. Cannibalism is the most detested of all crimes, therefore she is a cannibal; family ties are the most sacred of all ties, therefore she destroys members of her family; medicine and magic are the forces with which one can control the environment in the interests of one's society, therefore they become perverted in the hands of the witch; animals such as snakes are dangerous because they can kill; owls are feared because they fly when all other birds sleep, therefore the witch has these creatures as her familiars. She is associated with all that is feared and all that is detestable.

It is because witchcraft is both a theory of causation and a personification of evil that witchcraft obtains its social relevance. Conversely it is the social relevance of an event ascribed to witchcraft which determines how people will behave. If a man cuts himself and the wound festers the Shona is likely to think that the wound was caused by witchcraft. However interested he himself may be in the injury the community is unlikely to concern itself much with his plight. If he accuses another of witchcraft people are unlikely to pay much attention. So long as oneself, one's friends and one's kin are well, one is unlikely to be much concerned with witchcraft beliefs. However, the death of a child or its mother is a matter of concern to the whole community as without mothers and children the community as a whole cannot survive. It is the intense feeling of the community on occasions such as this which appears to give witchcraft its greatest social relevance. Parrinder (1958, p. 193) has already stressed the close link between child mortality and wizardry belief and this is shown in the present study where over forty-five per cent of the allegations examined by me resulted from the death of a child. A further twenty-three per cent originated with the death of an adult. There is no reason to suppose that these cases do not represent a fair sample of the more serious type of wizardry allegations —more serious, that is, from the point of view of the person named as a wizard. Even misfortune of a serious kind such as the death of a child is unlikely to be interpreted in terms of wizardry if there are no political, social or other conflicts in a village. In a number of cases examined by me a diviner was only consulted after repeated deaths; deaths only being interpreted in terms of wizardry, apparently, when some occasion arose which rendered these beliefs relevant. However, misfortune and social tensions are matters which are closely related. In a society which attaches a high value to the bearing and rearing of children the continued failure of a woman to rear children may lead to estrangement between the husband or his family and the wife and then to the attribution of the deaths of the children to their mother's witchcraft.

To sum up, wizardry beliefs have social relevance because they combine a theory of causation with a personification of those forces which the community detests. Further, wizardry allegations reflect the tensions and conflicts in the community which generates them. The pattern and nature of these conflicts will be discussed later in this work.

CHAPTER IV

WITCHCRAFT AND RELIGION

BELIEF in witchcraft is an attempt by man to rationalize and understand the malevolent forces of nature and the misfortunes of life. Among most peoples of the world one of the important purposes of religion and religious philosophy is to explain and make endurable these ills and it is, therefore, to be expected that belief in the nature of witchcraft should be closely associated with the religious beliefs of the people concerned. In mediaeval Europe with its beliefs in God and the Devil, the witch was, quite naturally, regarded as a creature of the Devil; in the polytheistic classical world witchcraft was associated with the goddess Hecate. The fact that Evans-Pritchard (1937) was able to describe beliefs in witchcraft amongst the Azande, a tribe of the Nilotic Sudan, without reference to Azande religious beliefs, illustrates that the *nexus* between religion and witchcraft may not be inevitable, but there is usually such a *nexus* and, among the Southern Bantu, it is impossible to describe their beliefs in witchcraft without some reference to their religion.

Evans-Pritchard states (1937, p. 21): 'A witch performs no rite, utters no spell, and possesses no medicines. An act of witchcraft is a psychic act. They (the Azande) believe also that sorcerers may do them ill by performing magic rites with bad medicines. Azande distinguish clearly between witches and sorcerers.' At first sight this distinction between witchcraft and sorcery is not applicable to Shona belief for, as Howman (1948, p. 9) has shown, the word 'witch' (*muroyi*) is used to mean, among other things, the true witch, the sorcerer who uses his powers to harm others, one who causes harm through breach of some taboo, the poisoner and even the troublemaker. Again, the distinction between a psychic act and an act of sorcery is not clearly made. The 'horn' which witches possess and which contains medicine to harm others ought to be real enough, but such a horn may be credited with the ability to fly through the air and, as if it were a familiar, to suck at the breasts of women and poison their milk. Witches may harm others by administering 'medicine' (*muti* or *mushonga*) which may well be derived from a plant that can be pointed out to an investigator (p. 56); but such a medicine may be administered during the course of nocturnal travels when the witch flies through the air or rides her familiar. This first impression of Shona belief is, however, misleading. The Shona distinguish between a 'real' witch and other sorts of witches. Only a 'real' witch is capable of psychic acts although, being a thoroughly malevolent person, it is not to be expected that her activities should be confined only to the world of the psyche. A 'real' witch is a person possessed by an evil ancestral spirit (*mudzimu*) or an evil spirit of human or animal origin derived from outside the family circle (*shave* spirit). It is in possession by the *vadzimu* or the *mashave* that the Shona explain many unusual characteristics or capabilities in a person. Thus a *nganga* (doctor-diviner) or a craftsman such as a smith owe their abilities to these same spirits. The difference between the abilities of these men and a witch lies in the qualities of the particular spirit possessing them. The Shona distinguish between a 'real' *nganga* and a mere charlatan on the same basis that they distinguish between a 'real' witch and any other evilly disposed person. The one is possessed, the other is not. Just as a *mudzimu* can possess successive generations of the same family, so a *shave* can be inherited from an ancestor.[1]

Middleton and Winter (1963, p. 10) explain the coexistence of witchcraft and sorcery beliefs as being 'due to the idea that witch-

---

[1] Among the Ndebele the *holi* or *lozwi* part of the nation believe in possession by the *amatjukwa*, *amatshave* and *amashumba* spirits (Kuper *et al.*, 1955, p. 106) and their beliefs as to the nature of witchcraft appear to be very much the same as the Shona peoples. The upper class, the *zanzi*, on the other hand appear to regard witchcraft as purely a manifestation of ancestral spirits (*amadhlozi*) which were, themselves, witches. Beliefs in the avenging spirit, the *uzimu*, are similar to Shona beliefs in the *ngozi*.

craft is usually confined to members of one sex' therefore 'sorcery beliefs fill a gap in the total system of thought dealing with the causation of misfortune.' I think that this is at least a partial explanation of the coexistence of witchcraft and sorcery beliefs among the Shona. It is true that the Shona, or at least many of them, believe that there can be a male witch; but they also believe that there are very few of them compared with the number of female witches. Indeed some say all witches are women. With the Shona, as in other societies, envy relationships arise between persons of the same sex and not between men and women. 'It follows', to use the words of Middleton and Winter (p. 10) 'that if a man believes another envies him and is attempting to harm him, he must suspect the latter of practising sorcery since, by cultural definition, in this society a man is thought to be incapable of practising witchcraft'. If we substitute 'unlikely to practise' for 'incapable of practising' we have, in my view, a fair reflection of the attitude of the Shona. I have, however, been unable to find any evidence which supports the further suggestion of Middleton and Winter that witchcraft explains generalized misfortunes while sorcery provides the explanation of particular misfortunes. The Shona regard witchcraft as causing both generalized and particular misfortunes. It is, however, true to say that witchcraft and not sorcery is the most likely explanation a Shona would offer for a generalized misfortune or a series of misfortunes. Whether a misfortune is generalized or particular depends on the standpoint of the observer.

According to Middleton and Winter (1963, p. 11ff) in many societies accusations against specific wizards tend to be expressed either in terms of witchcraft or sorcery. They associate witchcraft accusations with societies in which unilineal kinship principles are employed in the formation of local residential groups larger than the domestic household while sorcery beliefs tend to be similarly utilized when unilineal principles are not so used. They contrast the Lugubara of Uganda, where accusations are expressed in terms of witchcraft and the local group consists of groups of agnates together with their wives and children, and the Nyoro, also of Uganda, whose accusations are expressed in the idiom of sorcery and whose villages consist of a group of people who are heterogeneous in terms of lineage affiliations. Obviously this suggestion requires further investigation; but it is, perhaps, a point of interest that the Shona, who express their accusations against individuals both in terms of witchcraft and of sorcery, live in villages which conform neither to Nyoro nor the Lugubara type. Shona villages not only contain a nuclear core of persons agnatically related, but also a large number of persons who are heterogeneous in terms of lineage affiliation.

The distinction between witchcraft and sorcery is vital for the understanding of Shona witchcraft and, in particular, for understanding the pattern of witchcraft allegations. This will be elaborated later. At this stage it will suffice to say that to allege a person is a witch is to allege that she is morally evil and, to all intents and purposes, incurable. For one lineage member to make an allegation of this sort against another will have not only the effect of alleging an enormity so great as to render ordinary relations between agnates impossible, but may reflect on the person alleging witchcraft since witchcraft is inheritable. Allegations of wizardry against agnates are normally, therefore, expressed in terms of sorcery and not witchcraft. The contrary is the case where allegations are made against persons other than agnates. Marriage being exogamous and virilocal the most important groups of persons in a village who are not lineage members are their wives. It is against this category that witchcraft allegations are made, often with the deliberate intention of driving them from the community. An allegation of sorcery is less serious than an allegation of witchcraft as a sorcerer is not inherently evil. Although the deed ascribed to him may be serious enough, he does not represent the standing and isidious source of danger that a witch does. A sorcerer is only likely to harm a person with whom he has quarrelled. One is safe from sorcery if one avoids situations in which sorcery is likely to be used. One can never know who and when a witch will strike. By ensuring that allegations against lineage members are made in the idiom of sorcery and not witchcraft, Shona society does much to ensure the stability of the lineage.

Although Shona does not distinguish linguistically between witchcraft and sorcery, although *chipotswa* is sometimes used as a specific term for sorcery, it will be seen later that, when an allegation of witchcraft is made, it is often accompanied by a statement indicating the manner in which the witchcraft has been performed or alleging that certain attributes, such as the eating of human flesh or the possession of familiars, belong to the supposed witch. It is clear that the purpose of these statements is not merely to elaborate on the allegation that the person accused is a 'witch' but to make it quite clear that the allegation is one of witchcraft and not sorcery. There would be little point in making this clear were the importance of the distinction a matter of no moment.

The following is a brief description of Shona religious beliefs in so far as is relevant to the present study. For further details Dr. Gelfand's works should be consulted (1956, 1959, 1962 and 1964). Minor differences of belief exist between the various Shona groups, but they are comparatively unimportant and, for the purposes of this description, will be ignored. It is not necessary, either, to discuss the nature of the Shona belief in God. This is a difficult subject to investigate after some seventy years of missionary work in the country and sporadic missionary activity on the borders of the country for many centuries, and is not really relevant for the present purposes because, to the extent that the Shona had any belief in God, that God was, in the main, of the passive Bantu type who concerned himself little with the affairs of the world except, probably, with rain. Shona belief centred on the activities of certain spirits, some benevolent, others ambivalent or malevolent, of which the principle categories are:

THE VADZIMU

The ancestral spirits *vadzimu* or, as Gelfand (1962, p. 51) would prefer to call them, the spirit elders are, perhaps, the most important of all the spirits. The unity of the lineage which, in life, is so impressive persists after death. A married man or woman becomes a *mudzimu* after death and takes as active a part in the affairs of the family as if he or she were still alive. In practice only the names of the persons who were personally known to the living are recalled in the family rituals, other *vadzimu* being referred to collectively. The *vadzimu* of parents and grandparents are regarded with very real affection by the living and, in return, these spirits are thought to take an interest in, and promote, the welfare of the lineage. However, a spirit is upset if proper respect has not been paid and may bear a grudge if he or she has been badly treated by his or her children during life, e.g. if a woman has not received the *mombe ya amai* (beast of the mother) when her daughter marries. If a spirit is annoyed it will make a member of the family ill. In the case of illness a *nganga* (doctor-diviner) may be consulted to diagnose the cause of illness. If he states the illness was caused by a *mudzimu* he will explain what the spirit desires, whether it be beer, a blanket or an animal. In a number of the court cases doctor-diviners charged with indicating a witch confessed to the divination, but claimed that they had indicated an ancestral spirit and not a witch as being responsible. Apart from the ordinary *mudzimu* there is the spirit known amongst the Vazezuru as the *mudzimu mudiki wapamusha*. This is the guardian spirit of the extended family, the spirit of the ancestor of the lineage—a person who often lived some generations ago. This spirit may, like any other *mudzimu*, make a person ill to indicate its desires but more often, and in particular on occasions where the *vadzimu* are propitiated, it will possess a medium and give instructions or express its desires through his mouth. Those *nganga* who divine by means of their ancestral spirits are similarly possessed. Witchcraft may be ascribed to possession by a *mudzimu*, itself a witch.

I will later describe the manner in which this possession first manifests itself. Generally in accusations of witchcraft the diviner does not state what particular spirit is responsible for the witch's condition but in two of the cases under consideration it would seem that a *mudzimu* is what was implied. In one case the *nganga,* after indicating a certain woman as a witch who had sent a snake to kill a child, told the persons present that there was a spirit at the kraal which was working through the witch and that it was necessary to make some beer and brew the beer for this spirit. The other case will be discussed in more detail later.

As in the case of all other *vadzimu,* the *mudzimu* of a witch demands to be propitiated with sacrifices. In *R v Sophie* (tried before the High Court Salisbury 28.9.60) a woman living in the Mhondoro Tribal Trust Land, who undoubtedly had been dabbling in sorcery and may well have regarded herself as a 'witch', poisoned a child. She threw the bottle which had contained the arsenic into a hole. The bottle was subsequently found by the police to be resting on bones from at least two chickens. Some of the bones still had dried flesh on them and thus probably originated from a sacrifice. In addition, there were two *ndoro* (the polished ends of conus shells, of great value in the past) and fragments of a number of bead ropes (*mikonde*). The opinion of Africans who saw this exhibit was that it was a sacrifice made by a witch to her evil ancestral spirit. Certainly this is the sort of sacrifice expected from a witch. If it was indeed such a sacrifice, the *ndoro* and the *mikonde* presumably belonged to the person whose spirit was inherited.

The *mudzimu* which possesses a witch is thought to be the driving force behind her. On occasion the spirit of the witch may act independently of the witch and become a vampire. A spirit of this sort will be described later in the extracts from the case of *R v Tachinson* (p. 209). In common with all forms of spirit manifestation the *mudzimu* of witchcraft may speak through a medium. The following story, which is said to come from a qualified African nurse in a Gwelo hospital, illustrates this and is also of interest as illustrating the type of story which is told among Africans and which makes disbelief so difficult.

'A young girl became ill and a *nganga* was consulted. He stated that a *mudzimu* wished to possess her and make her a witch and that unless the appropriate ceremony was performed to enable her to accept the spirit she would die. The ceremony was performed and she recovered. This incident was forgotten and the girl grew up and married. She bore her husband seven children who all died, including the eldest. When the sixth child became ill it was taken to hospital. While on her death bed she became possessed by the *mudzimu* of her mother which spoke through her. The child suddenly sat up and talked saying, "Do you think you are likely to succeed in competition with me, you white man (i.e., the European doctor) feeding my child with your white *muti* (medicine). I will not be so-and-so's (the mother's) spirit if she recovers".'

The child having said this fell right out of bed and died. The story was reported to the father who consulted a *nganga*. The *nganga* related how the mother of the deceased had been dedicated to her evil *mudzimu* when a child. The parents of the witch were taxed with this and admitted the truth of the *nganga's* statement. The husband of the witch then tried to get a divorce from the Native Commissioner but was unable to do so. The parties returned to the *nganga* who revealed there was a secret box kept at the bottom of the witch's trunk and that if the parties were interested they should examine it. They went home and the box was found and it was full of witchcraft paraphernalia. Thereafter a divorce was granted.

The dividing line between living and dead is not clearly drawn. Very old people are believed to be in communication with their *vadzimu* and to partake of their nature. They may thus demand that a beast be sacrificed to them and may cause their *vadzimu* to hurt people in the village if they themselves are slighted. For this reason elderly people are feared and seem to acquire some of the characteristics of witches. This may be one of the reasons why in the cases of wizardry accusations examined by me a fairly high proportion of elderly people, mainly women, were involved. An elderly person may even deliberately exploit the situation by claiming to be a witch.

If the *vadzimu* are properly respected they will protect the people of their lineage from witches, although on occasion witches may succeed in entering despite this protection, for how then could the children become ill? If a *mudzimu* is angry, however, it may be deliberately remiss in its duties and allow a witch to enter and harm the people.

A major reason why the cult of the *vadzimu* is so important from the sociological point of view is because of the close association between the cult and the lineage structure of the community. The lineage we are here concerned with is the agnatic lineage which forms the basis of the kinship group and of the geographical group, the village or cluster of villages. On the one hand the cult of the *vadzimu* is the religious sanction which furthers the unity of the lineage, which in this context is the minor lineage. If a member of the lineage misbehaves and refuses to recognize the authority of the lineage head, the lineage head may invoke the *vadzimu* to punish the offender or, perhaps more important, may refuse to propitiate the *vadzimu* if the offender or members of his family are made ill by them. On the other hand, it is the recognition by members of a minor lineage that a certain person is entitled to sacrifice on their behalf which validates that person's claim to be head of that lineage and which finally determines whether an attempt by a person to become lineage head in his own right has succeeded. The cult serves to resolve conflicts between agnates since the co-operation and assistance of agnates is required when the *vadzimu* are propitiated. Lack of harmony may indeed be the reason why the *vadzimu* are angry and require propitiation.

Later I shall attempt to show the effect of the lineage structure on the pattern of wizardry allegations in the community. If the wizardry allegation is one of the forces, or a sympton of those forces, which disrupt the unity of the lineage, it is, on the other hand, the cult of the *vadzimu* which is one of the major forces counteracting the forces of disruption and which ensures the stability and continuity of the lineage. Maternal as well as paternal *vadzimu* can cause illness to a person. Although one informant claimed that a lineage head can propitiate the *vadzimu* of persons not related to him, e.g., the spirit of his child's maternal grandmother, the better view seems to be that a person can only propitiate the spirit of a person who in life was agnatically related to him. It is, however, more important that the spirit be propitiated than that the right person perform the function. After all, the spirits are related to one and cannot expect the impossible, one merely does what one can.

THE MASHAVE

The *mashave* are believed to be spirits originating from outside the patrilineage, including the spirits of animals, which possess people in various ways. They are sometimes known as alien spirits in contradistinction to the *vadzimu*, the spirits of the lineage.

The *shave* spirits normally confer upon their host some particular skill or ability. They may possess both men and women although the ceremonies or seances associated with the cult would appear to centre more upon men. There appears to have been no sociological study of the *shave* cults in Mashonaland but the analogous *mazenge* cult of the Western Shona, among the Kalanga of the Plumtree area, has recently been studied by Werbner (1964, p. 206ff). Werbner found that having women to act as *mazenge* hosts is crucial for controlling norms where there is opposition between categories of persons. These areas of opposition are not controlled by the religious structure of elderhood (i.e., the cult of the *vadzimu*) alone as this structure may be too limited or rigid to cope with the various patterns of settlement or with certain forms of conflict arising within the community. Apart from members of wife-receiving lineages who are obliged to perform certain mystically polluting or dangerous ritual services which men cannot perform for themselves, the cult of the ancestral spirits need not include diverse categories of affines or cognates who may have, through women, opposed interests in property. The attonement rituals of guardian spirit possession (i.e., *mazenge* possession) bring together the more diverse congregation centred on women and stress rank order between kinsmen. The cult serves *inter alia* to stress the rightful order between wife-receivers and wife-givers and tends to be primarily focused on women in structurally critical positions. The atonement rituals tend to dramatize conflicts within the community. Relations between close kinsmen may be amended by fulfilment of ritual obligations towards the spirit host.

I think that Werbner's account of spirit possession among the Kalanga is, broadly speaking, true of the Eastern Shona also, although the position there is somewhat more complex in that *shave* hosts include men. Although, however, skills of various sorts are conferred upon men, in Shona belief, by *shave* spirits— and many men possess them—my impression is that men do not play any very great part in the atonement rituals associated with the cult.

A woman's position in the home of her husband is one of subordination. This position is entirely reversed during the period when she becomes possessed by a *shave* spirit. The *shave* cult, however, confers no permanent status upon the host in the way that the cult of the *vadzimu* does upon the lineage head, the host being treated as an ordinary person except when possessed. This is dramatized by the practice of keeping the various objects worn or carried by the host when possessed concealed from her except when she is possessed.

It seems that the popularity of the *shave* cults has tended to increase and diminish cyclically in the past. They seem to have been particularly prevalent during the years following the occupation of the country by Europeans, being presumably associated with the social changes of the time. At present they are losing ground to the prophets of the Pentecostal Churches. The *shave* cult resembles that of the Pentecostal Churches in some ways. Both are cults of spirit possession and both make use of colourful rituals and costumes which contrast strongly with the drabness of everyday life. The excitement produced by the rituals in both cases has a cathartic effect and provides some measure of release from inner tensions. This, the more sober and decorous rituals associated with the cult of the *vadzimu* fail to do.

The *shave* most closely associated with witchcraft in Central and Northern Mashonaland is the *mazenda shave* or, according to Gelfand (1959, p. 129), one of the varieties of this *shave*. The following extracts from the case *R v Zindoga alias Nice* (85)[1] illustrates the manner in which this spirit is supposed to behave. A man had died and a number of women washed the body and then guarded it overnight, as is customary to prevent witches interfering with it. In the morning there was blood on the pillow on which the head of the corpse had been resting. The women who had watched the corpse were Sanga, Nyamita and Maida. The accused, Zindoga, was a prophet of the Apostolic Church. A witness's account of what took place afterwards is as follows:—

'I went to the accused's kraal with Sanga, Maida, Beni and Nyamita. Accused was preaching. He later came over to our group and we said we had come about a "case". Accused said that God was not permitting him to say anything as he saw bad things between these three women. He said Nyamita and Maida were "clean" (*machena*). He mentioned the blood from the body and questioned Sanga about it. He accused her of taking it. Sanga replied. Accused said Sanga had a "*shave* of Zenda" and the spirit of a snake and baboon. I asked accused when the blood was removed and accused said it was taken at the time of the star *Nyamatsatse* (Venus). Accused said the blood was taken as a love potion (and also to ensure good *rapoko* crops). Sanga was attempting to defend herself. She was upset.'

Another case illustrating beliefs in the witchcraft *shave* is *R v Modas* (83). In this case the senior wife of a certain Mushawe died. Suspicion fell on her co-wife, Modas. Mushawe's evidence is as follows:—

'My first wife was Murushaya who died on the 8th January, 1956. My first wife had been sick for three weeks previously. On Friday before she died Modas made a report to me. She said, "Some of the women are asking me to accompany them to kill and eat your first wife". I asked her how this could be done. She replied that they had spirits (*mashave*) which told them to eat. I decided not to question her further at this time, but to refer to the kraal head, which I did on the next day, Saturday. The kraal head sent for the accused and spoke with her, he asked "What worries you?" Modas replied, "I am worried because the others asked me to accompany them to kill and eat my elder sister". She used the words "elder sister" in reference to my first wife. She said "I am refusing, they said that they would kill me". The kraal head

[1] Numbers refer to Table of Cases in Appendix I.

asked whether, were he to call the other women together, she would repeat this. She replied "Yes". The kraal head asked the accused the names of the women concerned, she mentioned the names of Magderina, Sarah, Seti, Redi and Chitsaka. These I can remember, others I have forgotten. Magaya sent for all these women. There was no compulsion used. She voluntarily pointed out each woman in turn naming them, and saying to Magderina "You are the one who asked these others to accompany you to kill and eat my husband's first wife." In front of the kraal head she said that she had refused to accompany them. The kraal head then dismissed everyone.'

Modas made a similar accusation of witchcraft to the police, adding 'I . . . am a witch.' At the end of the Preparatory Examination she said:

'I wish to state that I pointed the women out because they asked me to lead them to kill my husband's first wife. I refused. We were attacked by the spirit. They said they would cause me to die and my child also. I reported to my husband's wife and then to my husband. I told the kraal head that I was worried. Magderina thought my husband's first wife was proud. I named Magderina, Chitsaka, Redi, Seti and Sarah to the kraal head. I pointed to them as witches.'

Evidence was led that the spirit referred to was a *'shave ro uroyi'* (a witchcraft *shave*). It is fairly common for a person accused of a crime such as murder or rape to allege that he was 'attacked by the spirit' so the explanation given by Modas of her conduct is only abnormal in so far as she alleges that the 'spirit' drove her and her companions to commit what, objectively speaking, was a psychic act. The 'spirit' on which people put the blame for their own anti-social conduct becomes, in the case of the Christian Shona, the devil.

The manifestations of the *mashave* are in many cases so bizarre, at least to a European, that it should not occasion surprise that persons such as Modas should genuinely believe they are possessed by a witchcraft *shave*—such a belief is, after all, no more difficult than believing that one is possessed by a baboon spirit. Mang Shona claim to be possessed by baboon and other animal *shave*.

Shave spirits may not only possess a person of their own volition, they may also be given to a person by a previous 'owner' or may be inherited from an ancestor. Unlike the ancestral spirits, which are usually propitiated by offerings of meat or beer, the *mashave* generally demand dances in their honour in which persons carry or wear the regalia demanded by their *shave* and become possessed by it, usually in the small hours of the morning. While possessed they do whatever the spirit demands of them. For example, those possessed by the *shave* of a European wear European dress and eat raw eggs; those possessed by baboon *mashave* wear fibre eyebrow ornaments and behave like baboons; those possessed by a dog *shave* eat filth, etc. Much of Shona music is associated with these *shave* rituals and since most of the varieties of *shave* demand articles of traditional form—axes, beaded aprons, etc.—they play a part in preserving some of the fast vanishing material culture. The baboon *shave* particularly is associated with various skills and the following is an account of a diviner possessed by such a *shave* taken from the case of *R v Mubiwa* (81) from the Madziwa Reserve. In this case the witness had lost four of her children. She asked a certain Chitema whom she should consult:

'As a result of Chitema's words I went to the accused. No mention was made of money. Chitema and I saw accused in his hut in our kraal, we went there long after dark, people were about to go to sleep. When I saw accused he appeared to be possessed by a spirit and was sitting dressed in a pair of shorts and a jacket and was wrapped in a blanket which completely covered his head. Accused was making a whistling sibilant noise, something like "whoo" and also was grunting like a baboon. In my belief accused was possessed then by the spirit of a baboon. Accused then spoke to me, after I had addressed him and told him I had visited him because of my trouble. I mentioned the fact that I did not know the reason why my children had died. Accused then said "The people who killed your children are Jairos and Chutare". Both these live in the Madziwa reserve. Then I left the hut weeping. As I left accused made similar baboon-like noises.'

THE MHONDORO

Concerned with the welfare of the tribe as a whole and,

in particular, rain and the affairs of the chieftaincy, are the great spirits—often termed the *mhondoro* or lion spirits. Some of the greatest of these spirits and, in particular, the *mlimo*, speak oracularly without the intervention of a visible human medium or *svikiro*. The centre of the *mlimo* cult is the Matopos and is of importance here in that the effect of this cult, which is of Kalanga origin, has been to restrict the role of the Ndebele *isangoma* amongst the Kalanga (see p. 187). Generally, however, these spirits possess a human medium or *svikiro*. Some of these *svikiro* are very powerful and a section of the Budjga tribe of Mtoko is virtually ruled by Charewa, the *svikiro* of their *mhondoro*. These spirits ordinarily do not concern themselves with matters such as witchcraft and I shall try to show that their main interest here is the effect that belief in the *mhondoro* has had on the beliefs of the African Christians. For a person who believes in the *mhondoro,* the possession of a Prophet of the Pentecostal Churches by the spirit of God, Christ or the Apostles, appears in no way untoward. Texts of statements of witnesses who have witnessed divinations by such prophets will be given below (p. 221) and, for purposes of comparison, include an account from the case of *R v Magwenzi* (Bindura 27.10.60) the possession of the *svikiro* by his *mhondoro* spirit. It will be noticed that, as in the case of the spirit consulted by Gelfand (1962, p. 46), the utterances of the spirit have a markedly political character which is, indeed, why the case was brought to court. The evidence was given by a village head:

'I was called to the kraal of Chief of Musana. When I got there I found that all the headmen had been called and also the heads of kraals. Some were missing, but there were a lot there. In the kraal of the Chief there is one hut which is for the *svikiro* (of Chief Musana's tribal spirit). We all gathered at this hut. We were invited by the Chief to enter the house. A man who I know as Magwenzi, whom I know as the *svikiro,* was sitting in the hut on a reed mat. We were all instructed to clap our hands (a token of respect). The Chief was there as well. Then Magwenzi, who was covered with a white cloth, started to move up and down in a bouncing movement, he was shaking his body. He started to shout very loudly and said, "What I have called you here for is—cattle have been destocked, lands have been cut (i.e. divided under the Land Husbandry Act), now what do you want?" I remember the people answered that they wanted more cattle and more land to plough. Magwenzi then said, "I don't want cattle to go for dipping, even demonstrators must not be allowed to come (agricultural demonstrators), they are people who are cutting our lands—when you leave here tell the others who are not here what I have said. Tell them that this has been said by the Chief . . . Anyone who does not do as I say, I will not have him in my country." I remember someone asked about what we should say when asked by people why we were not taking our cattle for dipping. Magwenzi asked something and then said, "You will not be asked first." Then Chief Musana said, "I will be the one who will be asked first." The Chief then said, "All right my children, whatever I am told, I will tell you." I then left to go back to my kraal, all the other people left with me. This meeting with the chief lasted for one complete night. There was dancing for the *svikiro* and many meetings when the same words were said.'

THE NGOZI

The *ngozi* is a spirit with a grudge, determined on vengeance. If a man murders another the spirit of his victim may become *ngozi* and cause death and illness in the family of his killer. Again, an ancestral spirit may bear a grudge and become *ngozi*. It is from fear of the *ngozi* that the body of a murdered man may be mutilated, the purpose being to keep the *ngozi* in the victim's body so that it may be buried with him. Amongst the Budjga of the Mtoko district ways of avoiding the *ngozi* include eating part of the victim's *muputi* (string worn round the waist), and the eating of the blood or flesh of the victim taken from the private parts, the little fingers, the little toes, the ears, tongue or heart. Only a little blood or flesh is taken. Zezuru informants state that the portion removed must be mixed with medicine by a *nganga* and eaten with the medicine. Should an *ngozi* cause deaths at a kraal a *nganga* may advise that a woman has to be given to the family of the deceased to raise a child in the place of the person killed. Amongst the Manyika this may develop into a form of 'ghost marriage' (Crawford, 1963, p. 27).

The *ngozi* is of great importance in witchcraft in that, being a malevolent spirit, it is a ready-made tool in the hands of a witch and I am told by informants that it is one of the most frequently used tools and one of the most feared. The *ngozi* may possess its victim and the victim's ravings and delirium may be attributed to this cause. In cases which will be discussed more fully later the *ngozi*, speaking through the mouth of its victim, named the witch who had sent it. Informants deny that a witch may herself kill a person to obtain his *ngozi* but in the case of *R v Mathias and Kariba*, (17) involving *Ndau*, this was alleged. In this case a man's child had died and as a result of what his father said, he blamed it on his father. Eventually, with the aid of a hired assistant, he killed his father the alleged witch. Apparently the father had, prior to his grandson's death, told his son that he would see an anthill (i.e., a grave) and had stated that some years ago, in Kimberley, he had murdered a person and that it was this person's spirit (*ngozi*) which had killed the child. He said to his son that he had a medicine and it was this medicine, he thought, that had assisted the spirit of the murdered man to kill the child.

A further reason why the *ngozi* is of importance in the study of witchcraft is that it may, itself, if it is the spirit of a man killed by a wizard, reveal its killer. An example of such an indication is given below. Furthermore, fear that the deceased may become *ngozi* is said to be a patent force in driving people to consult a *nganga* to ascertain who the killer of a person was, so that the death of that person may be avenged. In the words of one woman who was asked why she went to a *nganga*, 'I was afraid that the child's spirit would return to the kraal.' This, however, is not the only reason why a *nganga* is consulted about a death. Far more potent is the desire to remove the source of danger from the kraal and to prevent further death.

Not only man, but certain animals such as the eland, may become *ngozi*. Shona belief is here very similar to Tsonga belief as described by Junod (1913, I, p. 453, II, pp. 57-62).

The *ngozi* plays a part in vengeance magic (see below Part IV) and also gives rise to various forms of spirit possession (Gelfand, 1962, Chap. 5) which are not here relevant. It is of importance in

Shona law, particularly where the distribution of the estate is concerned. Holleman (1952, p. 357) states that disputes concerning the distribution of the matri-estate seldom came to court. Fear of the woman's *ngozi* is sufficient to ensure a proper distribution.

SHONA BELIEFS TODAY

In some parts of the Shona area there have been over seventy years of missionary activity. That Christianity should have had a very great impact on the Shona is therefore to be expected. Again, close contact with the increasingly agnostic European society has not been without its effects. The *shave* cult is less popular than it used to be. When one enters Tribal Trust Land seeking examples of the traditional material culture one is fortunate if the articles demanded by the *mashave* or, for that matter, all examples of traditional arts and crafts whatsoever, have not been burned at the instigation of some religious sect. However, wherever the Shona lineage structure remains intact, as it does to a great extent in most tribal areas, beliefs in the *vadzimu* are still of significance. Some Christians will refuse to take part in the rituals of ancestor worship; but many do, and in such cases Christian beliefs supplement but do not supplant traditional ways of thought. Later, in Part III, I shall endeavour to explain how in the Pentecostal Churches Shona beliefs have altered and transformed the Christian faith.

In the towns, with the disintegration of the lineage structure, traditional religious beliefs are of little importance, although if a *nganga* is consulted about illness or death he may try to impress on his clients the necessity of properly respecting the *vadzimu*. Many people are Christians; but many others have abandoned their traditional faiths without embracing Christianity. The rise of African Nationalism has, however, led to a deliberate attempt to revive certain selected elements of the traditional culture and, among the elements so selected, has been the cult of the *vadzimu*. As a result, certain families, mainly urban, which had abandoned the rituals of ancestor worship are once again, and rather self

Witchcraft and Religion

consciously, propitiating the *vadzimu*. The growth of state education is also weakening the power of the missions and increasing the trend towards the secularization of Shona society. Many people, however, who forget about their *vadzimu* when times are good will remember them when their luck changes. It is said that a man who loses a job and who is unable to find another will often return home to his relatives in the Tribal Trust Areas and ask them to placate the *vadzimu* on his behalf. Thereafter, it is said, he seldom fails to find employment.

Witchcraft belief and superstitions have not suffered to the same extent as religious beliefs. Life in the towns is often insecure and, if anything, the fear of witchcraft and sorcery has increased or, at any rate, not diminished. Some Shona profess not to believe in witchcraft but, on the whole, I have been impressed by the obvious belief of my informants who came mainly from a class which is comparatively well educated, speaks English fairly well and which professed Christianity.

The *Weekly Mirror,* the short-lived successor to the Saturday edition of the banned *Daily News,* invited its readers, who were predominantly African, to express their views on the subject, 'Do your family spirits help you?' The letters received were published in the editions of the 23rd and 30th of October, 1964. They are of great interest in the light they throw upon the beliefs of the paper's readers who belonged to the more literate section of the African, particularly the Shona, population. The arguments for and against the existence of the family spirits, that is the *vadzimu,* are interesting particularly as they closely resemble the arguments used by literate Africans when discussing witchcraft beliefs. There is a strong tendency to use arguments which it is thought would not appear ridiculous to a European and which are based, for example, on the Bible or on Shakespeare. This desire to justify African belief in European terms is one of the aspects of the inferiority complex that appears to be inevitable in a country where the vast mass of the population is dominated by a group that is not only politically but culturally felt to be superior. All the letters except one were written by Africans. The remaining letter was written by a European spiritualist and is only of importance in so far as not all Europeans express sceptical views in regard to African belief; this fact has not escaped African notice and suggests to them that the attitude of the rest is partially accountable to wilful perverseness. Only three of the remaining eleven letters express disbelief. One of these simply asserts that the spirits do not exist and that one must follow 'what our European counterparts have done to us.' The other two point out that belief in the spirits is incompatible with Christianity. One of these writers points out that witchdoctors have a vested interest in promoting belief in the ancestral spirits and that people are 'mammals like cattle.' Can it seriously be suggested that the spirits of cattle return to earth to protect their calves?

Of the remaining letters, one is simply an assertion that the spirits exist and that the reason why Africans do not prosper is because they disregard the spirits. Civilization cannot stop the trees growing or spirits existing. Another voices a complaint that the spirits are a nuisance and bring unhappiness and poverty. Troublesome people will become troublesome spirits. The spirits of rich people will demand their property rights and the spirits of poor people demand the return of credit. Doctors (i.e., doctor-diviners) cannot necessarily stop the troublesome spirits and one has to go from doctor to doctor until one's wealth is dissipated. The other letters all adduce evidence in favour of the existence of spirits. One states that the writer knows that the spirits guide us because they appear to us—and he has experienced this himself—in our dreams. Two writers tell the usual sort of story that one hears in such discussions. The one relates how his grandfather was ill and asked his father to kill a bull so they could eat together 'and rejoice'. His father refused as he did not believe in the spirits. Before his grandfather died he told his son, the writer's father, not to go to his burial place. The warning was disregarded. The week thereafter the bull disappeared. It was found dead on the grave. The other writer tells the story of a man dying in a hospital who asked to be buried there and not at home. His relatives disregarded this and took him home in a jeep. On the way the jeep stuck in the mud and even oxen could not move it. Then one of the relatives pointed out that the deceased did not want to be buried at home. When the vehicle was put into reverse it came out with ease. The writer ends off by affirming that even 'church people' believe in the spirits.

The remaining letter writers argue the case, the one by referring to the ghost scene in Hamlet and stating that Shakespeare knew all about spirits and could not have learned this from Africans; the other by referring to Jesus who cast spirits out of living people. Further 'our fathers' prayed to the spirits and they were answered. Another says that people, which in the context clearly includes Europeans, put flowers on the graves of their loved ones. Any living person has an instinct 'which shows him that there is something more important in the dead than what they can make up differently.'

This correspondence reveals the literate African re-examining his traditional beliefs and, as often as not, reaffirming their validity. It does, however, seem that even though the ancestral spirits may still be believed in, their rituals are less socially relevant in the towns and outside Tribal Trust Land than they used to be and, because of this, belief in the ancestral spirits will probably eventually become mere superstition, playing little more part than ghosts do in the thinking of a European village community. Acceptance of Christianity does not mean that old beliefs are abandoned and, indeed, much can be found in the Bible that can be used to support belief in both the spirits and witchcraft. The relevant passages are well known to many Africans.

CHAPTER V

WITCHCRAFT AND MISFORTUNE

JUST as witchcraft is closely associated with religion, it is also closely associated with beliefs relating to the cause of disease and misfortune. It is, indeed, believed to be one of the more important causes of afflictions of all kinds. For this reason it is necessary to say something as to Shona beliefs as to the cause of such evils. The person who ascertains the cause of disease or misfortune is the doctor-diviner who does so by means of various techniques of divination which will be discussed later. That different diagnoses are possible is a factor of great importance to the diviner as it assists him to produce a popular verdict or to avoid an unpopular one. A diviner may avail himself of these beliefs in court before a European magistrate and, on a charge of indicating a witch as causing misfortune, will often raise the defence that he indicated a *mudzimu* as the source of the trouble.

Minor ailments or misfortunes such as the common cold or a petty scratch or bruise are accepted as natural hazards of life unless complications arise from the injury or the victim is searching for an excuse to accuse someone of witchcraft or sorcery. Apart from these petty matters the principal causes of misfortune are as follows:

WITCHCRAFT

It is thought that this can cause practically any misfortune from the cutting of a shoe strap to the death of numbers of people. However, certain diseases and particularly those of a rather 'uncanny' nature are regarded as clear indications of witchcraft. Thus if people suffer from *mamhepo* where people become delirious, then clearly there is a witch in their midst, if people are looking for a witch. Again a series of deaths is unlikely to have any other cause. Lightning striking a hut, the appearance of the will-o'-the-wisp or antbears are again obvious signs of witchcraft, at least if persons' thoughts are directed to the possibility of witchcraft.

THE SPIRIT WORLD

As mentioned previously a spirit, *mudzimu* or *shave,* may make a person ill to indicate its wants or to indicate that it has been neglected. An *ngozi* is believed to destroy from motives of revenge. If, when misfortune occurs, a diviner is consulted in time he can give instructions as to the proper manner of placating the spirit which is causing the trouble, so causing the spirit to remove its influence.

SORCERY

Although the Shona distinguish between witchcraft and sorcery a sorcerer is also called a 'witch' (*muroyi*). Among allegations of sorcery in the cases examined were the following:

'The accused told me that the cause of her childlessness was the fact that someone had taken her underpants away. He then added that my senior wife also had her petticoat removed.' (*R v Brown* (33)).

'I had to come to find out what was wrong with me since I had no children since 1958. The witchdoctor told me that another man had sent a woman, Cecilia, to come and collect the cloth I used for my monthly periods and had put a spell on this cloth. Cecilia had also taken some of my urine.' (*R v Kateya* (29)).

'You are the one who will die from bleeding, you will die and this will be caused by a relation of yours. This relation of yours collected some urine of yours and put it in the hoof of an animal. He then picked up the hoof and placed a needle on each side. He then tied a string on these needles. When your relation stirs the urine you will die.' (*R v. Makina*. Filabusi 25/2/62).

In yet another case a similar allegation was made, to the effect that the 'witch' had taken urine from her victim and cooked it in a pan. However, this allegation was coupled with another 'You have the portion of the head of the child (another alleged victim) and have eaten a bit of it. You have a snake at your kraal. You have evil spirits which strike your husband.' *R v Chemere alias Mahondoro* (15)). The coupling of these two allegations illustrates that the Shona do not always sharply distinguish witchcraft and sorcery although, as stated previously, only a 'real' witch is capable of psychic acts.

It is widely believed that 'witches' who, in this context, include sorcerers, use evil medicines to injure people. Such medicines are frequently produced by diviners, particularly the prophets of the

Pentecostal Churches. Medicines such as *divisi*, to make crops grow, obtained by murder or through incest are inherently evil; and because their use brings misfortune to the family of the person using them or to other people the user is a sorcerer. However, the object for which this sort of *divisi* is used is eminently desirable. The owner of the medicine is regarded as a sorcerer not because he intends to harm people but because he does not care, being avaricious, whether such harm results or not. There is nothing wrong in the use of legitimate medicines to make *divisi* although, if crops prosper unduly, envy will suggest illicit medicine.

The usual material of sorcery is something closely associated with the victim as, for instance, his urine, nail parings, under garments stained with sweat or a woman's menstrual blood, etc. The Ndebele kings, Lobengula and Mzilikazi, had attendants whose duty it was to dispose of the king's sputum so that no sorcerer could harm him by obtaining possession of it.

Attempts at sorcery take place. A good example is the case of *R v Aaron and Siliva Matshuma* (75) originating from the Kalanga of the Plumtree area—a group under strong Ndebele influence. In this case evidence was led that a certain Petro had become ill and his paternal uncle gave him medicines. Instead of getting better Petro got worse and accused Pukunyoni, his father's elder brother, of bewitching him. There seems to have been some sort of cattle dispute in the background and in addition Petro's father was dead and Petro apparently resented the authority of Pukunyoni. Siliva, Petro's sister, became drawn into the quarrel and accused Pukunyoni of not taking proper care of her brother. Petro then died. Siliva was convinced that Pukunyoni had killed him. Various events took place to confirm that suspicion. Thus, Pukunyoni stayed away from the *kalufu* ceremony at which the deceased's property was distributed. This was particularly surprising as being the eldest of the lineage it was his duty to distribute the property. Again Pukunyoni, probably annoyed with Siliva's allegations, was said to have threatened to kill her by lightning. At some stage a diviner in Bechuanaland was consulted; but although witnesses said that he exonerated Pukunyoni, Siliva remained convinced that he had killed her brother. She importuned several of her friends to obtain for her the urine of Pukunyoni in order to enable her to kill him, but they refused to do so and reported the matter to the village head. A *dare* was held and Siliva told to behave herself. Siliva's attempt to kill Pukunyoni by sorcery was, therefore, frustrated and she and her half brother Aaron who (being the son of her mother's sister and co-wife was almost in the position of a uterine brother) then decided to kill Pukunyoni by physical means. Aaron had, apparently, already tried to burn Pukunyoni's huts. The two of them then waylaid Pukunyoni and killed him with an axe. Evidence was, during the course of the examination, led on Kalanga belief. The following is an extract of the evidence of a village headman:

'I am a Kalanga by tribe and I am familiar with Kalanga tribal customs and witchcraft beliefs. There is a Kalanga belief that a person can be killed by witchcraft (i.e. sorcery) by taking the urine of the person who is to be killed. This is mixed up with some other medicine and is kept. This has the effect of stopping the victim from urinating or relieving nature. The stomach swells up and the person dies. The method of killing by means of urine is the most widely known method and is often used.'

Later I shall give a description of an attempt to kill a person by putting medicine in his snuff—the use of any medicine is, of course, sorcery, when it is used for a purpose not socially approved of. Cases of attempts at poisoning and poisoning using arsenical cattle dip occur occasionally. There can be little doubt that persons do attempt to injure others, on occasion, by means of sorcery.

Certain medicines are believed by the Shona to be used by sorcerers. 'Real' witches may resort to sorcery and use the medicines too. Perhaps the most feared are those which cause *chitsinga* and *chipotswa*. *Chitsinga* is believed to cause paralysis of a limb. The most usual sign of *chipotswa* is said to be that every time a person eats he vomits. All sorts of stomach and intestinal troubles can be blamed on *chipotswa*. According to an urban informant, if a sorcerer wishes to kill you, he may cause *chipotswa* to blind or befuddle you so that you are run down by a car when crossing a road or accidentally touch a live electric cable. He will obtain the medicine from an *nganga*. The sort of occasion which is said to be dangerous is when you go to fill a kettle at the tap and go away for a while while the water is running. Your enemy may, while you are away, place *chitsinga* in water. When you try to lift the kettle on your return your arm will become paralysed. *Chipotswa* may sometimes be used as a general term for sorcery.

In country districts it is thought that if a sorcerer wishes to harm others by means of *chitsinga* he will bury the medicine at the cross-roads telling it the name of the person whom he wishes to hurt. When the victim passes over the medicine it is believed he will become afflicted by the *chitsinga*. A story told me, which is alleged to be of events which took place recently in the Shamva area, illustrates the belief. It is said there were two brothers and the younger committed adultery with the elder's wife. The matter was taken to court and the adulterer was ordered to pay three head of cattle as damages. He refused to do so. The elder brother became angry and threatened the adulterer saying '*Ti cha sangana*' ('we shall meet'—this expression and also 'we shall see' are often construed as threats of supernatural harm). The adulterer lived in a farm compound. Some weeks later people in the compound saw the elder brother in the middle of the night. It was not clear what he was doing. Thereafter the adulterer wished to return home and passed over the spot where his brother had been seen. Immediately he fell down with a swollen leg. His European employer wished him to go to hospital but he refused; so his father took him home. After a few days he died. On his deathbed he stated he had been killed by his brother. Later the alleged sorcerer was charged with killing his brother by his brother's friends and told that he had been seen in the compound. He admitted that he had been in the compound and said nothing more, so it was assumed he was guilty.

If this story is true and I think, at least in outline, it is, it may well be an instance of a person dying as a result of being convinced he had been ensorcelled—I was told that the adulterer had been informed of the nocturnal visit of his brother prior to his death.

Witchcraft and Misfortune

Such deaths are said by both Europeans and Africans to be common.

A case of the alleged use of *chitsinga* occurred on my own property. This case will be discussed in more detail later (p. 175). *Chitsinga* is still greatly feared. Some areas have a particularly evil reputation for using it. For example, the Northern Zezuru think the Karanga of the Enkeldoorn district are prone to using it. It is one of the medicines which transform themselves in the bodies of the victim and, turning into the creatures the sucking doctors remove, may thereafter possess a doctor (see Davies, 1931, p. 41).

In Matabeleland salt is feared as an instrument of sorcery. It is thought that salt taken from someone after dark can be used to harm people. It is said that anyone asking for salt after dark is likely to be treated as a sorcerer.

In view of the belief that faeces can be used for the purposes of sorcery it was a matter of some surprise to me the ease with which it was possible to collect faeces from pupils (mainly Zezuru) at my wife's school which was close to the Chinamora Reserve. The specimens were required for the purposes of Bilharzia research. There was an initial reluctance to bring specimens but when the purpose of the exercise was fully explained there were few who did not co-operate. While it is true that Europeans are not usually thought of as sorcerers the attitude of the pupils suggests beliefs in this type of sorcery are only relevant when tensions have produced what one might call an 'atmosphere of sorcery' and that unless this atmosphere exists no particular significance is attached to the fact that one's excreta may get into the hands of other people—as, indeed, a walk in the veld will also reveal.

BREAKING A TABOO OR OTHER PROHIBITION

Certain taboos are enforced by the spirits. Gelfand (1962, p. 16) states that amongst the Korekore it is believed that a person committing incest will anger the tribal *mhondoro* and that, as a result, drought will ensue. Usually, however, where a taboo is broken misfortune will result simply as the natural consequence of the breach and no spirit intervention is involved.

Amongst the Shona some of the most important taboos are associated with the sexual act. If a man commits adultery and thereafter touches his child, the child will become ill. The social relevance of this taboo as a social sanction in ensuring proper conduct need hardly be stressed. This belief appears to be universal amongst the Shona and, unlike some other taboos which are losing their force, is still of importance. The evil can be averted if one confesses one's adultery to one's wife. If one's wife has a jealous disposition this is not easy but fortunately this difficulty can be overcome by handing one's child a stick from the hearth when one's wife is not looking. If this is impossible, for example, because one has an electric stove in the house, then an object taken from the spot where the adultery was committed will, if handed to the child, avert the evil. A woman's adultery will cause difficult labour and will be dangerous to the life of the newly born child. If childbirth is difficult a woman is made to confess her infidelities. Intercourse with a woman who is having her menses is dangerous, as it is with a woman who has had a miscarriage or with a newly widowed woman. It is said that if one has intercourse with one's sister-in-law (*muramu*) and thereafter eats meat which has been salted by the *muramu* with one's own wife then one's own wife will have a sore back or become blind. The only way of curing this illness is said to be to call in the wife's maternal aunt (*ambuya*) who must give the husband and wife meat salted and medicated by her. Husband and wife must put their knuckles together and eat this meat off their knuckles. This belief is, I believe, confined to the eastern districts. Again, the person who discovers lovers in the veld is likely to have ill luck unless he takes two stones and spits on them. He must then put the stones on the spot where the lovers had intercourse. Other persons passing the spot must do likewise unless they also wish to have ill luck. As a result, they say heaps of stones called *hambakwe* have grown throughout the country on which passing travellers throw stones

Witchcraft and Misfortune

for luck. Similar heaps of stones exist throughout Southern Africa although beliefs as to their origin may differ.

Apart from the taboos associated with sex the Shona have many other taboos. Throughout the world corpses are usually considered to be unlucky and the same is true in Mashonaland. If children of women with babies see a corpse it is believed that they may get ill. For this reason they hide, or used to hide, when the corpse is removed from a village for burial. It is forbidden to eat certain parts of one's totem (*mutupo*) animal and if one does, either one's hair will turn grey, or the teeth fall out. If one's wife is pregnant one must not kill a snake otherwise the new born child will become blind. It is said, however, that the latter danger can be averted if one keeps a small bit of the snake and, when the baby is born, mixes it with the baby's bath water. The birth of twins brings misfortune and, in the past, necessitated their death, or the death of one of them. Even now twins are often so badly neglected that they die.

I shall deal later (p. 103) with the concept of 'medicine' but an important taboo exists in connection with destructive medicines. It is possible for a man to possess medicines such as *chitsinga* and *chipotswa* for a socially approved purpose, for example, for the purpose of avenging a person killed by witchcraft, but should one not confess to one's family the possession of these medicines, members of the family will become ill and the possessor is, in such a case, no better than a witch himself—as indeed is anyone else who wilfully breaks a taboo and thereby causes harm to others. The taboo in this case is not on the possession of destructive medicine but on the secret possession of the medicine.

Certain taboos clearly serve a social function in ensuring proper standards of conduct. It is, for example, socially undesirable that footpaths should be fouled. The Shona believe that should a person urinate on a footpath, or should his urine flow onto a path, he will not have children. The evil here can be avoided—as is usually the case. You must take the wet dust from the path and smear it on your forehead and navel. This will ensure that you become the object of ridicule but it is better than taking a risk. Another taboo is on seeing a woman naked, at any rate if she is not your wife. If you break the taboo you will suffer from a growth (*choshiro*) upon your eyelid. Anyone who has the misfortune to have such a growth is in for a lot of good-natured ribbing. Here, again, the social function of the belief, which is to protect women from molestation when washing and performing other necessary acts, is obvious. Women may be found washing at most times in most rivers so when a Shona man approaches a river he calls *'tipindayiwo'*—'may I pass?'—lest he see a naked woman. If women are present he waits for the reply *'pindayi'*—'pass!'—before crossing.

There are a large number of prohibitions which do not appear to be enforced by any specific sanction. Thus one must not tell *ngano* (stories) in the daytime or in summer. The reason here is probably because they are too distracting. Again, men must not be present when water is put into a newly made pot. Pots are made by women. Again, a man must not eat the first relish cooked in a new pot. A man must not eat the new season's groundnuts (*nyimo*) or pumpkin leaves unless these are prepared by his girl friend. In none of these cases does it appear that any very clearly defined harm will follow upon the transgression of the taboo.

Sometimes the sanction behind the observance of a prohibition is not supernatural harm, but the intervention of the chief and the formal trial of the matter in his *dare*. One such taboo concerns the edible tuber called *tsenza* by the Shona (*Coelus esculentus*). A man is forbidden to eat a tuber which has been cleaned by a married woman unless that woman is the wife of a classificatory brother. In particular, you cannot eat the tuber if it has been cleaned by the wife of your brother-in-law or any woman whom you would call *ambuya*. The reason why this taboo is, or was, the concern of the chief is that a breach of the taboo is only explicable on the basis of sexual familiarity between the woman preparing the vegetable and the man who eats it.

Not all taboos are of equal seriousness. The taboo against incest is, of course, an important one and the transgressor is a wizard.

Others are much less serious. The person with a growth on his eyelid 'caused' by seeing a naked woman is merely laughed at, although here good manners ensure obedience to ordinary accepted standards of conduct even if the supposed sanction does not. Some avoidances are hardly worthy of the name taboo, being mere superstitions which none but the most superstitious would take seriously.

A state of affairs which is inherently risky, in that the desired outcome may fail to eventuate, is almost bound to attract taboos which, if respected, will ensure success and, if neglected, bring disaster. Pregnancy (see Gelfand, 1964, Chap. 12) and the activities of the craftsman are examples of such a state.

New taboos have been created by the Pentecostal Churches and not only is the breach of such taboos vested with spiritual sanctions but the person breaking the rule of the church may become physically ill. I shall discuss these matters in Part III.

MEDICINES

Medicines may cause and cure disease and misfortune and bring good fortune. Medicines (*miti* or *mishonga*) play a large part in Shona wizardry beliefs as it is believed that not only a sorcerer, but also a witch, uses medicines to harm others. I shall in Part III describe the part possession of medicines plays in wizardry denunciations by prophets of the Pentecostal Churches and a similar attitude is found, although it is less pronounced, amongst traditional diviners.

Amongst the Shona, medicine is used not only to cure disorders of the body but to achieve almost any end that requires for its success control over forces which would otherwise be uncontrollable. Medicines are used to protect one against witchcraft; to pass examinations; to win the love of an unwilling woman; to see in the dark; to grow crops successfully; to dispel the *ngozi* and to raise it; to create or cure a witch; and for many other purposes. To categorize the purpose for which medicines are used is impossible. The use of medicines is only limited by the imagination of the user or if there is some other socially recognized means of gaining the end desired. For example, if illness is stated to be caused by the ancestral spirits, the proper method of curing the disease is to propitiate them; I have not come across a suggestion that the *vadzimu* may be coerced by means of medicine. More faith may be reposed in medicines that are demonstrably effective, e.g. a purgative, than in those which are not, e.g. a love potion; but no clear distinction is made between 'medicine' in its medicinal sense and the broader sense which includes charms and periapts of various sorts.

Gelfand (1956, p. 176ff, 1964, Part III) lists many roots, barks and other remedies used as medicines but unfortunately does not state why particular substances have been chosen as remedies. Some, no doubt, have been chosen for their proven therapeutic properties but it is clear from information I have obtained from *nganga* in the Chinamora Reserve that much of Shona medicine is of sympathetic nature (see also Gelfand, 1964, p. 25). Thus *mangoromera*, a medicine which gives strength, is obtained from the rhinoceros and elephant. Medicine which makes a man patient is obtained from the sluggish python. Medicine to close the fontanel of an infant is obtained from the hornbill (*hoto*) because the closing of the fontanel is likened to the way the male hornbill walls up the incubating female in a tree. For swiftness you must kill a swallow (*nyenganyenga*) on the wing and eat it. Crocodiles are evil so their bile (*nduru*) is believed to be one of the most dangerous of all poisons, but they are also strong and *mangoromera* may be obtained from the sand on which they lie. The *ngozi* which hovers over the body of the dead man is conceived as a thick shadow. To dispel it substances such as burning bee's wax, which produce a thick smoke, are used. If you want to dream true dreams because you want to know the racing winners or become a *nganga* you must eat a mixture of the flesh of certain parts of the vulture, which can find its food from afar, of the hyena, which can find its food without seeing it, of the antbear which can see in the dark, and of the cockerel which always knows the time. Other reasons for the selection of medicines probably include verbal similarities between the name of the medicine and the misfortune or object desired. Thus a root called *chiunga* (gathering) attracts custom to a *nganga*; but in such a case it is difficult to exclude the possibility that the root was given its name because of its supposed properties. Much medicinal lore is handed down from generation to generation. A medicine is often used simply because tradition says it can be used in a certain way. Other medicines are revealed to doctor-diviners in dreams.

Even where a medicine could conceivably have some definite medical value it is frequently administered in some way which clearly renders its use ineffective, e.g. by burning it and then rubbing it in incisions (*nyora*) over the affected part of the body. It is important that a medicine be used with the correct ritual, e.g. a patient may be told to lick the medicine from one side of a plate or repeat certain words when taking it. A medicine may on occasion only be effective if used or administered to or by a certain person. In one case before the High Court the accused was charged with murdering a child by administering cattle dip. The accused admitted she had been given the dip by another to kill the deceased's mother and had given it to the child, but claimed that she had no ground for believing it would harm the child as it was intended to harm the mother only. The court rejected this defence; but it would not have been advanced had the accused not thought it had some chance of success.

There are legitimate and non-legitimate medicines. Medicine is not legitimate if it secures an unfair advantage for its owner. A medicine which is not legitimate may involve the use of such forbidden medicines as human flesh or medicinal incest. A person who uses such medicines is a sorcerer. Medicines which are used to capture thieves or exact vengeance where vengeance is justified are not, however, illegitimate even if they cause harm to the person against whom they are directed. The person who uses such medicine is not a sorcerer. To understand the attitude of persons when a man is found in possession of evil medicines, which is exemplified in the case of *R v Mison and Others* (p. 177), it is important to realize how closely medicines, and especially the socially more important medicines, are associated with ideas of morality. A description of the medicine *mangoromera* as given to me by an informant will serve to illustrate that there is as close a connection between a good medicine and ethical concepts as in the case of a bad medicine.

Mangoromera is a medicine which gives a person the power to knock out or even kill a person he strikes. There are many varieties, including the type boxers use to enable them to win their fights, but the type my informant was principally describing was that carried by the law-abiding citizen to protect himself against the hazards of life in the urban townships where violence is seldom far from the surface. The medicine may be obtained in a number of ways, but the types obtained from snakes or from electric wiring are popular. This, incidentally, is a good example of sympathetic magic. The medicine obtained from electrical wiring is said to be the most dangerous. The medicine may be rubbed by the *nganga* into medicinal *nyoro* (cuts) or carried in a cloth armlet (*zango*) or in his pocket. If the owner of this medicine uses it, not to protect himself when attacked, but to attack people, to rob them, or for any other anti-social purpose he is said to become mad and may even wander around striking trees in his frenzy.

A number of medicines have both good and bad forms—I have already mentioned *divisi*. Another is *rukwa* used both to protect and harm property (Gelfand, 1964, p. 72).

SUMMARY

Diseases and afflictions may be caused in many ways but frequently involve a human being as the conscious or unconscious agent of harm. In general, anyone who deliberately causes harm to others in a way which is not socially approved of is a witch or a sorcerer, even if his act is not a psychic act. An act which harms another is not necessarily wizardry, for to constitute wizardry an act must be anti-social and disapproved of. Thus a woman who does not make a confession in childbirth which would save her child is a wizard (see Holleman, 1958, p. 102) although, strictly speaking, she is neither a witch nor a sorcerer as these are terms used by Evans-Pritchard. A man who uses medicines to trap a thief is not a wizard. In addition to being anti-social, for an act to be wizardry there must be something mysterious about the way in which the victim is harmed. A person who kills another with a knife is not a wizard in the ordinary sense of the word, at least if his motive is hate or revenge, although he might be if the motive were to obtain medicine for *divisi* or gambling. Secrecy is not peculiar to wizardry as many forms of magic involve secret actions. In its wider meaning the word 'wizard' (*muroyi*) in Shona can, however, be applied to almost any anti-social person. According to Hannan (1959) the Shona word *chikambi* may mean both a witch and an anti-social person. Clearly, to a Shona, wizardry and anti-social acts have a great deal in common.

CHAPTER VI

THE MAKING OF A SHONA WITCH

As explained previously, a witch is a witch in Shona belief because she is possessed by a spirit which gives her both the ability to perform psychic acts and which drives her to evil. Generally a person possessed by such a spirit is a woman. A witch may, it is believed, become a witch either because a spirit wishes to possess her and she decides to accept that spirit, or because she has been made a witch by another witch. In the former instance it is said she may be possessed by either a *mudzimu* or a *shave* spirit; in the latter instance she will receive a *shave* spirit from her sponsor. Witchcraft is regarded as being frequently hereditary in the female line of the family. Gelfand (1956, p. 52) calls an hereditary witch an *utaka*. I have not, however, heard this word and informants suggest that it might be a corruption of the Ndebele word for witch, *umtakati*.

SPIRIT POSSESSION

If a spirit wishes to possess someone in order to make that person a witch it is said to make that person or her children ill or, perhaps, barren or to cause some other misfortune. If a diviner is consulted he will ascertain that there is a spirit in the village which wishes to make the person afflicted into a witch. The Karanga case of *R v Shango and Mudzingwa* (20) illustrates this belief. Signs of witchcraft (probably *mamhepo*) had been present at the village. Suspicion fell on strangers, Rungano and his wife, probably because they *were* strangers. The suspicion was confirmed because they had good crops, a sign of the use of *divisi,* while others in the village had not. The Shona, as previously mentioned, believe there is both good and bad *divisi*; but once an unfair advantage is thought to have been obtained it will be assumed that bad *divisi* was used. The following is an extract from a witness's evidence. Shango, referred to by the witness, was the *nganga* who divined in the matter:

'In December 1960 we had a *dare* at the kraal. All the men of the kraal were present including Rungano and the kraal head Mudzingwa who is actually the deputy kraal head. The kraal head asked us all to pay money so that we could go and ask the advice of a witchdoctor. We all paid 1s. 3d. The kraal head then said he would send someone to call the witchdoctor. A name of a certain witchdoctor was mentioned. Later that same month Shango came to visit us. He wanted maize. Before he left the kraal on the following day Mudzingwa saw Shango. Mudzingwa said, "Shango I have ten shillings given by the kraal head to give to you to come to the kraal and throw the bones (*hakata*)". Shango replied that he did not have his bones with him. Mudzingwa replied that Shango could use his. Mudzingwa then gave Shango ten shillings. Shango then called all the people around him at Mudzingwa's lands and he said, "Each one of you will have to pay a shilling." He called each person one by one and each paid a shilling. He threw the bones, looked at them and said, "You are innocent." He did this with us all, one by one, until he threw the bones for Rungano. He was the last one. Shango then said, "I have discovered that your wife is possessed by evil spirits. If these are not appeased your wife will be a witch." Rungano asked for advice from the bone-thrower and was told that she should be taken back to her kraal where the spirit could be appeased. Shango then told the gathering, "You can disperse—go back to your lands".'

Another witness in the above case stated that the diviner had said that Shango's wife was possessed by three spirits; so it is probable that the woman was afflicted by the witchcraft *shave*.

According to a Zezuru informant from the Msana Reserve, if a person wishes to get rid of a spirit which wishes to make her into a witch she must consult a *nganga* who will tell her to buy a female sheep. A man would buy a male sheep. The *nganga* will then order her to go into the bush with the sheep together with her elders. She is then made to ride this sheep, which has to be accompanied by a black hen. She gets off the sheep. The sheep and hen are abandoned and medicines have to be buried where they are abandoned. In this way the witchcraft (*uroyi*) is transferred to the animals. When the woman gets off the sheep she must not turn her head to see what is happening and she must go home without thinking of what has taken place. My informant said he had heard of this on a number of occasions. Such treatment is said to be frequent where a woman is barren or if a spinster is not proposed to. If a man takes possession of an animal abandoned in this manner he may become a witch. People are therefore said to be loath to seize stray animals, and the belief serves as a social sanction against the appropriation of stray animals. Animals are often allowed to stray in the expectation that no one will interfere with them. Thus I have been told that amongst the Kalanga donkeys are allowed to stray in the bush during that part of the year when their services are not required. The Shona are reluctant to appropriate abandoned property of any sort. Apart from spirits of witchcraft, abandoned property may harbour an *ngozi* as may, for example, the equipment of a deceased diviner abandoned in the veld.

The above account as to the manner in which a woman can get rid of the spirit which wishes to make her a witch is similar to an account given by Gelfand (1956, p. 56). Various informants 'knew' that something of the sort happens.

A woman may decide to accept the spirit and become a witch.

An account of this was given me by an informant from Manicaland. Let it be supposed that a woman or her children fall ill or that the woman is barren. The woman will consult a *nganga* who may tell her that the *mudzimu* of her grandmother, who was a witch, wishes to possess her. She will then discuss the matter with her elders and these may agree to her accepting the spirit as they may feel it would be worth the price of having a witch in the village if it will cure the affliction, for example, if it will enable a barren woman to bear children. If the elders are all agreed, it is said they will go and look for a black fowl or goat which will then be brought into the hut. One of the elders will then mention the name of the *mudzimu* causing the affliction saying, 'So-and-so is suffering from barrenness (or whatever is the matter), and she has now decided to comply with your request. Here is the offering.' He will then pour water on the back of the animal which must then shake the water off. If it does so it shows that the spirit has accepted the offering and will possess the woman who will, thereafter, be a witch. If the offering is not accepted then the *nganga* must again be consulted. The ceremony can take place at any time of the day or night but must take place indoors. I asked my informant if he knew of any instance of such a sacrifice being made and he told me that he knew of an instance where he thought it had been. A young man in his home district had asked his uncle for a black goat. When asked why he wanted it he replied that it was because his wife wanted to refuse to accept the spirit of witchcraft. His uncle told him not to be silly, one does not refuse to become a witch by means of a black goat. He told his nephew that if he wanted to look for a black goat he must do so secretly. Another informant told me a rather similar story. He said that his uncle, a Zezuru, had married a woman who was barren. The grandmother of the woman informed my informant's uncle that a *shave* of witchcraft wished to possess the barren woman. Her husband refused to let the *shave* possess her and, instead, divorced her. The woman remarried and her new husband is said to have allowed her to accept the *shave*. As a result she now has children.

THE MAKING OF A WITCH BY ANOTHER WITCH

Somewhat surprisingly, amongst the cases examined were a number in which women gave accounts of the manner in which they became witches. The relevant passages of evidence have already been quoted—*see Dawu's case* (pp. 45, 47), *Mazwita's case* (p. 52). Not only does a witch receive a spirit from the person who makes her a witch but she also receives her familiars from the same source—*see Rosi's case* (p. 57). In a number of the passages referred to the suggestion was made that to be a witch it was necessary for the witch to kill her own children or, at least, the first child. Muhlava's illness (p. 47) was presumably a sign of spirit possession.

CHAPTER VII

BELIEFS IN THE MANIFESTATIONS OF WITCHCRAFT

THE forms of witchcraft are believed to be as protean as the forms of evil itself. There is scarcely a calamity or misfortune of any sort which may not be attributed to a witch; she can ride by air at night or bind the lightning to her will; she can use her familiars as vehicles of her power; she knows the secrets of all medicines; she can make the snake strike or the elephant kill its hunter. Whereas beliefs in the nature of witchcraft must differ among peoples whose religions and philosophies differ, beliefs in the forms of manifestations of witchcraft are remarkably similar in outline, even if differing in detail, throughout Southern Africa and, indeed, many close parallels to European belief can be noted.

Although not all witches are believed to be equally destructive, the Shona and Ndebele believe that usually a witch has to kill and is driven relentlessly to perform her misdeeds. Above all, she will seek to destroy people against whom she bears a grudge.

Thus, in the case of *R v Joshua Taruwodzera* (38) it was alleged that the witch's enmity had been caused through a quarrel about fowls. In *R v Elias alias Elijah* (35) the witch was alleged to have been angry because an ant-bear, her steed at night, had been killed. As often as not, however, she bears no grudge against those she kills; but a witch who bears no malice against anyone is unlikely to harm people unless she is angered. The concept of the 'white' witch is familiar to the Shona.

The following are some of the more important beliefs as to the manner in which witches are believed by the Shona and Ndebele to behave—I shall often here quote the words used by various people in making allegations of witchcraft. As pointed out previously, detail accompanying the allegation is frequently essential to the allegation in order to make it clear that it is one of witchcraft and not of sorcery.

CANNIBALISM AND THE USE OF HUMAN FLESH

If you ask a Shona what a witch does the most likely answer you will receive is, 'A witch eats people.' It is believed that they exhume the bodies of the newly dead and eat the flesh. They also make use of this flesh as one of the most powerful of their medicines. One of the commonest allegations, among both Shona and Ndebele, against a person accused of witchcraft is that she has eaten, or is using, human flesh. The horror in which a cannibal is held is as great, if not greater, than the horror our own society feels. Cannibalism, outside the realm of witchcraft and magic, is completely unknown in Southern Africa today and only occurred in the past in time of famine such as that caused by the wars of Shaka in South Africa. The following is a selection of allegations in which this belief is referred to:

'Grandmother you walk about carrying two pieces of human flesh with which you bewitch people.' (*R v. Ruka* (60)).

'You bewitched my child, you no longer go to the butchery to buy meat, you eat the meat of my child which is still in your quarters.' (*R v. Mack alias Chowa* (91)).

Beliefs in the Manifestations of Witchcraft

'He said . . . I wanted to kill Lilian and eat her flesh because she was being protected by Mildred.' (*R v Kufa* (32)).

'You are a witch and always sit on the grave of Makati at night. You have some part from a dead person's body which you put on your hands and you place your hands on people at night.' (*R. v. Mapfumo Mufonganyedza* (4)).

'You ate your daughter's child . . . you have the arm of that child, a hyena, owl and snake.' (*R v. Paradza* (37)).

'You, grandmother, are a witch . . . you have a portion of the head of a child and have eaten a bit of it. You have a snake in your kraal, you have evil spirits which strike your husband.' (*R v Chemere alias Mahondoro* (15)).

Perhaps, however, the best account of witchcraft beliefs in this matter, at any rate as far as the Shona are concerned, is to be found in the passage (p. 47ff) of the case of *R v Dawu*. In this case the self-confessed witches Muhlava and Tsatsawani alleged that they had ridden their hyenas to the grave of their victim Chidava and had exhumed the body and eaten a part of it. The body was actually exhumed by the police and later subjected to a post-mortem but no trace of any interference with the body was found. This is as one would expect. As Parrinder (1958, p. 142) has shown, the eating of the body by witches is, throughout Africa, a psychic act. Many informants, however, insisted that the eating of the body was not a psychic act but an actual physical eating. The better view, however, seems to be that expressed by a witness in the case of *R v Modas* (83)—'I know of a native superstition to the effect that if a person is possessed of certain spirits (*shave ro uroyi*) he can eat the flesh of a dead and injured person, yet there will be no visible signs of injury to the body.' It is because of the fear that witches interfere with the bodies of the newly dead that the corpse and grave were, and in places still are, watched by the relatives at night to ensure that no one comes near. That this is not entirely without danger to the watchers is illustrated by the case of *R v Zindoga alias Nice* (p. 84) where one of the watchers was herself accused of witchcraft. According to Gelfand (1959, p. 156) if the watchers at the grave can catch a witch at the grave and drive a nail into her head, or rather into the head of the psychic body of the witch, some days later the witch herself will die. Any interference with a grave, in particular by an animal such as a hyena, may be regarded as proof of witchcraft.

If a person wishes to prove she is a witch the most obvious way to do so is to eat human flesh. Sporadic cases of this nature are reported from time to time in the press of various African territories. A Northern Rhodesian example is described by White (1947, p. 10). One such example in Southern Rhodesia came to light in the case of *R v Zalepi* (committed for trial at Tjolotjo 2.11.59), an Ndebele case. Zalepi, a woman, had been charged with infanticide and it was, therefore, essential for the prosecution to prove that her child had been born alive. This is normally done by leading medical evidence to show that the lungs of the infant were expanded with air. However, in this instance, the police recovered only the lower portion of the infant's body. Further investigation revealed that the upper portion of the body had been eaten by two women who stated that they were 'witches'. One of these women—who must surely be one of the most extraordinary witnesses ever to give post-mortem evidence before a court—was called by the Crown to testify as to the state of the lungs when she ate them. As a result of the indecisive nature of her evidence the Attorney-General declined to bring Zalepi to trial. The witness's name was Mdingelwa and her evidence was as follows:

'I live in Mazini kraal in the Gwaai Reserve. I am a witch, I bewitch people. During the last ploughing/planting season the accused came to my kraal. She asked me for a love potion. I told her I could obtain some for her, but first I wanted some menstrual blood. Accused told me she had missed a period and thought she was pregnant.

After threshing and harvesting this year accused came to see me at my kraal and she said, "I gave birth on Monday night." (After that she indicated where she had hidden the child.) I went with my sister Neiwa to the accused's kraal in the night when people were asleep. The accused came to call us. We went to the spot indicated by the accused. We found a dead baby. We cut the child in half at the waist. We left the lower portion of the body in the pit and covered it up again as we had found it. My sister and I took the upper portion of the child. We had used a

Beliefs in the Manifestations of Witchcraft

knife to cut it in half. We went back to Masusu line to my sister's kraal with a portion of the child's body. When we cut the body in half, I collected some of the blood in the shell of a kaffir orange and handed the blood to the accused who said she wanted it. My sister and I had already mixed some medicine with the child's blood that we handed to the accused. She was to anoint herself with this medicine. On reaching my sister's kraal with the upper portion of the body we cooked it all and ate it. The bones were soft, we were able to chew them.'

This case is of very great interest in that, as mentioned earlier (p. 59) it is one of the few cases where the reason for a confession of witchcraft seems reasonably certain. In view of the evidence of the supplying of medicine to Zalepi for a love potion it would seem that Mdingelwa and her sister were in the process of establishing themselves as *inyanga* (doctor-diviners).

The flesh of a man is regarded by the Shona as one of the witch's most potent instruments of evil. It may be administered by the witch herself during the course of her nocturnal travels or she may send a familiar to administer the poison for her. Sometimes witchcraft allegations refer to this belief. In the accusations mentioned above it will be noted that the possession of human flesh is put in the same category as the possession of animal familiars. An example of the belief in the potency of human flesh as a poison is in the case of *R v Muteto* (62) where evidence was given that a certain Tsatsavani was accused of giving human meat to another woman and so causing her to miscarry.

THE WITCH'S FAMILIARS

Every 'real' witch is believed to possess her familiars which are called *zwidoma* in Shona and *imikoba* in Ndebele. The words *zwidoma* and *imikoba* do not, however, refer to all familiars but only to those which can be sent to cause harm. The animals which a witch rides on her nocturnal excursions, such as the hyena or ant-bear, are simply regarded as the steeds of witches. Possession of familiars is frequently alleged in accusations of witchcraft although, unfortunately, court interpreters often translate the word into English by means of the ambiguous word 'spirit' or even as a 'fairy' and it is thus sometimes difficult to understand precisely what is being referred to. The following are examples of such accusations:

'Stand up you are a witch and have *zwimwanana* (dog-like familiars) which you have in your hut.' (*R v. Peter alias Lelizwe* (77)).

'The accused then said to me that when I was pregnant my breast was sucked by some things which are seen at night; when I gave birth my child sucked the dirt which was left by those things on my breast.' (*R v. Moses* committed for trial at Bulawayo 5.8.61).

'The illness of Pikita was caused by the old woman Ncoto through the agency of small wild animals.' (*R v. Mandebele* (45)).

'Accused said that I rode an ant-bear together with Mtswulani. He said that the ant-bear was Tshandita whom we turned into an ant-bear and rode at night.' (*R v Madubeko* (73)).

Shona witches are believed to possess a number of such familiars. It will be recalled that Rosi (p. 57) possessed a *chitukwani*, a crocodile, two snakes, a pole cat and a hyena. Amongst the Shona the animals most popularly believed to be the familiars and steeds of witches are ant-bear, hyena, owl and crocodile.

In *R v Dawu* (p. 45) evidence was led that the hyenas were ridden and tied up very much in the manner of horses. In the case of *R v Mazwita and Others* (p. 49) on the other hand, the familiars were treated as pets, being fed and given names. Gelfand (1959, p. 167) records the feeding of owl familiars and states that a witch rides 'the hyena, pig or sheep in order to reach the abode of her victim' and she holds 'in the palm of her hand the owl (*zizi*) which is her messenger'. It is the smaller, more domestic familiars which it is believed will suck the milk of a nursing mother and cause death to the child she is suckling and will suck a man's saliva or the mucus of his nose and so destroy him. Because of their association with witches, animals such as the ant-bear, hyena and crocodile are greatly feared. In an inquiry into the death of a certain *Bhuja Amos* (died 28.8.60), a Kalanga from the Plumtree district, it was thought possible that the deceased had committed suicide because ant-bears had visited his hut and,

Beliefs in the Manifestations of Witchcraft 117

accordingly, evidence was obtained from a Native Department Messenger on Kalanga belief. His evidence was as follows:

'I am a Kalanga by tribe and qualified to give evidence on their customs. The Kalanga have a fear of the ant-eater and regard it as being associated with evil. Like some of the Mashona tribes (i.e. the Eastern Shona) they believe that it is used as a steed at night by witches. The fear of the ant-eater is so great amongst the unsophisticated Kalanga that even to see it at day in the the veld is regarded as a premonition of evil and bewitchment. Should an ant-eater visit a kraal during the night it is considered a very bad omen and is an indication that the owner or occupier of the kraal has been bewitched. Normally when this happens the occupiers of the kraal will immediately seek the advice of a witch-doctor. Bones are thrown with a view to ascertaining who is responsible for bewitching the occupier. If no immediate satisfaction is obtained from the throwing of the bones the kraal concerned is normally abandoned and the people move to another area. In my opinion, the visit of an ant-eater to a kraal at night is sufficient cause for a person to take his own life. The fear in which the unsophisticated Kalanga regard the ant-eater cannot be overstressed and of all the animals it is regarded as being the most closely associated with witchcraft. I am myself afraid of it. Should one visit my kraal whether by day or night I should definitely move my kraal elsewhere. I would not consider it unusual for a person to take his own life without bothering to first seek advice from the *inyanga*.'

The witness undoubtedly overstresses the fear in which ant-bears are held. It is not, for example, a common cause of suicide that ant-bears have been seen in the village, although the ordinary man seeing or hearing an animal he thinks is a familiar will make use of the appropriate medicines or take other measures to ensure that no harm comes of it. Nevertheless, his evidence does illustrate the very real fear in which the animals are held. Killing an ant-bear is an act which it can be expected its owner will avenge. In the case of *R v Elias* (35) evidence was led that shortly before his death the deceased had killed an ant-bear. A prophet of a local church was called in to divine and a woman, Madende, indicated as a witch. As one might expect the accusation took the following form:

'Your father was killed by his female relatives. Your father killed an ant-bear. A female killed your father because he had killed her horse. This (indicated) is the woman who killed your father.'

In a number of Shona cases a familiar called a *chitukwani* is mentioned. Not all *zwitukwani* belong to witches but many do. A *chitukwani* is said by my Zezuru informants to be a familiar in the form of a maimed and disfigured child, although others say he is tall and thin. He may sometimes be seen in the form of a will-o'-the-wisp. He strikes people who wander alone in the veld. These will die thereafter unless they obtain medicine from an *nganga*. Many people wear a *zango* (cloth armlet containing medicine) to protect themselves from the *chitukwani*. A witch may obtain a *chitukwani* by raising the spirit of someone who has died. Some say that the *chitukwani* can be heard roaring at night but in this case it may be confused with *chimbwanana*, a small, dog-like, familiar. In some areas, probably under Ndebele influence, the *chitukwani* seems to have acquired some of the characteristics of that 'lecherous little beast' (Ashton, 1952, p. 295) the *thokolosi* or *tokoloshe*, so universally believed in in South Africa, but several of my informants strongly denied that the *chitukwani* interfered sexually with women in any way. Others said it might do so.

Witches may acquire familiars either by inheritance, or from another witch. Rosi (p. 57) was alleged to have been given quite a menagerie by Ngurirayi. In *Mazwita's case* Netsayi told the police that she has not yet been given any (p. 56). Further they may be obtained by capture. The following is a statement from an Ndebele witness in the case of *R v Kani* (49) which illustrates this belief. Shona belief is very similar:

'I am of the Ndebele tribe and *umkoba* (familiar) should be interpreted as the witch's messenger or tool of the witch. It is, in fact, the spirit of a dead person which has been awakened or captured by other *imikoba*, these *imikoba* being, in turn, sent by a witch. The witch sends the *umkoba* to a person he wishes to harm or kill. This *umkoba* is said to be able to speak with the voice of its earthly body and is generally associated with death or some terrible happening. If the *umkoba* speaks to a person, that person knows that something terrible is going to happen to him. Both members of my tribe and the Kalanga tribe are frightened of the *Umkoba* which is a thing to be feared.'

The witness in the above passage is apparently referring to the type of familiar known as the *izituhwane*, which are the same as the *zwitukwani*. According to Kani, the accused, the familiar appeared to him in the form of his dead child.

Some African peoples, e.g. the Kaonde of Northern Rhodesia (Melland, 1923, p. 204ff) believe that the familiar will eventually destroy the witch. The Shona or, at least, the Zezuru do not think this is inevitable or even likely but state that if the familiars are really annoyed, for example, by being sent to a village where the protective magic is too strong for them, they may turn on their owner and destroy her.

There are a number of accounts of Ndebele beliefs in familiars. One of the earliest is Carnegie (1894, Chap. III) who mentions a number of the animal familiars well known in Shona mythology. Garbutt (1910, p. 46) mentions, in addition, the *isituhwana*, which are clearly the Shona *zwitukwane*, and *dzijga* or *simbuwanana*, an imp the shape of a human being with only one leg. All these familiars are apparently of Shona origin. Bullock (1950, p. 172) mentions the *zwizha* as a Shona familiar—although it was unknown to my informants—and the *chimbwanana*, which is an animal familiar, is well known throughout Mashonaland. Hughe's description of Ndebele belief (in Kuper *et al.*, 1955, p. 107), again conveys the impression that Ndebele belief is almost entirely of Kalanga origin. This is not a matter which I have been able to investigate fully, but my few Ndebele informants certainly knew the *tokoloshe*, which plays its usual lecherous part in Ndebele belief, and co-exists with the belief in the *izituhwane*. Again they knew that a witch might invoke *izulu* but they regarded *izulu* as being the powers of the elements and not, as the Zulu know it, the lightning bird (Schapera, 1937, p. 244). Further investigation in regard to Ndebele beliefs is required. Two types of *tokoloshe* are recognized by the Ndebele. The one sort is sent by a witch to cause trouble and the other is kept to protect its owner and has the usual sexual attributes. As in the case of the *madzimudzangara* (goblins) in Shona belief, when you meet a *tokoloshe* in the veld and he asks 'When did you see me?' as he is accustomed to do, you must reply, 'A long way off.' The *tokoloshe* is sensitive about his short stature and if one fails to give a proper reply the *tokoloshe* will be offended and will harm you. This belief is, of course, well known in various forms throughout Southern Africa and may, perhaps, be a folk memory of the Bushmen who previously occupied the land. The *madzimudzangara* are frequently associated with caves containing paintings of the late Stone Age.

There is little that is overtly sexual in Shona witchcraft beliefs. There was, however, a reference to a witch having sexual intercourse with an animal familiar in the case of *R v Shonayi Chipembere Juwere* (committed for trial at Fort Victoria 20.6.64). The accusation in this case, which was made by a prophet of one of the Pentecostal Churches took the following form—'You, wife, are a witch. You have three *zwidoma*. You have got an owl. You also have a snake which you keep in a pot and also a crocodile has sexual intercourse with you and this crocodile stays in the pool of water.'

It is of some interest that the Shona words used for certain familiars are etymologically related to similar words used in the language of other Southern Bantu peoples for the ancestral spirits. Thus the Lovedu word *zwidajani* would appear to be the same as the Shona *zvitukwani*. The Tsonga word *shikwambo* is clearly the same as the Shona *chikwambo* which is a familiar used not by witches but by the *nganga*, the doctor-diviner, who has, however, many of the aspects of a witch. While it is possible that the *chitukwani* and the *chikwambo* may be in origin merely 'worn down' ancestral spirits it is more probable that they originated as inversions of the benevolent ancestral spirits. Here again one finds the characteristics inversion in witchcraft beliefs of the order of things which are regarded as right and proper.

Although many of the houses in which the Shona and Ndebele now live have glass windows, the fear of the *zwidoma* is still sufficiently general and widespread to ensure that they are normally kept shut at night.

THE NOCTURNAL TRAVELS OF WITCHES

Witches are believed to travel at night to carry on their nefarious calling. The three cases discussed at length in Part I are good examples of Shona belief. In the case of *R v Dawu* it will be remembered that evidence was given as to how the witches travelled at night on hyenas. In *R v Mazwita and Others* the witches were said to have stripped themselves naked and smeared themselves with ointment so they could fly through the air or, as they put it, 'travel by night.' Although the passages quoted do not make it altogether clear that the nocturnal travelling involved flight I understand that this emerged clearly from the evidence given before the High Court. As far as I know the belief that witches may travel through the air without a steed has not so far been recorded from the Shona, whose witches are generally supposed to ride their familiars, but the belief is widespread in Africa. Thus Basuto witches are believed to be able to fly at night through their knowledge of the appropriate medicines and to foregather in secluded dongas where they disport themselves naked (Ashton, 1952, p. 249).

A Shona witch and, apparently, also an Ndebele witch is enabled to travel at night through the agency of the spirits which possess her, be they *vadzimu, mashave* or their equivalent. This belief may, on occasion, be referred to in witchcraft allegations, thus in the case of *R v Dumbu* (65) from Nuanetsi the allegation took the following form:

'The accused said that Nyadzi got up at night and travelled with evil spirits. He said he saw that Nyadzi had an evil spirit which caused her to get up at night and had killed Mahlupe's child, a baby girl.'

While the Shona picture a female witch as riding her steed at night, whether it be an ant-bear or a hyena or some other animal, the male witch is imagined by those who consider a man can be a witch, as a warlock walking forth at night carrying his spear or battle axe and accompanied by his familiars which follow him like a pack of dogs. He carries with him the medicines he uses to create the weird and hideous shapes he uses to frighten people.

Junod (1913, p. 463) states that the Tsonga believe that a 'true unsheathing' of the personality takes place when a witch travels at night, for when a witch flies away his *'ntjhuti'* or shadow remains behind him, lying on his mat. The Shona have no such belief. They believe that when a witch travels at night she goes entirely, leaving nothing behind except a medicine to stupefy her husband or other occupants of her hut and to ensure that no one wakes and finds her missing.

THE CONTROL BY WITCHES OVER THE FORCES OF NATURE

Not only may a Shona or Ndebele witch injure a person by means of her familiars or during the course of her nocturnal wanderings, but she may use the forces of nature, animate and inanimate, to execute her evil purposes. That a person is killed by a snake or elephant does not exclude the possibility of witchcraft. The problem is then who 'sent' the animal. So too, lightning may strike because it has been sent by a witch, or a tree may fall because a witch wills it to do so. This attitude was expressed in the case of *R v Machuchu* (92):

'We went to a witchdoctor to find out from him what had caused the death of Levi. We knew a snake had bitten him but according to our custom (i.e. belief) we had to find out through a witchdoctor what had caused the snake to bite him.'

The elements which an Ndebele witch invokes to strike her victim, and more particularly the lightning, are called *izulu*.

A witch may even cause soil erosion. In the case of *R v Sihwanda* (90) it was alleged that a witch had threatened to cause this. Curiously enough Native Department Agricultural Demonstrators were credited with causing erosion. The reason is probably that their interference in farming operations was resented and because they were introduced at the time when the necessity to prevent

Beliefs in the Manifestations of Witchcraft

erosion in the tribal trust land first became apparent because erosion was occurring.

Perhaps the most frequent tool of nature which witches are believed to use is the lightning. I am told by a European doctor who used to practise at Harare Hospital that the patients frequently diagnose the cause of their illness as due to lightning. Since few who are struck by real lightning live, one may presume that a witch's lightning is often a psychic variety that may strike its victim in his sleep. Lightning is visualized as a bird which lays its eggs where it strikes. The sending of the lightning bird is no more difficult for a witch than is the sending of any other familiar.

There is a type of doctor who specializes in protecting people from lightning. The case of *R v Kwame* (committed for trial at Selukwe 8.4.58) will serve to illustrate both beliefs concerning lightning and the manner in which these practitioners operate. Kwame was an old Karanga of about seventy. The case contains one of those coincidences which makes it so difficult for the Shona to disbelieve in witchcraft. The extract below is taken from the evidence of a certain Jeka:

'I went to a beer drink at Makwarera, Selukwe Reserve, where I saw the accused. He told me he had been to the Matopo hills where he had heard my name mentioned (by the Mlimo). He told me that lightning was going to come to me and that it was being sent to me by other people who disliked me because I am a kraal head. He told me that the spirits had given him this information. Accused then said that if I had 15/- he could fix it up for me and prevent the lightning from coming to my kraal. I refused to agree to this. On the 19th February (i.e. about a month later) lightning struck my young brother whilst he was in his hut. He was killed as a result. Towards the end of February I went to accused at his kraal and asked him to come and fix my kraal. Accused asked me for 5/- saying it was for coming to my kraal. I paid accused the 5/- when he arrived at my kraal in the evening. He slept the night at my kraal. Next morning he dug a hole in the floor of my deceased brother's hut. Accused then said he had found the lightning eggs. Accused then asked for a small piece of iron sheeting which I gave him. He placed the eggs on this sheet. They looked like mushroom roots but I did not touch them. Accused then asked if there was a river nearby. I told him where it was and I accompanied him there. We went to a pool. Accused got into it until he was waist deep. Accused then put the eggs into the water with the iron sheet and then walked out of the pool. We returned to my kraal. Accused then said, "I have fixed the lightning from coming to your kraal again." He then asked me for £1. Rudowo handed £1 to the accused. Accused then asked for meat and I brought a goat. He told me to skin it, which I did. Accused then told Rudowo and myself to cut the goat across the waist. Accused then took the lower portion of the body and we took the top. After he had eaten he said he wanted a beast and that if I could not get one I would have to pay him £5. I promised to sell my grain and pay him £5.'

Many evil omens are attributed to witches. Their medicines can create phantasmagora of all kinds. Should any unnatural occurrence take place a diviner should be consulted. He will instruct his clients how to protect their village. The eclipse of the moon may even be interpreted in terms of witchcraft. Thus when in 1885 the Ndebele army was sent to attack the people in the Lake Ngami area an eclipse took place. This was interpreted as a sign of witchcraft and the damage to morale so caused probably contributed to the disaster that ensued (Carnegie, 1894, p. 45).

THE SENDING OF THE NGOZI BY A SHONA WITCH

The *ngozi* is a spirit of a man who died with a grudge and, being malevolent, is a ready-made tool for a witch to use. The witch may send an *ngozi* in the manner in which she sends a familiar. The ability of the *ngozi* to speak through a medium is, according to Gelfand (1962, p. 69), one of the most important characteristics of the *ngozi*. The *ngozi* sent by a witch may similarly possess its victim. An example of possession by the *ngozi* is the disease of epilepsy. While it is recognized that epilepsy may be hereditary, the Shona believe that non-hereditary epilepsy is caused by witchcraft. Some years ago a Manyika from Portuguese East Africa was found dead with a wooden nail in his skull which had been inserted after death. In his life the deceased suffered from epilepsy. An explanation of the nail was given in court by a labour recruiter and was amplified to me by an informant. It is,

Beliefs in the Manifestations of Witchcraft

as I have said, believed that a witch may invoke an *ngozi* in the family of her victim to cause epilepsy. The victim becomes possessed by the *ngozi*. When the epileptic dies it is necessary to ensure that the *ngozi* does not come out of the body but is buried with it. Therefore, a wooden nail is driven into the head in the same way that a murderer may drive a nail into the head of his victim to prevent his victim's *ngozi* from troubling him or, indeed, a nail may be driven into the skull of a witch (Gelfand, 1959, p. 156). I have previously mentioned various ways in which the *ngozi* may be laid (p. 88) but apparently a wooden nail is regarded as particularly appropriate where witchcraft is involved.

THE WITCH'S MEDICINES

Shona and Ndebele witches are believed to possess medicines which they administer during the course of their nocturnal wanderings. These medicines may be of such allegedly poisonous substances as human flesh or crocodile bile or else of plants known only to witches. One of the commoner forms of witchcraft allegation is to state of a person that she possesses 'medicines'. Examples of such accusations are:

'This person gave medicine to the child and it died.' (*R v. Ester Mancube* (69)).

'You are a bad old man, you have medicine for killing people.' (*R v. Mison and Others* (101)).

'You are a witch, you have bewitched the child of your other wife, you have cooked medicine and put it into the porridge. He also said I had small animals.' (*R v. Peter alias Lelizwe* (77)).

'You, old woman, you are the one who killed Konzapi's child. You killed this child by your spirits. There is another old woman who gave you medicines to kill the child.' (*R v. Aaron Ndhlovu* (88)).

'You are a witch, you wrapped medicines in a cloth.' (*R v Mapfumo & Mufonganyedza* (4)).

'This witch person has some roots which she keeps in her anus. You will see this person if I get up and dance.' (*R v. Maria* (18)).

While it is not clear in all cases whether an act of witchcraft or sorcery is alleged, in many of the accusations the giving of medicine is associated with other allegations which make it clear that the act alleged was one of witchcraft.

A witch may keep her medicines in a 'horn' (Shona *gona*) which, however, may not necessarily consist of an animal's horn. Indeed, the analogous 'horn' of the Shona doctor-diviner is almost always a gourd. This 'horn' may itself take on some of the attributes of a familiar. It may fly through the air and suck at the breasts of women. I shall give accounts in Part III as to the manner in which prophets of the Pentecostal Churches frequently produce such horns during the course of divinations. Diviners of traditional type may also produce horns, but apparently less frequently. However, in two of the cases examined the horn was produced dramatically by the diviner entering the hut and nodding, the horn then falling from the roof. Medicines are frequently carried in horns, a common charm consisting of a small antelope horn containing medicine hung on a string around the neck. This has its dangers since the finding of such a horn on a person suspected of witchcraft or sorcery, particularly if it appears to be secreted, will often be regarded as proof of witchcraft or sorcery, as in the case of *R v Mison and Others* (101).

I have previously described how a Shona sorcerer is believed to administer *chitsinga* and *chipotswa*. These medicines are also part of the stock in trade of a witch who travels by night. Suppose that a Shona witch wishes to harm you by using *chitsinga*. In such a case it is believed she will enter your house while you are sleeping and make *nyora* (cuts) on the limb she wishes to afflict in the same manner as a doctor-diviner cuts *nyora* on his patient. She will then rub the medicine into the cuts. When you wake up in the morning you will find the limb paralysed. You can tell that the affliction really is *chitsinga* because if you look closely you will find a slight swelling where the witch made her cuts. In passing, the similarity between the conduct of a doctor-diviner and the conduct attributed to a witch should again be noted.

Other medicines which a Shona witch carries with her at night can, they say, create huge and frightening shapes.

CHAPTER VIII

PROTECTION AGAINST WIZARDRY

NEARLY all children and many adults carry with them charms to protect themselves against wizardry. A frequent form taken by these charms amongst the Shona is a cloth circlet, the *zango*, worn around the arm which has protective medicine sewn into it.

Not only are individuals protected by means of charms, but it is necessary to protect the village as a whole against the machinations of wizards. A case illustrating the manner in which a village may be protected is *R v Jackson William Maseko* (committed for trial at Nkai 23.8.60). The persons concerned were, with the exception of the doctor, Ndebele-speaking. Although the doctor came from Nyasaland his manner of procedure resembles, in general, that of local doctors although, no doubt, each doctor's methods differ in detail from other doctors. The following is an extract from the evidence of kraal head Zhobolo:

'In July 1960 accused came to my kraal. With him was my brother-in-law Mtetwa. Mtetwa introduced the accused to me and told me he was able to perform magic. In my own language I would call him an *inyanga*. I asked accused to perform magic and by so doing to protect my kraal and cast out evil spirits from it. The accused said that he was without his apparatus but that he would return to perform his magic. He then left me. I went to the accused on Wednesday the third of August at Mapolisa kraal. I asked accused if he was coming to perform his magic at my kraal. He said he was and asked me to have two eggs ready for me at my kraal in the evening. He did not ask me to have anything else ready. I returned to my kraal and at about six o'clock in the evening accused came to my kraal. The accused arrived with a woman whom I took to be his wife. I know her by the name of Mamoyo. My brother Sikalongwe was with me and there were two other women at the kraal as well as my wife and my brother's wife with two small children. The accused offered to perform his magic for the payment of £7, but I told him I had no money. I offered him a beast instead and showed him a young ox in my cattle kraal which the accused accepted. I estimated the value of the beast to be £8. We returned to the kraal after arranging about the beast and accused asked for two eggs. He insisted on them being fresh eggs. After asking for the eggs he told me to go and fetch a fowl. He did not specify the type or colour of the fowl. I brought him a black hen of my own. The accused took the fowl and cut off one of its toes. He then painted the eggs with blood from the fowl's foot. The accused then asked all the people in the kraal to gather round. He had a haversack with him from which he took a small calabash which contained a black powder. He took a second small calabash from the haversack. This was decorated with beads. He asked me for an old razor blade which I gave him. He, the accused, then began making small cuts on the foreheads and backs of men and the backs of the women's hands. He then rubbed the black powder into these cuts. The accused then took the second decorated calabash and poured water into it and told us it was his magic instrument. He then took another calabash from his haversack. This had something inside which made it rattle. The accused then sealed the decorated calabash with wax and started to rattle the calabash with the things inside it. He was holding the decorated calabash upside down in his left hand while rattling the other in his right hand. The accused started mentioning all forms of evil that could trouble us and said if one of those troubled us the water would come out of the calabash, which it did do. I dug a hole in the centre of the kraal at the accused's request into which he put the eggs smeared with blood. The hole was filled up with soil again. It was a small hole about six inches in diameter and a foot deep. This took place before the accused filled the decorated calabash with water. This completed accused's performance for my beast. Sikolongwe then asked if accused could perform magic to show what was wrong with the small child of his. The accused agreed to do this for 7s. 6d. but Sikolongwe had no cash and offered a fowl worth 5s. to the accused which he agreed to accept. He asked for a small tin of mealie meal. He put medicine into the tin with the meal and made porridge which was given to the child. The accused and his wife then left.'

In answer to a question put by the accused in cross-examination Zhobolo added:

'I was satisfied with your magic up to the time you returned to the kraal with the police who dug up the eggs and now the evil spirits have all returned.'

In the case of *R v Brown* (33) evidence was led that an Ndebele called Mavoluntiya consulted the accused, an *inyanga,* about the whereabouts of his missing wife. The accused said that the woman was well and ascribed her absence to wizardry and, as Mavoluntiya's village was 'no good', he offered to cure it. He later agreed to protect the village for a fee of £10. To protect the village he put medicine in a dish and sprinkled this about the village. At the entrance of the village holes were dug and the medicine put into the holes. He then gave Mavoluntiya medicine, telling him to burn it in the village. He also gave him a duiker's horn containing medicine which was to be kept to protect the village. Some days later Mavoluntiya discovered that his wife had killed herself. Quite naturally Mavoluntiya then decided that Brown was a charlatan and went to demand his money back. Brown refused and offered to perform vengeance magic against the putative wizard who had caused his wife's death. Mavoluntiya was annoyed and refused to give Brown the goat which he required to perform this magic. The case was then reported to the police.

PART III

THE ALLEGATION OF WIZARDRY

CHAPTER IX
THE PATTERN OF ACCUSATIONS

OVER a hundred court records of accusations of wizardry were examined and, although this number is not really sufficient to enable one to come to any final conclusions, some guidance may be sought from these cases as to the manner in which, and the persons against whom, such accusations are made. Wizardry allegations result from social conflict; but it is clearly not every such conflict which results in an accusation. They do not, for example, occur where the conflict can be satisfactorily settled by the tribal courts, although they may occur when such proceedings become frustrated, as in the case of *R v Sengani* (p. 162), or where litigation is unlikely to provide a satisfactory remedy. Hogbin (1958, p. 112) has suggested that the existence of tribal courts reduces the number of wizardry allegations by resolving many of the conflicts in the society. Certainly, if the cases reported to the authorities be any guide, serious allegations among the Shona and Ndebele, who possess such courts which still function fairly efficiently, are not particularly frequent.

Wizardry allegations may occur as a result of two different ways of thinking. Firstly, because a person dislikes someone else, he may think that that person is a wizard and therefore likely to bewitch or ensorcel him or his relatives. Accordingly the accuser seeks for a misfortune to lay at the wizard's door—amongst the Shona this may be done literally by putting ash or a branch at the threshold of the wizard—and when a misfortune occurs the suspected wizard is then blamed. Secondly, a misfortune may occur and that misfortune, particularly if it is the death of a person and, more especially, a child, may be attributed to wizardry. The accuser will then seek to find who is responsible. He may turn to a diviner, but whether he does so or not, the person seeking to find the wizard will be guided by his knowledge of the situations in which the first mentioned type of allegation are known to take place. Thus, if the afflicted person is a woman, then certainly the fact that her co-wife bears her ill-will will be taken into consideration. It is well known that allegations of wizardry are common between co-wives. The situation is complicated because social tensions between two persons may result in an allegation of wizardry against a third. Also because what people appear to be fighting about may be only a symptom of a more fundamental underlying conflict. Unfortunately the material at my disposal is seldom sufficient to investigate the real sources of friction in the particular case, but some analysis is possible of the relationship between 'witch' and victim amongst the Eastern Shona and, to a lesser degree, the Ndebele-Kalanga. The apparent nature of the conflict which gave rise to an accusation of wizardry is listed in the Table in Appendix I. This is simply what the persons concerned appeared to be fighting about, deeper analysis being, from the nature of the material, seldom possible.

There were fifty-five allegations of wizardry amongst the cases examined which originated from the Eastern Shona groups and twenty-six such cases from the Ndebele-Kalanga. Unfortunately it did not prove possible in the cases examined to separate the Ndebele from the Kalanga. Both groups formed part of the Ndebele nation. Many Ndebele speakers are of Kalanga origin and even persons who are more properly Kalanga claim to be Ndebele (O'Neil, 1906, p. 146). Even where the Kalanga language survives, a Kalanga diviner such as Ester Ncube may divine entirely in an Ndebele idiom so that, notwithstanding that she is a Kalanga, she can only be regarded as an Ndebele *isangoma*—indeed she is one of the most famous of all such *isangoma*. The information necessary to separate the 'real' Ndebele and the others was seldom given in the cases examined by me. The primary value of the

Ndebele-Kalanga cases is, as a result as comparative material for the statistics relating to the Eastern Shona.

Many accusations involved persons of various tribal groups and I have included in the tables below such cases where the accuser, whether or not he was a diviner, was a Shona or Ndebele-Kalanga, as the case may be. An ordinary person makes an accusation in accordance with the norms of the society to which he belongs and cases such as *R v Kukubula* (p. 197) show that this is the case also with professional diviners. An Ndebele diviner would almost certainly have indicated fewer men and more women than Kukubula, a Zambian among Ndebele, did.

It would have been better, had the information been available, to investigate the matter as Marwick has done amongst the Cewa (1952, pp. 120 and 215ff) by examining, not the relationship of the alleged wizard to the victim, but the relationship of the accuser to the alleged wizard. However, much of my material is derived from cases where the accuser was a professional diviner and to obtain sufficient material for statistical analysis it has been necessary to adopt the less satisfactory approach. This, however, facilitates comparison with accusations amongst the Lovedu of the Northern Transvaal as described by the Kriges (1943, p. 264) and for this reason I have set out the tables in a similar manner to that of the Kriges. I have also included in the tables statistics relating to the Cewa derived from Marwick's paper (p. 343). Further information about the cases read by me and on which the following tables are based will be found in the Table in Appendix 1.

One disadvantage of the material I have used is that sometimes questions as to the relationship of the parties were not asked by the prosecutor. However, even if no questions are asked, witnesses usually state the relationship of the parties involved. A witness would not, for example, refer to his mother except in terms of the relationship. While the number of cases in category II—strangers—may be somewhat greater than it would have been had the relationships been fully explored during the course of a witness's evidence, I have no reason to suppose that this factor has seriously affected the validity of the figures given.

TABLE I. PATTERN OF ALLEGATIONS OF WIZARDRY: THE EASTERN SHONA

Category of conflict	wizard	victim	No.	E. Shona	Cewa	Lovedu
I. Relatives						
(a) House of co-wife against house or co-wife	co-wife of paternal grandmother	co-wife's grandchild	1			
	co-wife of maternal grandmother	co-wife's grandchild	1			
	co-wife	co-wife's child	2			
	co-wife's child	co-wife's child	1			
	co-wife	co-wife	4			
	co-wife's child	co-wife	1	18.2	14.3	24
(b) Wife against husband	wife of brother	brother's child	3	5.5	19	20
(c) Husband against wife	—	—		—	—	16
(d) Parent and own child	father	child	2			
	mother	child	2	7.3	4.8	6
(e) grandparent and grandchild	paternal grandfather	grandchild	1			
	maternal grandmother	grandchild	1			
	grandmother	grandson's wife	1			
	paternal great grandmother	great grandchild	1	7.3	9.5	0

10

Category of conflict	wizard	victim	No.	E. Shona	Cewa	Lovedu
(f) uterine brothers and sisters	sister	brother's child	1			
	brother	brother's son	1			
	brothers	sister's child	1			
	sisters	sister's child	1	7.3	47.6	4
II. Strangers	woman	lover	1			
	woman	child or children of community	10			
	woman	woman in same community	5			
	woman	child and mother	1			
	woman and son	2 children	1			
	woman	man in same community	2			
	5 women	woman in same community	1			
	Sena and Nyasa men	girl	1			
	Salvation Army Captain	school teacher	1			
	distant female relatives	child	1			
	Old woman	old man and others	1			
	man	child	1			
	'boss boy'	co-employees	1			
	kraal head's wife	child	1			
	distant male relative	child	1			
	builder	rival builder's employees	1	54.5	4.8	30

The Pattern of Accusations
TABLE II. NDEBELE AND KALANGA

Percentages

Category of conflict	wizard	victim	No.	Nd. & Kal.	Cewa	Lovedu
I. *Relatives*						
(a) House or co-wife against house or co-wife	co-wife	co-wife's child	3			
	co-wife	co-wife	1			
	co-wife's son's wife	co-wife's son's wife	1			
	co-wife	co-wife's grandchild	1	23.1	14.3	24
(b) wife against husband	—	—	—	—	19	20
(c) husband against wife	—		—	—	—	16
(d) parent and own child	mother	children	1			
	mother	son	1	7.7	4.8	6
(e) grandparent and grandchild	paternal grandmother	grandchild	2	7.7	9.5	0
(f) uterine brothers and sisters	sister	brother's child	1			
	brother	brother's child	1			
	brother's wife	sister's child	1	11.5	47.6	4
II. *Strangers*	elderly widow	2 women and child	1			
	4 women	several	1			
	woman	woman in same community	2			

Category of conflict	wizard	victim	No.	Nd. & Kal.	Cewa	Lovedu
	Chairman Farmer's Association	man	1			
	elderly widow	farm hand old man	1			
	wife of headman	child in village	1			
	remote female relative	child	1			
	man	woman and man in same village	1			
	woman	child in same line	1			
	father of girl seduced	father of seducer	1			
	woman and mother	child	1			
	remote female relations	woman man	1	50	4.8	30

If any meaningful analysis is to be made of the pattern of wizardry accusations it must be assumed that the figures given above reflect, to some extent, the pattern of wizardry allegations in the societies concerned or a particular aspect of such allegations. I think it is safe to assume that this is so; but it is necessary at the outset to say that there is a least one important discrepancy between the figures given and the observations of two competent observers, the one working amongst the Western Shona, the Kalanga, and the other among the Zezuru of the Mrewa district. Both these observers have remarked on witchcraft or sorcery allegations between brothers. Thus Werbner (1964, p. 120) states that seminal brothers are 'most likely to impute sorcery to one

The Pattern of Accusations

another' while Kingsley Garbett states that (1960, p. 4) among the Zezuru 'witchcraft' accusations occur largely between kin, especially brothers. This discrepancy is, I think, not accidental, and is, indeed, highly significant for the proper understanding of the nature of Shona, and presumably also Ndebele, wizardry allegations. I shall return to this question later, but in the interim it is clear that any attempt at an analysis of the figures given must bear in mind the probability that for one reason or another cases involving wizardry allegations have undergone a measure of selection prior to their being reported to the authorities. Before saying anything further on this point it will, however, be necessary to examine the figures given in more detail; but attention is again drawn to the fact that the wizardry allegations brought before the court have mostly originated from cases where the consequences to the person accused of wizardry have been serious and, also, to the word 'sorcery' used by Werbner and, I believe, correctly used by him. It is probable that in these facts the solution to the problem lies.

The tables show a certain similarity in the pattern of wizardry allegations in the patrilineal societies—the Eastern Shona, the Ndebele-Kalanga and the Lovedu. Thus allegations are as often as not made against a stranger living in the vicinity of the victim, the percentage of such accusations ranging from 30 per cent amongst the Lovedu to 54.5 per cent amongst the Eastern Shona. Again, if one examines the accusations within the family group, those falling within the category of 'house or co-wife' are commonest in all three societies, varying from 18.2 per cent amongst the Eastern Shona to 24 per cent amongst the Lovedu. These figures are, indeed, a little surprising in view of the supposed decrease in the incidence of polygamy. However, despite these similarities between the partrilineal tribes, there are also considerable differences between the Eastern Shona and Ndebele-Kalanga on the one hand and the Lovedu on the other. Thus 16 per cent of Lovedu accusations fall into the 'husband against wife' category. None of the Eastern Shona or Ndebele-Kalanga accusations do. Again, I have had to introduce a category not mentioned by the

Kriges, that of 'grandparent and grandchild', into my tables. If one examines the Kriges's category 'parent and own child' (op. cit. p. 266) it will be observed that in the three cases instanced by them the 'witch' is a man—the father or son. Amongst the Lovedu an accusation that a woman has bewitched her own child is, apparently, unthinkable. Such accusations are relatively common amongst the Eastern Shona and the Ndebele-Kalanga. As stated previously, the Shona believe that a witch must kill at least one of her own children. I shall later give an account of a Korekore case where a woman asked for the poison ordeal after her children had died in order to ascertain if she were a witch (p. 216). Stories of mothers killing their children by witchcraft are common amongst the Shona.

Cewa allegations follow a pattern which is very different from any of the three patrilineal societies although the figures given above should be read subject to the findings in a subsequent study by Marwick (1963, p. 18), where nearly one third of all allegations of wizardry among the cases then studied were found to be between affines as contrasted with none in the previous study.

It has been said that 'witchcraft is a reflection, not of tensions as such, whether open or repressed, but of tensions within the framework of cultural mechanisms for avoiding their being projected as witchcraft.' (Krige, 1943, p. 264). If this is true then differences in the pattern of wizardry allegations between various societies ought to be explained in terms of differences in social structure and the mechanisms created in the various societies to regulate the conduct of persons. It is, therefore, necessary to examine the kinship structure of the various groups under discussion in order to ascertain if the thesis can be supported.

In all four societies it would appear that wizardry allegations only occur commonly in rural areas within a single geographic community composed of a village or, perhaps, one or two neighbouring villages. People in such an area are generally closely related. In view of this the number of allegations made against persons not closely related to the victim is perhaps surprising in the case of the Eastern Shona, Ndebele-Kalanga and Lovedu and is worth stressing since much anthropological literature lays stress on wizardry allegations within the family group. Allegations against strangers can readily be interpreted in psychological terms as allegations by the 'in' group against the 'out' group. An examination of allegations within the family group could, on the basis of the statistics relating to the three societies which are given above, be interpreted in a similar manner. The principal social, economic and political unit in these three groups is the village. In the patrilineal societies under discussion, the nucleus of the village consists of a group of men who are patrilineally related to one another, normally persons who are the agnatic decendants of a grandfather or, perhaps, a great grandfather. This group has a strong feeling of unity and, indeed, one writer (Stead, 1946, p. 9) compares it to a partnership which usually acts through its senior members. The members of the lineage which, in this context, is the minor lineage, share various rights and privileges and may enter into legal relationships with other lineages, for example, by marriage. Since marriage is exogamous the wives of lineage members must inevitably belong to other lineages and, since marriage is virilocal, a married woman must inevitably be something of a stranger in her husband's village—at least until her children grow up. The children of such a marriage belong to their father's lineage. The father is their guardian and, except in the case of very young children, the custodian also in the event of a divorce.

A number of writers have remarked that allegations of wizardry in a patrilineal society of the type under discussion are frequently made by a member of the husband's lineage against the wife or her lineage. Thus Monica Hunter (1961, p. 307) says that amongst the Pondo 'a study of the accusations shows that they are almost invariably made against a woman of the *umzi* (village) who is a wife, not the daughter of the *umzi,* or against a former lover or a rival in love, or neighbour.' This is true also of the Shona and the Ndebele-Kalanga although if the cases studied are any guide, where a 'wife of the village' is named as a wizard it is seldom by her own husband. Gluckman (1955, p. 97) has attempted to explain the reason for this sort of accusation in psychological terms. He states that strong animosities may develop between lineage members for the misfortunes that occur and that they seek a scapegoat and blame the women who have married into the group, the daughters-in-law and sisters-in-law; or their mothers may blame their wives.

As the following table shows, a similar pattern of accusation occurs on the basis of the case material amongst the Shona, Ndebele-Kalanga and Lovedu, accusations within the lineage group being rare as compared with accusations against persons who are not members of the lineage. The figures are derived from tables 1 and 2.

TABLE III. PATTERNS OF ALLEGATIONS BY PERCENTAGES

Group	Accusations within family group	Accusations within lineage group	Total accusations by lineage members against non-lineage members
Shona (Eastern)	45.5%	9.1%	90.9%
Ndebele-Kalanga	50%	7.7%	92.3%
Lovedu (after the Kriges)	70%	10%	90%

It will be seen that in the three groups about 90% of all accusations are made on the assumption that it is a member of another lineage who has bewitched or ensorcelled the lineage member. Even assuming that the material used by me has somewhat exaggerated the pattern the figures appear too consistent to be due to chance. Gluckman's suggestion that conflicts within the group are, in the case of these three Southern Bantu groups, projected on the 'out group' is at first sight very attractive. Some doubt is, however, thrown on Gluckman's suggestion that, although allegations are generally made by a lineage member against a non-lineage member, these allegations are made against persons closely related in other ways or living within the same neighbourhood. Logically, if tensions between agnates are to be projected on to an 'out group' it would be better to project these conflicts on to total strangers. This is, however, not fatal to Gluckman's thesis as one can readily conceptualize the wives and cognates of lineage members living together in the same community as being members of an 'out group'. The real objection, however, to Gluckman's approach as far as the Shona are concerned, comes from the observations of Werbner and Kingsley Garbett who, as remarked previously (p. 137) found in two widely separated Shona groups that allegations were frequently made by one brother against another brother. These allegations would appear to arise mainly as a result of political rivalry within the village. It is obviously idle to seek any sort of projection in this sort of allegation.

If one sort of conflict between agnates is expressed directly in terms of witchcraft or sorcery, there is little reason to suppose that any question of projection arises in any other category of conflict. It will be recalled that Werbner referred to 'sorcery' allegations between brothers. This must be correct because the Shona believe that men are not normally witches in the true sense of that word. A man may employ, so it is thought, a female witch if he wishes to harm someone, and to that extent an accusation against a man may be one of witchcraft and not sorcery. An accusation of witchcraft is, inevitably, more serious than an accusation of sorcery. A witch is, as it were, a continuing source of contagion within a village. No one knows when, where or against whom a witch may strike, and strike she must, for her spirit compels her to do so. What is worse, she can iniate other people into witchcraft and, after death, her spirit may be inherited by others. A sorcerer, on the other hand, is unlikely to be a source of danger except to his enemy and however reprehensible an act of sorcery may be, it is, unlike an act of witchcraft, not the concern of any save the sorcerer's victim and possibly those who are on bad terms with the sorcerer. There is every reason to suppose that the cases which come before the courts are mainly allegations of witchcraft and not sorcery because the consequences of an allegation of witchcraft, which is believed, are more serious than an allegation of sorcery. Complainants in most of the cases which come before the courts are women, for it is women who have most to fear from an allegation. Such an allegation may be expected to be one of witchcraft and not one of sorcery.

The Allegation of Wizardry

If the above is correct it is apparent that the distinction between allegations of witchcraft, which are made against women, and allegations of sorcery, which are made against men, serves an important part in the maintenance of the lineage structure. The women of the lineage marry members of other lineages and, even if for geographical reasons alone, are not normally the object of a witchcraft allegation by an agnate. Thus, for all practical purposes, it can be said that allegations against agnates are expressed in terms of sorcery. The contrary is true in the case of allegations against the female members of the lineages into which lineage members have married. These allegations are normally allegations of witchcraft. A sorcery allegation against an agnate is serious enough, but it is hardly irreparable and, in any event, does not damage the relationship between other agnates. Witchcraft is inherited and to suggest that a lineage member is a witch, is to suggest that members of the lineage as a whole are witches. A witchcraft allegation against a woman who is one's own wife or the wife of an agnate may entirely disrupt the link between husband and wife; but the return of a woman to her parents does not affect the unity of the lineage and her children may be claimed by their father as soon as they are old enough to leave her.

It would seem, therefore, that the preponderance of allegations against non-lineage members as shown in the figures relating to criminal prosecutions is, most probably, to be attributed to the distinction made by the Eastern Shona and the Ndebele-Kalanga between witchcraft and sorcery. This in its turn, must be regarded as a social device designed to mitigate the social disharmony occasioned by allegations of supernatural harm made by one agnate against another.

I have stated previously that for one agnate to make an allegation of witchcraft against another agnate is to suggest that other members of the lineage also are witches. This must be qualified to some extent. The fact that normally women and not men are witches means that, where witchcraft is believed to be inherited, it must be regarded as being inherited from a woman. However likely it may be that agnates who are either uterine brothers and sisters, or related by cognation to the same lineage of wife-givers, may all be witches, an allegation of witchcraft can hardly suggest that a person not so related is a witch. The belief that witchcraft is normally inherited from a female relative serves, therefore, to limit the social consequences of a witchcraft allegation made between lineage members. One consequence of this belief, however, is undoubtedly to suggest that where an allegation is made against a woman or one of her children, for example by the child of a co-wife, all the children of that woman are, themselves, witches. Beliefs concerning the inheritance of witchcraft, therefore, present no barrier, and may even assist, in the segmentation of the lineage between the 'houses' of co-wives.

In the following pages it will not be possible to distinguish clearly between witchcraft and sorcery allegations because the same word is, in the court records, used for both. It should, however, be borne in mind that where mention is made of an accusation against a man, this is normally one of sorcery, where the Shona or Ndebele-Kalanga are concerned, while accusations against a woman are normally accusations of witchcraft. There is, however, reason to suppose that where relationships between agnates are more than usually embittered and where, as a result, the likelihood of the matter coming before the criminal courts is greater, the accusation is more likely to be expressed in the idiom of witchcraft than would normally be the case.

Among the Shona and the Ndebele-Kalanga most accusations are made against women. There is an interesting suggestion by Middleton and Winter (1963, p. 15) that accusations of witchcraft against specific women tend to occur only in those patrilineal societies characterized by the presence of a house property complex. The house property complex is reflected, for example, by the division of a man's herd of cattle between the houses of his various wives and by the inheritance by a son only of the cattle, or of a share of the cattle, of the house to which he belongs. This is said to be associated with the true levirate rather than widow inheritance, disapproval of divorce and the allocation of children to their sociological father and not their biological father. Middleton and

Winter say that in the case of societies with a house property complex a woman's reproductive powers are transferred entirely to her husband and his lineage and that she becomes incorporated in her husband's lineage as an integral part thereof and 'since her status in the lineage into which she married becomes an inalienable part of her social personality notions of witchcraft conceived as inherent and perverted tendencies of persons in ascribed positions become relevant.' (p. 16). This, it is said, contrasts with societies which lack the house property complex and 'since a woman's relationship to her husband is voluntary and contractual, ideas concerned with the perversion of inherent status are not relevant, and such women are accused of practising sorcery rather than witchcraft.' If there is substance in Middleton and Winter's suggestions then accusations against women in Shona society should take the form of accusations of sorcery since the Shona are not characterized to any great extent by a house property complex. Cattle, at any rate the economically important cattle of the patri-estate, are not divided between the various wives and are inherited by the general heir and not by the sons of the various houses. Of the associated characteristics it should be noted that widow inheritance, not the levirate, is ordinarily found among the Shona. Children may, however, be claimed by their biological father, but only if the sociological father is prepared to surrender them. What, however, Shona society shares with the postulated societies 'characterized by the presence of the house property complex' is a disapproval of divorce and a low incidence of it. One wonders whether, in fact, this is not what is of importance. If the incidence of divorce is low it is broadly true to say that a woman's status as a wife 'becomes an inalienable part of her social personality.' If the incidence of divorce is high, her status *vis-à-vis* the lineage of her husband is 'voluntary and contractual'. Mediaeval European society was not characterized by the house property complex but accusations against individual women were undoubtedly made. The incidence of divorce was, however, low and, indeed, save in the guise of nullity proceedings, virtually non-existent. Ndebele society is, as far as is known, and satisfactory modern accounts do not exist, a society 'characterized by the presence of the house property complex' and is, probably, very similar to the Zulu, from whom they are historically descended and whom Middleton and Winter cite as a characteristic society of this nature. In fact, as far as the evidence available to me goes, accusations of witchcraft among the Shona and Ndebele follow very much the same pattern. In both societies the incidence of divorce is low.

When one turns from the pattern of accusations among the patrilineal societies under discussion to the Cewa a very different picture emerges. Marwick states that in 60% of all accusations the victim is a matrilineal relative of the alleged 'witch' (op. cit., p. 217). He states (p. 123) that in certain societies such as the Navaho in North America tension between members of the community results in an allegation of witchcraft against an unrelated member of the community. In the light of what has previously been said it may be doubted whether this is in an entirely adequate explanation of the pattern of Navaho accusations. Marwick then says that amongst the Cewa the feelings of aggression are expressed 'in the relation in which it originated'. He goes on to state that the reason for the difference between the Navaho and Cewa is that 'witchcraft allegations are, amongst the Navaho, a serious threat to subsistence but not amongst the Cewa'. Whether Marwick is right or not, this does not take one very far, for it does not explain why wizardry allegations should be in one society a threat to subsistence, and not in the other. The economy of the Shona is very similar to that of the Cewa. Both Shona and Cewa societies are organized on the lineage principle. Yet the pattern of accusations is entirely different. Again, there is a definite pattern to Cewa allegations; they do not occur haphazardly within the lineage but in the main fall into the 'uterine brother and sister' category. There is no reason to suppose that Cewa feel less strongly than the Shona that the unity of the lineage should be maintained intact. That, in fact, they find it less easy to maintain it, as is shown *inter alia* by the number of accusations within the lineage, suggests that the Cewa matrilineal lineage is structurally weaker and the opportunities for open conflict proportionately greater than is the case with its Shona patrilineal counterpart. A weakness in matrilineal systems is that a man's heirs are usually his sister's sons and not his own children. Many men feel their obligations lie rather to their own children than to their sister's children and should they, as a result, try to favour their own children at the expense of their legal heirs the latter are likely to object. However, while I think that the above may be a partial explanation of the difference between the Shona and Cewa pattern of accusations it seems clear from Marwick's study that the major conflicts within the Cewa lineage relate, not so much to rivalry connected with the law of succession, but to political rivalry for position within the lineage. Very few of the wizardry allegations amongst the Eastern Shona and Ndebele-Kalanga, which were examined by me, could be classified under this heading and this suggests that there is a social mechanism acting within the lineage structure which tends to inhibit (but not always prevent) conflict of a political nature between lineage members in these societies which is absent in the case of the Cewa lineage. Both Cewa and Shona kinship structures are organized on hierarchical principles, although these are more strongly stressed amongst the Shona. However, the differences between the nature of the conflicts as expressed in wizardry allegations between the two kinship systems cannot be accounted for in the differing emphasis on the social hierarchy. The weakness of the Cewa lineage structure appears to be more fundamental and arises from the inherent weakness of the matrilineal system itself. In a patrilineal system such as the Shona where marriage is virilocal, in any conflict for status between members of the lineage group, a man's primary support is likely to come from his own sons, their wives, children and dependants. The political allegiance of most dependants belonging to the patrilineage is thus fixed in Shona society by the accident of birth and, furthermore, there is little conflict of allegiances involved as a man has only one father and only one grandfather agnatically related to him. The structure of the natural family, of parents and children, is thus the primary buttress of the Shona kinship system. The position is otherwise amongst the Cewa, for as is common in matrilineal societies, political power rests in the hands of the men. This means that a man's primary support comes not from his own children, who belong to a different lineage, but from his sisters and their children. This problem so created is this, that a woman is likely to have not one, but a number of brothers and although she should, no doubt, give her support to her most senior brother, she is likely to feel more affection for a brother nearer her own age. The conflict between the tie of affection and the rules of seniority enables brothers to vie with one another for the control of their sisters and it is the tensions created by this rivalry that would appear to generate accusations of wizardry. Amongst the cases listed by Marwick nearly 77% of accusations within the lineage can be classified as falling into the 'uterine brother and sister' class so this is clearly the relationship which creates the greatest difficulties. Cewa society is very similar to the neighbouring Yao in structure and the sort of situation which arises has been described by Mitchell (1956, Chapter VI). The sorority group is termed the *mbumba* and brothers compete with one another for the control of the *mbumba*. Mitchell describes (op. cit., p. 149ff) the manner in which the *mbumba* may transfer its allegiance from one brother to another according to the fortunes of the moment and it is hardly surprising that one informant should tell him 'to live with a sorority group needs courage'. Mitchell adds (p. 157): 'The threat which lies over the head of an inefficient warden of a sorority group is that of losing them to his younger brother, and it is scarcely possible to exaggerate the frequency with which this takes place in Yao society.'

If my argument is correct the inherent strength of the Southern Bantu patrilineal lineage and the inherent weakness of the Cewa matrilineal lineage is reflected in the pattern of wizardry allegations in the respective societies.

Turning now to wizardry allegations within the group of agnatic kin composing the lineage, these will be found to belong to various categories. Perhaps the least dangerous to the solidarity of the lineage are those expressions of tension which result in an accusation against the child of a co-wife that he or she has bewitched another co-wife's child. Such an accusation is but an extension of the notorious sexual and economic rivalry between co-wives. The process whereby a lineage may divide has been described above (p. 30). It will be noted that one of the most important lines of division after the death of the 'father' of the lineage is between the houses of co-wives. At worst then, such an accusation may lead to the fission of the lineage either now or at some time in the future; but the fission, or rather the tensions which create it, does not seriously damage the foundation of the lineage system as such. More serious than an allegation between half brothers and sisters are those tensions which result in an allegation between uterine brothers and sisters. The relationship between uterine brothers and sisters is supposed to be particularly intimate and, in fact, allegations of wizardry between such people are comparatively rare on the evidence of the court records, ranging from 7.3% of accusations amongst the Eastern Shona to 11.5% amongst the Ndebele and Kalanga. Not all of these cases, however, were in the form of a direct conflict between siblings. While the father is alive it would seem that accusations are more likely to be made against an uterine sister than against her brother. Serious though an allegation against an uterine sister may be, being a woman she will marry a member of another lineage and so live elsewhere. The expression of hostility against such a woman is therefore not as likely to destroy the solidarity of the lineage as it would were such allegations made against her brother. Also, unless the father is dead, one brother is not economically dependent on another nor is a sister on her brother. A man, however, may have to depend on his sister's bridewealth for his own marriage, particularly in the case of a cattle-linked sister and, again, if a sister is divorced and the bridewealth refunded the father may be less able to assist his son to obtain a wife. It will be noted that in one of the cases of this type listed by the Kriges (op. cit., p. 266) the accusation arose partly from bridewealth trouble. Probably for these reasons, although a man's relationship with his sister is supposed to be particularly intimate, allegations of wizardry against an uterine sister occur. After the father's death his senior son or his senior surviving brother may step into his place as head of the minor lineage. When this happens the possibility of the lineage segmenting exists and conflict of a political nature for the control of the lineage or segment thereof or for the village of which the father was the head can result. The only Eastern Shona case amongst those examined of an allegation of wizardry between brothers or their children is *R v Matumbu* (54) and is apparently of this nature. The Kalanga case of *R v Aaron and Siliva Matshuma* (75) is similar although in this case it was not the lineage head but the lineage head's younger brother who died. This, however, brought the deceased's children under the immediate control of the lineage head and this was resented by them. When one of the deceased's children died the elder brother, the lineage head, was blamed. It is also probable that the elder brother had made use of his position to make use of the cattle belonging to the deceased for bridewealth purposes. Evidence on this point was not, however, clear. Certain relationships which in our society are regarded as particularly intimate are, in the case of the Rhodesian peoples we are concerned with, not of this nature. Gluckman (1955, p. 58) explains this by suggesting that European society is divided into 'functional single interest groups' with a high measure of social attachment between its members. African society lacks such groups and 'hence they have to draw the members of various families together by driving wedges into the family itself'. One such wedge is driven between husband and wife and another between father and son. To prevent conflict between such persons custom dictates an elaborate code of behaviour between the parties concerned. Thus, among the Shona a wife must respect (*kutya*—literally, to fear) her husband, a man must respect his elder brother, his father's brothers and his father. Stead (1946, p. 13) describes how a man must not enter his father's hut but must huddle humbly at the door until told to enter and must thereafter show respect by clapping hands. This extreme show of respect is, in many areas, a thing of the past, but illustrates clearly the nature of the father-son relationship. The relationship between grandfather and grandson is, on the whole, fairly intimate and the only grandfather-grandson allegation listed by me took, in fact, the form of an accusation by a son against his father alleging that the father had killed the son's child. Is is clear that the traditional behaviour patterns towards persons of one's lineage, together with the distinction drawn between witchcraft and sorcery, do, on the whole, prevent serious wizardry allegations arising between lineage members and therefore the question as to why father-son accusations may come before the courts, even if only occasionally, is of some interest, particularly in view of the attitude of respect which the son has to adopt towards his father, which is designed to prevent overt conflict. The answer would appear to be that father and son are, in a polygamous household, potential sexual and economic rivals. This appears most clearly in the bridewealth transaction. A father should provide bridewealth for his son among both Shona and Ndebele; but bridewealth handed over when the man's daughters marry belongs to the father and may be used by him to obtain another wife, as may the other cattle at his disposal. Father and son are thus in direct competition for bridewealth that will secure them wives and, since the father has the legal right to appropriate the cattle to himself, resentment on the son's part is to be expected if this happens or if the father is tardy in assisting with the bridewealth. The fact that two of the accusations listed by the Kriges originated as a result of the son's cohabitation with his father's wives is a reminder that sexual rivalry may sometimes take a more direct form than rivalry over the bridewealth cattle. Particularly when the father becomes old, father and son may come into conflict if the son attempts to obtain more power of a political nature than the father is willing to relinquish. However, a son is not likely to make an accusation of wizardry against his father lightly, for a conflict which results in such an accusation tends to destroy the foundations upon which the agnatic lineage is built. It is not without significance that both the cases known to me amongst the Shona where a son accused his father of witchcraft—in the

The Pattern of Accusations

case of *R v Mathias and Kariba* (17) alleging the death of his son, and in the other, *R v Mudzingwa and Tanda* (12) alleging the death of his brother—were murder trials in which the son was charged with killing his father because he thought he was a wizard. It would seem that where a wizardry allegation occurs in a situation where the structure of the society is designed to prevent overt conflict emotions are likely to get out of hand. It is only if feelings are really intense that such an accusation could be contemplated. At least one of these accusations was definitely of witchcraft and not sorcery.

Whereas in studying accusations within the agnatic lineage differences between the Eastern Shona and Ndebele-Kalanga, on the one hand, and Lovedu on the other, were not of significant importance, in studying accusations within the family, but outside the lineage groups, differences between the various societies are of paramount importance. It is, therefore, necessary to examine the position of the wife in the homestead of her husband in the three societies.

Amongst the Shona a man cannot marry anyone with the same *mutupo* and *chidawo* (clan and sub-clan names as himself nor can he marry any person with whom there is agnatic relationship, or any member of his mother's clan. Amongst the Manyika a form of reciprocal marriage alliance exists; but it would seem that this sort of marriage is only possible where the parties are not close blood relations. A woman is, therefore, not related by any recognized blood ties to her husband or her husband's parents and she is not, therefore, related to those persons who concern her welfare most directly. She comes in close daily contact with these people and generally manages to get on fairly well with them; but it can happen that her in-laws become jealous of her because her husband is devoting all his attention to her or she may otherwise irritate them. Her in-laws will then start complaining about her and, particularly if her children die, a witchcraft allegation is likely to result. An allegation that a mother has killed her children usually takes the form of an accusation by the husband's lineage against the wife. A child would not ordinarily accuse its mother. As I remarked previously, tensions which result in an allegation against a woman by her husband or his relatives do not seriously affect the solidarity of the lineage group or the father's rights to his children and, while it is true that an allegation of witchcraft may lead to a divorce, this may well have been what was intended. It is easier for a man to contemplate the loss of bridewealth which he has already paid, if a divorce ensues, and the husband's action cannot be justified, than to be in the position of the father-in-law who, unless he can show his son-in-law was at fault, must refund part or all of the bridewealth which, by that stage, would probably have been dispersed far and wide and be no longer in the possession of the father-in-law. The wife, on the other hand, is in a difficult position if she feels she is being bewitched or ensorcelled by her husband or his relatives. She has often no one of consequence to argue her case in her husband's village and, unless she has been notoriously ill-treated by her husband, her own family is unlikely to support her, since to do so might lead to a divorce and the refund of the bridewealth. There is, indeed, little reason why she should make an allegation of wizardry. If her position is intolerable an accusation would only make matters worse and, if intolerable, the sensible thing is to return to her parents. If the above is correct then, among the Shona allegations of witchcraft against a wife should be common, whether in the form of an allegation that she has bewitched her husband, her children or co-wife's children, while allegations by a wife against her husband or his group should be rare. The cases examined by me show that this is probably the case although cases in which a woman was accused of bewitching her husband were, somewhat surprisingly, absent.

Cases which I have classified in the Ndebele-Kalanga group originate on the whole from persons speaking Ndebele and probably represent the pattern of Ndebele rather than Kalanga society. Fortunately, however, the differences between these two societies in so far as the position of the wife is concerned do not seem to be of great importance. As in the case of the Eastern Shona an Ndebele man may not have sexual relations with a

The Pattern of Accusations

member of his own clan (*isibongo*) or of his mother's clan or with anyone with whom a blood tie can be traced. While Hughes states (1956, p. 48) that there is a 'somewhat vague theory that one should marry into the same clan as one's grandmother', he says that such marriages are not particularly prevalent and, in any event, this is presumably only possible where no blood tie can be traced. As with the Shona, so also with the Ndebele, a wife is, therefore, not related to her husband or his uterine brothers and sisters or parents. Again, marriage amongst the Ndebele, as amongst the Shona, involves payment of a considerable amount of bridewealth. As a result the same mechanisms exist to secure the stability of the marriage. It is therefore to be expected that wizardry allegations among the Ndebele should, here, follow the same pattern as amongst the Shona. This, indeed, would appear to be the case. In view of Gluckman's statement (1955, p. 92) that amongst the Zulu an accusation that a mother has killed her child is unthinkable, such accusations amongst Ndebele speakers should probably be ascribed to Kalanga influence.

When we turn to the Kriges' descriptions of Lovedu society a very different pattern of marriage emerges. A man is, as far as possible, linked with a particular sister for bridewealth purposes and uses the bridewealth obtained from his sister's marriage to obtain a bride for himself. Such linking exists amongst the Shona and Ndebele but amongst the Lovedu this linking has led to a strongly preferent marriage between a man and his mother's brother's daughter and a woman and her father's sister's son. It is not any such relation a man or woman must marry. A man must marry the daughter of the brother who used his mother's marriage cattle to obtain a wife for himself (Krige, 1943, p. 142). A woman should similarly marry the son of the sister to whom her father was similarly linked. The effect of this system is greatly to enhance the position of the mother of the bridegroom who is also the sister of the bride's father. The Kriges, indeed, describe the 'sister', who in this context is the bride's mother-in-law, as the 'centre of the social system' (Chap. V). The Kriges state that a man's sister wields a certain amount of authority in the house of her brother and hence over her brother's children. They (p. 75) give an example of the sister intervening in a quarrel between the man of the house and his wife over an uninvited guest. If the wife obtained by means of a sister's cattle is badly treated by her husband she may run away to this sister. Again, the influence of the 'sister' is enhanced by her religious position. The result of preferential marriage amongst the Lovedu is thus that, in any dispute between husband and wife, the wife's position is very strong, particularly if she can get her father on her side and her father is the brother of her husband's mother. The husband's position *vis-à-vis* his wife is, of course, correspondingly weakened. It is therefore hardly surprising that nearly as many cases were found by the Kriges of accusations against the husband (16%) of 'bewitching' his wife as against the wife (20%) of 'bewitching' her husband (op. cit., p. 264ff). The absence among the Lovedu of allegations against a mother of killing her own children by wizardry is perhaps to be explained by the greater importance of the mother's group in the upbringing of children amongst the Lovedu than amongst the Shona and also the close links of consanguinity between wife and husband. Thus, conflicts which result in an allegation of wizardry which damages the links between mother and child are far more destructive than in Shona society. I know of no case amongst the Shona and Ndebele where an accusation was made against a father or mother-in-law, presumably because the traditional attitude of respect is sufficient to prevent such accusations. There is little reason for the son-in-law, except in the near-extinct service marriages, to come into close contact with his affines after marriage if he does not want to. Very often, however, the relationship between father-in-law and son-in-law is very intimate, particularly in the case of chiefs who find it safer to rely on their sons-in-law for support than on their own blood relations. Among the Lovedu the links of kin bring a man into close contact with his in-laws. The Kriges give two examples of accusations against the husband's mother-in-law.

At first sight it may seem surprising that 19% of the cases listed by Marwick fall into the 'wife against husband' category, that is,

The Pattern of Accusations

in the class of conflicts which ordinarily take the form of accusations by the husband against the wife. Since the Cewa husband is a stranger in the village of his wife, one would expect that accusations, on the Shona analogy, would be by the wife against her husband and not vice-versa. However, if the suggestion that it is not so much the effect of patrilocal marriage but the effect of bridewealth payments on the stability of the Shona marriage which makes it difficult for a woman to accuse her husband of wizardry be correct, then the Cewa accusations by the husband against his wife become comprehensible. Marriage amongst the Cewa is notoriously unstable and, although bridewealth may pass, it passes from the husband's group to the wife's group as among the patrilineal Shona. This means that, though a Cewa husband is in much the same position *vis-à-vis* his wife's group as a Shona wife *vis-à-vis* her husband's group, his family have no similar interest, based on their reluctance to return the bridewealth, to ensure the stability of the marriage. As a result, if a Cewa man wishes to put an end to the marriage by accusing his wife of wizardry there is little to stop him. The divorce rates show a very great difference between the stability of the Shona marriage and that of the Cewa type. Holleman (1952, p. 155) found in the Sabi Reserve, a Shona-speaking area, that the divorce rate was about ½% increasing to 2% near Buhera and a big mission. Among the Yao, whose social structure is similar to the Cewa, Mitchell (1956, p. 186) states that eight out of ten men and women over the age of forty have been divorced; there is no reason to suppose that figures from the Cewa would be significantly different.

It must not be supposed from the above that wizardry allegations are in any sense predetermined. Whether friction arises between two persons depends on their emotional make-up, social interests and character. It is easy to love some people and dislike others; there is certainly no inevitability about an allegation. What, however, is shown by the evidence is that whether tension or dislike is expressed as an allegation of wizardry or in some other way is, if not determined, at least regulated and influenced by the structure of the society concerned.

In her description of Pondo society Monica Hunter (1961, p. 494) remarks that the incentives to witchcraft and sorcery are believed to be 'sexual rivalry, jealousy over children, friction in the *umzi* (village) and, occasionally, economic rivalry.' This, no doubt, is so also in Rhodesia, but 'friction in the *umzi*' is a very wide concept and such friction can arise in many ways. Over forty-five per cent of the wizardry allegations examined by me arose from the death of children. While allegations of wizardry can be made for the most trivial reasons, the cases examined are probably a fair sample of the more serious type of allegation. There is no reason to suppose that the death of a child is not one of the major occasions which give rise to the more serious types of wizardry allegation, more serious, that is, from the point of view of the person accused as a wizard. Among both the Shona and Ndebele, although where a child dies the mother is not usually named as a wizard, this can happen. In a society which attaches a great value to fecundity and where it is important for religious reasons for a man to have children, the failure of a mother to rear children is a very serious matter indeed. In polygynous societies a man can find sexual satisfaction outside marriage and a man does not usually look to marriage for companionship. As the reason for the existence of marriage is thus, mainly, the procreation and rearing of children, the failure of a woman to rear children means that she has failed in her obligations to her husband and his group. I would suggest that it is from this failure of a woman to perform her obligations to society that the allegation of wizardry often arises. Usually a scapegoat can be found, whether in a co-wife or some other woman; but if no scapegoat can be found the blame may well be laid at the door of the woman whose children have died. The same is true also if she is barren. The fact that allegations frequently originate from failure to perform one's obligations to society is also illustrated by the fact that a large number of elderly people, mainly women, are named as wizards. When a woman becomes old she can no longer grow her own crops without assistance—women being, of course, the main producers of agricultural produce—and otherwise perform

The Pattern of Accusations

her obligations. While an accusation is unlikely to be made by a child against his or her own mother, accusations against elderly people by persons not closely related to them and who live in the same community are common, and whatever the expressed motive for the allegation it probably reflects the annoyance of the community in having to look after a person such as this.

Parrinder (1958, p. 187) has listed sexual antagonism as one of the sources of witchcraft allegations. This is probably so to some extent, but does not explain why witchcraft allegations are made against certain women and not against others. It is the social patterns of society which determine whether or not one may be inimate with a particular woman. Sexual antagonism cannot be seen as a cause of allegations separate and distinct from those patterns. It is, of course, true that women are feared at certain times as, for example, when menstruating or after a miscarriage. This fear could conceivably be reflected in witchcraft allegations. The fact that witchcraft is, throughout much of Africa, generally conceived of as being hereditary in the female line indicates that women are to some extent regarded as the possessors of mystic powers that are to be feared. There is, however, little that is overtly sexual in Shona witchcraft beliefs although the same is probably not to be said of Ndebele belief. A Shona witch does not usually, it is thought, consort sexually with her familiars. The *chitukwani,* which is in some ways similar to the *tokoloshe,* generally lacks the *tokoloshe's* lecherous nature. A far stronger case for a sexual background to witchcraft allegations could be made in regard to Pondo society where most familiars have an overtly sexual character (Monica Hunter, 1961, p. 275ff) or for mediaeval Europe with its beliefs in the *succubus* and *incubus.* This difference in emphasis on sex probably represents differences between the nature of the various societies. There is no recognized institution such as the Pondo *amadikazi* (loose women) or practice of *ukumetsha* (external intercourse) among the Shona and, although prostitution is rife in the towns, a prostitute is not accepted socially but stigmatized as a *muhuri* (from Afrikaans *hoer*) or a *mufambi* (traveller). These opprobrious epithets are, indeed, applied to women whose morals are merely loose, but are by no means prostitutes in the English sense of the word.

Wilson (1951, p. 312) has sought to explain the sexual aspect of Pondo witchcraft by comparing Pondo society with the Nyakyusa of Tanganyika. She found that among the Pondo the patrilineal lineage, which is exogamous, tended to be localized and that for any given man or woman a large number of neighbours of the opposite sex fell into the category of those with whom sexual relations are forbidden. Those who are forbidden to marry are naturally sexually attracted and the familiar can be regarded as a symbol of this sexual attraction. Amongst the Nyakyusa the local community is based, not on the patrilineage, but on the association of age-mates. Most of a person's neighbours of the opposite sex do not fall within prohibited degrees or relationship and there is not the same problem of suppressing sexual desires in regard to forbidden partners. Witchcraft beliefs have not, therefore, the same sexual aspect. If Wilson is right, since Shona society is, in its relevant aspects, similar to that of the Pondo, the Shona witchcraft beliefs might be expected to have a markedly sexual character. This is not the case. I do not mean by this that sex plays no part at all in Shona witchcraft beliefs; but the sexual aspect of Shona witchcraft beliefs is not very prominent. I am very doubtful if the degree to which a society is obsessed with sex can be related quite as simply as Monica Wilson would have it to the social structure of the community. The history of our own society shows great changes in the attitude to sex over comparatively short periods of time. It is not entirely easy to relate these changes directly to changes in the social structure although it is reasonably clear that a relationship exists. The practice of *ukumetsha* among the Pondo and their *amadikazi* should mean that they have a greater opportunity than persons of many other societies of relieving themselves of sexual repressions and inhibitions and the Pondo should be, therefore, less obsessed by sex than is Shona society, which lacks these. This is not the case.

It must not be supposed that all wizardry allegations result

The Pattern of Accusations

from the complex interpersonal relationships of communal life. Some result from jealousy or envy, relatively uncomplicated by other factors. Thus, at a school run by my wife, a pupil alleged that a group of brothers was using wizardry to cause him to fail his examinations. It appeared that he was jealous of them because he had to pay full school fees while they had had their fees reduced. In the towns the wealthy are envied and are sometimes even hardly regarded as members of the African community as the increasing tendency to refer to an African employer as *murungu wangu* (My European) illustrates. Wealthy persons are alleged to have obtained their position through wizardry and stories of their misdeeds circulate. Thus one wealthy bus owner is alleged to have killed his brother by means of sorcery. He is said to have requested a doctor to assist him to accomplish his ends. The doctor did so by making the face of the brother appear in a medicated broth. The bus owner pricked out the eyes of the image and, as a result, his brother died. These allegations may not always be without foundation. Some years ago a bus owner was charged with killing a man and using the flesh in the radiator of his bus to ensure success in business. Although the bus owner was acquitted the fact that the case was brought at all—and it reached the High Court—is of interest. Many businessmen pay very high prices to purchase medicines to achieve success. That the ordinary man in the street should suspect that these medicines are bad and that the owner is, therefore, a sorcerer is not surprising.

These days, and particularly in and near the larger urban centres, it is dangerous to accuse some one of wizardry because it is so easy for the person accused to go to the police. Because of this persons who believe they or their relations are bewitched or ensorcelled may call a *dare,* or take the opportunity of a public gathering, to announce that there is a wizard in the gathering. If the accuser has not yet been to a *nganga,* and if the wizardry is not removed, a *nganga* will be consulted or, if a *nganga* has been consulted and the accuser knows who the wizard is, action will be taken against her unless the wizardry is immediately removed. Such conduct is stated to be very common and, since no offence is committed unless and until a wizard is named, unlikely to come to court.

The comparatively small number of wizardry allegations examined by me and the near dearth of allegations from the main urban centres illustrates that the Witchcraft Suppression Act is, very largely, successful in the prevention of wizardry allegations against named individuals although there is no reason to suppose that belief in wizardry has greatly lessened. One cannot regard Bullock's statement (1950, p. 169) that 'we have put a stop to witch-finding' as being anything but false, but it is undoubtedly true that the witchfinder has become more circumspect.

There are a number of aspects of the wizardry allegations which I have not touched upon in the preceding pages and which I shall not discuss until the end of the book. One problem is the extent to which fear of an allegation of wizardry assists to ensure conformity with the social norms of the community. Another, and perhaps greater problem, is whether allegations of wizardry are mere manifestations of social tensions or whether they are something more than this. Some social anthropologists write of wizardry allegations as if they were of little more significance than signposts to social friction—almost like a rash in the case of measles. On this aspect of the matter I shall let the case material speak for itself. Over and over again it is difficult not to come to the conclusion that the sequence of events related could not have come about had the accusation which was made not been made in the idiom of wizardry. Then there is the question as to whether persons deliberately or unconsciously make use of the wizardry allegation in the manipulation of the structure of society to their own advantage. Are wizardry allegations, in other words, 'merely a stereotyped response to misfortune' or are they 'an instrumental technique'? (see Beattie in Middleton and Winter, p. 31). Do wizardry allegations resolve social tensions or intensify them? There are no doubt many other questions also. To some it is possible to suggest an answer, but more often the material at my disposal is insufficient or ambiguous. It may, perhaps, be wrong to assume that there is any very clear-cut answer. It is probable, for example, that among the Shona an allegation of wizardry is often no more than a stereotyped response to misfortune. It would, I think, be quite wrong to deduce from this that it can never be used as an instrumental technique. In certain circumstances, for example, in the case of rivalry for political office, accusations of wizardry are clearly used as an instrumental technique.

In the following pages I shall give an account of a number of wizardry allegations, mostly taken from cases which have come before the courts. The accounts will give an illustration of the nature of the material used by me, the manner in which accusations may take place and, I hope, something of the atmosphere surrounding an accusation. It is very easy to discuss wizardry accusations in the clinical atmosphere of a sociological study, but it is as well to keep in mind the emotions of hate and terror, the feelings of doubt and of certainty, the moments of rationality and irrationality which accompany an allegation and of the brutality which may eventuate. I have only once personally played a part in one of these dramas, but it is something which I shall not easily forget.

CHAPTER X

WIZARDRY ALLEGATIONS WHERE NO DIVINER WAS PRESENT

A DIVINER was not present or immediately responsible for comparatively few of the wizardry allegations known to me; but although the number of cases where no diviner was involved is comparatively small, such cases are of importance. Where a diviner is involved, the reason why a person is named as a wizard, at least as far as the onlookers are concerned, is simply because the diviner says she is a wizard. It is true that divination techniques may enable a diviner to discover the sources of friction and tension in the community; but this is not realized by the diviner's clients and usually no very great amount of the background information of the sort that an anthropologist would like is given in those cases where a witness describes a divination and its consequences. Rather more information is, however, given in those cases where no diviner is involved for, often, the immediate reason for the allegation is apparent to witnesses and regarded as relevant by them when they give evidence.

It would appear to be realized by those concerned that a wizardry allegation may originate in malice and, as a result, the consequences to the person named as a wizard by a person other than a diviner are likely to be less serious than if she had been pointed out by a diviner. Such a person, that is a person accused of wizardry, is normally entitled to insist that a diviner be consulted to clear her name or, in the past and still to some extent amongst the Korekore, that she should undergo the ordeal.

The sort of circumstances which generate a wizardry allegation is illustrated in the case of *R v Sengani* (6). The accused was a Venda in the Beit Bridge area. He accused three people, Manda, Maruri and Mbuyaleni of wizardry. Some four years prior to the allegation Sengani had committed adultery with Manda's wife. Manda had claimed damages from Sengani and received three head of cattle. It is not clear from the record of the case whether this claim was taken to a headman or merely settled informally between the families involved. Manda then sold a cow and its calf, part of the compensation paid by Sengani, to Maruri. Sengani was dissatisfied with the award of damages and appealed to the headman Siyoka. Siyoka decided that the cow and calf should be returned to Manda 'so that he could try the case'. Some four years later Maruri still had neither the cow nor the money he paid for it, nor was the dispute between Sengani and Manda settled. As a result of all this Sengani had a grudge against Manda and Maruri. Mbuyaleni, Maruri's sister, was included in the allegation of wizardry because one day, when she was in the company of her brother's wife, she swore at Sengani or, at least, Sengani thought she had sworn. Four days after this incident Sengani's leg, which had been troubling him for years, began to swell. It was this swelling which occasioned the allegation. Had legal proceedings

Wizardry Allegations where no Diviner was Present

not become bogged down in the manner in which they did there is no reason to suppose that an allegation would have been made.

Another case which was connected with a lawsuit was *R v Sihwanda* (90), an Ndebele case from Tuli. The statement made by the accused to the police explains the background to the case, although it will be noted that he denied naming anyone as a 'witch':

'When I went to Masole I was accompanied by Nyagwe and while we were talking about this matter Masole's two sons and Nyagwe were witnesses. I told Masole that I had met his wife at a beer drink at Majoni's and that she had said to me that she had received a letter from Zezane Mission telling her that her daughter was pregnant and that the person who had made her pregnant would have to pay £25 damages or the stores would be broken down. I remember seeing a letter written in English by Masole's daughter to my son in which she said that she was not pregnant and telling him not to deny making her pregnant or it would cause soil erosion. Those were bad words said by Masole's people. I deny that I indicated Masole as a wizard. He is making the allegation up by saying this. The reason I told Masole about these bad words was because at the time this pregnancy was being discussed his daughter and my son were called together and the matter was discussed and my son denied being the father of the child and then the lightning struck my son's hut. The lightning struck the hut three times and killed a dog which fell on the children in the hut and died there. I buried the dog the next day and two days later another storm brewed up and when I went into my son's hut I found a dove inside. It was alive when I first saw it and it died when I was watching it. It died because it stood in the hut for two days and then I threw it away. After that Masole called me to his kraal and told me to pay £25 damages. He did not discuss the matter in the presence of other people but merely stood up and passed sentence. That is all in connection with witchcraft. I wish to add that Masole's wife told me that in a letter they had received from Zezane the person who was responsible for making her daughter pregnant was named.'

Witnesses who were present when Sihwanda went to Masole's village state that he called Masole a 'witch' and explained how Masole had sent the lightning which had killed the dog.

An interesting case is that which took the form of two trials, *R v Mateyo* and *R v Macheka* (59), originating from the Budjga of Mtoko. Apparently the kraal head Macheka had, although he denied it, consulted a diviner about the deaths of people in his village and had been told that an elderly woman, Vamsiku, was a witch. Probably because he stood to lose his position as kraal head if he made an allegation of witchcraft he induced Mateyo, a young man, to make the accusation. The following is the statement made by Mateyo at the close of the preparatory examination:

'On arrival home at Chiutsi kraal last November I found my father had been stung by bees. His hand had decayed and he is still in hospital. Then January, a young boy straight from school, became ill. I took him to hospital at Mtoko and he died following an operation which revealed that his intestines had decayed. Vamsiku was not at the mourning party. We went to Chiutsi and, on arrival, I found that no sacrifice had been made to appease January's spirit. Subsequently Macheka, the kraal head, called me and said we would all die because of Vamsiku. He said he intended to call a meeting and asked me to make an allegation of witchcraft against Vamsiku at the meeting. As my kraal head had ordered this, I did it. After the meeting was over I arose and said, with emphasis because Macheka had promised to make me an assistant kraal head if we succeeded in getting rid of Vamsiku, that Vamsiku was a witch. I wanted that promotion and did not realize that I was getting myself into trouble. Later we heard from Macheka that Vamsiku was going to the police and he advised me to run away to Salisbury, which I did.'

According to Simon, Macheka's nephew, Macheka spoke to Mateyo and asked him to denounce Vamsiku. He promised Mateyo the witch's lands as a reward.

In the last case Vamsiku, the witch, was an old woman living alone with her children. Another case where an old woman living alone, this time without children, was charged with witchcraft was *R v Chemwe* (61), a case from the Nuanetsi area. In this case the old woman, Machiveyi, was reputed in the neighbourhood to be a witch and, when charged with witchcraft by the accused, did not deny the accusation, probably because she knew a denial would not be believed. However, she was so upset by it and the general hostility towards her that she hanged herself. Women without husbands living alone are undoubtedly misfits in Shona and Ndebele society. Ordinarily a woman will always have someone to look after her for, on divorce, she returns to her own family and, if widowed, she would be inherited by a member of her husband's family—amongst the Shona—or might enter the levirate among the Ndebele. If these arrangements are unacceptable she returns to her own family. It is understandable that a woman who does not, or cannot, do what is expected of her should be the object of suspicion.

From my brief account of Shona belief as to the causes of death and misfortune it should be clear that when misfortune happens the usual reaction, at least if men's thoughts turn to wizardry, is not to inquire what caused the illness, but who caused it. There is, therefore, a tendency to call to mind any expression of enmity by any person to the victim or any unusual event which would give a clue as to the identity of the wizard. This sort of *post hoc ergo propter hoc* reasoning is well illustrated in the case of *R v Zwichayira* (42) which comes from Gutu. In this case two children, who were on their way to the veld to collect mushrooms, passed by the house of a woman called Pedzai. Pedzai had been giving ground beans to her own children. When the passing children asked for beans she gave them some to eat. Afterwards in the veld it would seem that one of the children must have eaten a poisonous fungus, from the effects of which he later died. However, this explanation of the child's death seems never to have occurred to anyone. Everyone considered the fact that Pedzai had fed the deceased shortly before his death and this, for no very apparent reason, proved her guilt. It is, of course, possible that Pedzai was, in any event, disliked. As a result Pedzai was called a witch, ostracized, and her hut burnt.

A distinction must be drawn between the origin of the friction between persons and the event which occasions the accusation of wizardry. However, it is usually the latter event with which witnesses in court cases are concerned. In *R v Rori alias Vincent* (47), an Ndebele case, the accused was the son of the step-father of the woman named as a 'witch', who was called Elina. It is probable that the origin of the trouble lay long in the past and in the friction between Elina's and Rori's mothers who were, apparently, co-wives. Be this as it may, the immediate cause of the accusation was the sickness of Rori's wife and his sister-in-law. Rori then remembered an event which, to his mind, indisputably proved Elina's guilt. Elina, some time before, had sat on the legs of these women. According to Elina this had been a bit of tom-foolery. Elina had entered a hut and, to get past Rori's sister-in-law, this woman would have had to move her legs aside. As she did not, Elina sat on them. Elina did not remember sitting on the legs of Rori's wife, but thought she might have done so while drunk. Although Elina sat on the legs unthinkingly it was, as the headman Matchina and others explained, a gross breach of etiquette. Elina's action was something which 'has never generally happened before'. Under the circumstances, then, it was not surprising that Elina should have been charged with wizardry when the woman she sat on became ill.

The Ndebele case of *R v Kani* (49) illustrates the sort of atmosphere which can build up in cases where accusations of witchcraft are involved and which can result in a major tragedy. Kani was committed for trial on a charge of murder. The deceased, Gora, was one of his father Gwakuba's three wives. Gwakuba lived at his village in the Semokwe Reserve and with him lived Kani's wife. At the time of his child's death Kani was away from home in Johannesburg. In May, 1961, a message reached Kani telling him that his child had died. Kani came home, and thereafter, according to his father, there was increasing tension between him and his son. It soon became apparent that Kani was blaming his father for the death of the child. To continue in the words of Gwakuba:

'In our custom it is a bad omen for a father and son to quarrel. I decided to call three relatives to discuss the matter and I hoped that this would be a way of communicating with my son who would not speak to me direct. On the morning of Sunday the 4th of June, 1961, I went and called these three people—Tshibilo, Filisi and Dingani—and we returned to my kraal at about 10.00 a.m. in the morning. I then called

Wizardry Allegations where no Diviner was Present

to the accused to come and eat with us. I started explaining to these three relatives that the accused had accused me of causing the death of his child by witchcraft. I told them that he had refused to speak to me about this matter. I also proposed that we take the case to the headman that he should send us with a messenger to the witchdoctor. The accused agreed to this and said nothing more. Filisi said "The heart of a person who is crying, you don't have to go around it", which I think means that a person who has lost a child is liable to be upset. It was then agreed that we should go to the headman the following Wednesday, the 14th June, and Dingani, Tshibilo and Filisi left the kraal. It appeared to me that the accused still held me responsible for the death of his child.'

After this Gwakuba went for a walk in his fields and otherwise occupied himself till nightfall. That night he slept in a hut with his wife Gora, the deceased:

'I was awakened during the night by accused pushing the door open. It scraped on the floor and made a noise. I knew it was the accused by his voice. He said, "You are sending your *mukobas* to my hut." I replied, "What are *mukobas*?" and he said, "A snake has entered my hut. You come and sleep in my hut". The accused was angry . . . he was carrying a knobkerrie.'

Gwakuba had gone outside the hut at this stage to talk to the accused. He decided to go into the hut to get dressed since the accused was in a fighting mood. At this stage, Gora went outside to see what was happening and, according to Mlimo, the elder sister of the accused, Gora spoke to the accused saying:

' "Witchcraft, you do not have to fight for it." The accused then hit deceased with the knobkerrie . . . she had her head bent down to avoid the thatch when he struck her on the head with the knobkerrie.'

In his 'warned and cautioned' statements made to the police the accused, Kani, explained his action. The fullest of these statements reads:

'It has been two weeks since my child died. I was called by telephone that my child is dead. When I married here at home I quarrelled with my parents as to how the child had died. My parents did not reply to me in this quarrel. I went and slept on the following day with my family and the deceased did not speak to me. It stayed like that until yesterday when my father came with three men to ask me whether I had said that my father was a witch and that it was he who had killed my child. The elders said to my father, "your son did not mean that you were a witch, he was only grieving for his child". The elders said, "We will go to the headman on Wednesday." When I was asleep something cried at the door with the voice of that of a dead child. I then got up feeling as though something was strangling me. I went to wake up my father. I said to him, "The witch's messenger has come into my room. You go and sleep there." He made no reply. Then the deceased came out. She said, "Though your child has died, what are you going to do about it?" Then I hit her. That is all.'

In another statement to the police, commenting on the words that were spoken by the deceased before he hit her, the accused said, 'It showed me that all the time she did not speak to me she well knew how my child had died.'

Sexual antagonism can be a source of wizardry allegations. An example of such a case is the case of *R v Ndomene James* (78). In this case evidence was led that a married man had seduced a girl living at Hartley. Later the two parted. The accused, the seducer, went to Salisbury and brought his wife to live with him in Salisbury. Shortly thereafter he became impotent. He blamed the jealousy of his former girl-friend for this condition, probably on the advice of a *nganga*, and summoned her to Salisbury by means of a letter. When she arrived he charged her with wizardry and was extremely unpleasant. Fortunately for the girl she had a brother in Mabvuku and she persuaded the accused to take her to him. The brother reported the matter to the police.

Urban informants, when asked about instances of wizardry accusations, often said that they knew of none and if I wanted information I must ask people in the country districts. It was clear, however, that the informants in question strongly believed in wizardry. The relative uncommonness of accusations in towns is not, apparently, caused by any great decrease in belief and may even influence the thinking of a social reformer. Thus in a letter to the Daily News dated the 13th of October, 1962, a woman campaigning for the right of women to inherit from their deceased husband's estate and who was sufficiently literate to quote

Christina Rossetti, included in her argument the following passage:

'This custom (the inheritance of widows), tended to force women to remarry relatives of their deceased husbands in many cases. Right from the beginning, the custom was full of faults. It encouraged witchcraft in the communities. Say, for example, a man was rich; the relative who by custom would inherit after his death, would sometimes bewitch him so that he might inherit his belongings as soon as possible.'

Although belief in the towns is still great, wizardry allegations which are brought to the courts from these areas are surprisingly scarce, although one or two examples are listed in the table in Appendix I. This scarcity is not caused merely because such cases are not taken as preparatory examinations. I prosecuted for about a year in the Salisbury magistrate's court and never prosecuted a case in which a person was accused of naming a 'witch'. This is no new phenomenon. I have examined records in the Attorney-General's office for the years 1928 and 1929 and ascertained that already, at that stage, cases of indicating 'witches' did not originate from the towns or their immediate surroundings. The reason for this is probably, in the words of Monica Hunter (1961, p. 494), that 'The magistrate is near and the danger that the accuser will be punished for imputation of witchcraft or sorcery is too great for him to risk trying to drive away those whom he believes to be harming him.' For this reason I am told that where wizardry allegations are made in town they are often made by innuendo, a person being said to 'possess a spirit' or the like. I think, however, that even were the authorities not near wizardry allegations would be less common in towns as infant mortality rates are lower there than in the country. Further, I have shown that amongst the Shona and Ndebele serious allegations of witchcraft are generally made by the agnatic lineage against persons not of that lineage. In town the family unit tends to be the simple and not the extended family. Women do not normally have to live with their in-laws. It is, therefore, difficult for the traditional pattern of accusations to occur in an urban area. Wizardry allegations, however, tend to recur in conditions of economic competition and in the other situations of conflict created by town life. An example of an accusation occurring under these new situations is the case of *R v Abner Phiri and Others* (93) which comes from the Rhodesia Railways compound at Wankie, a coal-mining town. This compound is controlled by the railways administration by means of compound police, who are responsible to a European supervisor. However, in addition to this formal pattern of authority, the railwaymen have elected various persons to the local committee of the Wankie Branch of the Rhodesia Railways African Workers' Union. These persons constitute what one might term the informal leaders of the community. The possibility of conflict between these two patterns of authority clearly existed. The person denounced as a 'witch' was Shoniwa, a compound policeman. His accusers were Abner Phiri, the Chairman of the Wankie Branch of the Union, Morrison Kamanga, a committee member, Kasoka, another committee member and Simon Nguluwe, a labourer. Abner Phiri and Morrison Kamanga were employed as clerks in senior positions. All the accused were of northern origin and most of the people in the compound were also from Zambia or Malawi. Shoniwa was a Shona. The event that occasioned the accusation was the death of the 'head police boy' whom Shoniwa assisted. The account of the trouble that ensued is best given in Shoniwa's own words:

'I have been Assistant Head Compound Police Boy at Wankie for three months and fourteen days. During the period I had occasion to make reports on people living in the Railways Compound in connection with illicit beer brewing. Beer was also being brewed in excess and assaults took place at beer drinks. There were also cases of checking up on loafers and prostitutes. As a result of reports made by me I became unpopular with the people in the compound. Most of the people in the compound come from Northern Rhodesia. I am from Hartley, Muzezuru by tribe. There are less than ten Vazezuru in the compound. It is a big compound, perhaps 450 people. On the 30th May, 1957, Kachenjela, the senior police boy, died. Next day I attended a funeral at the Railway African cemetery. I saw all the accused there except Simon Nguluwe. While I was at the funeral Kasoka and Mazambani approached me. Kasoka said, "You are a witch and you have caused the death of Kachenjela". Mazambani also said, "You are a witch, you have caused Kachenjela's death". There were a lot of people there. Kasoka and Mazambani were angry; they were talking very loudly. Some of the people round about heard but some could not hear—there were too many of them. This gave me pain and I was afraid. I left the scene of the funeral. On the 3rd of April a meeting of all the people in the compound was called by Abner Phiri. It was my duty to be there and I attended the meeting. I did not know what was going to be discussed. Abner Phiri was the Chairman of the meeting and I also saw Morrison and Kasoka. The meeting was held in the open. Abner Phiri opened the meeting and he said, "This meeting I have called today is about the death of our Sergeant, Kachenjela. If there is anyone here who knows something about the death of Sergeant Kachenjela he must speak out". Morrison Kamanga stood up. He said, "I, Kamanga, say that I agree with what Abner has just said and I would like everyone here attending the meeting to write a note on which the name of Shoniwa would be written and these notes should be taken to the Area Controller's Office" (the office of the European in charge). Then Kasoka stood up. He said, "This man here, Shoniwa, is a witch and will finish us here. If I were a more responsible man in the Rhodesia Railways I would not keep him here, I would have him transferred somewhere else or have him discharged". On the 18th of April a further public meeting was held with Abner as Chairman. Simon Nguluwe was there but not the remaining accuseds. Abner opened the meeting. In his address he said, "You people all in this compound must thank us leaders because we have made this witch leave this place." The name Shoniwa was mentioned. One or two people addressed the meeting and then Simon Nguluwe got up. He said, "Shoniwa is travelling about the compound saying he has killed a dog" (meaning Kachenjela). After addresses by other people the meeting was closed by the Chairman, Abner Phiri.'

The express purpose of the accusation of wizardry was to secure the removal of Shoniwa. In this his accusers were successful since, as a consequence of the trouble, Shoniwa was transferred to Umtali. It would seem that, in the main, the attitude of the people reflected the attitude of their leaders. One witness remarked:

'The people generally were against Shoniwa. I don't know if it was because he was stopping beer brewing and prostitutes and loafers. He was doing his work well. I think he was unpopular because of this.'

Another witness said that he only began to feel strongly about Shoniwa after he had been told that Shoniwa had caused Kachenjela's death. There seems, however, little doubt that there was widespread resentment of the action of the police in enforcing the rules against beer brewing, prostitutes, etc; but this does not entirely account for the action taken by the accused. There seems to have been a definite attempt by the accused to obtain a recognition of their political power in the community. It was, no doubt, hoped that by removing the Zezuru, Shoniwa, the compound might obtain a more sympathetic police 'boy', perhaps of Zambian origin like the deceased. The use of the trade union machinery to denounce Shoniwa as a 'witch' is, perhaps, surprising but illustrates clearly how the trade union officials at Wankie form the popular leaders of the community and are expected to take action in cases affecting its general welfare.

In the case of *R v Mack alias Chowa* (91) from Sakubva Township, Umtali, the allegation of witchcraft, according to the Crown witnesses, arose consequent to a quarrel between neighbours. According to Enesia, a neighbour and the wife of the person named as a witch, the accused was party to a fight in which Enesia's husband intervened to separate the contestants. Some time after this incident Mack's child died. He laid the blame for this on his neighbour and told Enesia that her child resembled its father 'who eats human beings' and added rather colourfully, 'You are no longer go to the butcher to buy meat, you eat the meat of my child which is still in your quarters'. According to the accused, who denied that he called anyone a witch, but who admitted there was ill feeling between the families, the trouble arose, not because of a fight, but because of an incident in which a fowl had been borrowed and not paid for. After the borrowing, Enesia's husband had been heard to remark that he did not want to live near 'a Sena person who cries for money.' The reference to a 'Sena person' is apparently derogatory. Persons from the Sena area[1] have, on the whole, a very low social status in Rhodesia. It would therefore seem that apart from the superficial causes of con-

---

[1] cf. Moçambique.

flict the growing class consciousness of the urban areas played a part in the conflicts which led to the accusation.

At first sight it may seem surprising that wizardry allegations should occur among school teachers, but it must be remembered that primary school teachers are, due to the shortage of well educated men, often persons of standard six or even less (i.e., primary education only) and, in rural areas, such a man cannot live apart from the community whose children he instructs. That he does not entirely abandon his beliefs in wizardry is to be expected.

A very interesting case, *R v Kufa and R v Chingono* (32), originated from schools in the Sabi North Reserve. The persons who were the accused were, respectively, the heads of St. Cyprian's School and of Daramombe Primary School. Mildred, the victim of the putative witch, was a teacher at St. Cyprian's school and related by marriage to Chingono, the headmaster of Daramombe. Staying with Mildred was a child, Lillian, one of the pupils at St. Cyprian's. There seems to have been trouble between Lillian and a girl of about seventeen called Emelia and Emelia's mother, Sikayi. Emelia was not a pupil at St. Cyprian's but attended the services on Sunday. One day Mildred became ill. She went to the European superintendent and to the clinic but they were unable to help. She became unconscious and was taken home. In her delirium she made allegations of witchcraft. Chingono, who was present, seems to have thought the spirits afflicting here were speaking through her. At all events when Mildred recovered, Chingono gave her the following letter to take to her headmaster, Kufa (my translation):

> 'Daramombe Mission,
> P.O. Daramombe.
> 13th April, 1958

Dear Mr. Mapeza,

I am sorry to inform you that your Mistress has become ill and that she is here at Daramombe. What makes her ill is not the illness of God but the illness of the earth (i.e. witchcraft). Your Mistress has evil spirits (*mamhepo*). I was surprised when I heard her telling me a lot of things. Those *mamhepo* told me that they are the children of the mother of Emiriya and Betty. They said "We have come with our elder sister, Emiriya, and were in a letter. We were sent by our mother who said, "You (Mildred) are much too conceited when with your uncle, Mujuru. You prevent him from courting our elder sister, Betty. Again, why do you stay with Lillian, whose flesh we want to eat?" " When I heard all this I saw that this was the sort of thing that could not be cured by the Europeans. Thus I have sent her home. When I have heard what is going to happen I will let you know again.

Give my regards to all and to Mr. Mujuru and Jaja,

I am,

A. M. R. Chingono'

When Kufa received the letter he sent instructions to Emelia to come to church on Sunday. On Sunday after the service, and in the presence of the African preachers, Kufa announced that he wanted to tell the congregation how it was that the schoolmistress, Mildred, had become ill. He told them that Emelia had written a letter which Mildred had taken to Daramombe Mission for posting and that Emelia's mother had put 'magic' into the letter and this magic had attacked Mildred. After this, Mildred ran home to her mother and accused her of witchcraft. Sikayi was upset and reported the matter to the headman. Next day she saw Kufa who informed her that she wanted to kill Lillian and eat her flesh because Lillian was being protected by Mildred. After giving evidence in court to this effect Sikayi was cross-examined by Kufa and admitted that on one occasion she had called Lillian a 'whore'. This point seems to have been regarded as important by Kufa. Chingono's letter also suggests that sexual rivalry played a part in the accusation.

Unless we suppose that the allegation contained in the letter of the 13th April was a concoction of Chingono—and Chingono at his trial insisted that 'the contents of this letter are not of my own making, it is a recording of what this mad girl was saying'—we have the somewhat remarkable situation that two headmasters, both of some education, were prepared to denounce a woman as a witch merely on the basis of the ravings of a delirious woman. No doubt the notorious enmity between Lillian and Sikayi's family was regarded by the headmasters as strong evidence of the proof of the witchcraft allegation. Kufa clearly regarded it as important that he should bring this enmity to light at the preparatory examination; but, even so, the credulity of the persons involved is astonishing. Kufa, of course, stood to lose his job by acting as he did and that he did so means that he could hardly have realized that he was doing anything of which his superiors would have seriously disapproved. His actions were those of a man seeking to do what was proper in the circumstances. In his own words:

'As the parents were worrying me I thought to tell them why the mistress was absent. I decided to call the parents together and tell them. I did this but I did not know I was committing a crime.'

The fact that the Anglican preachers who were present at the denunciation did not intervene indicates that they saw nothing untoward in Kufa's behaviour.

A case of alleged sorcery occurred on the small-holding I used to occupy which is not far from the Chinamora Reserve. My wife ran a small school of her own for African children in the neighbourhood. The alleged sorcerer's victim was a newly employed school teacher whom I will call Gideon. We learned later that this was not the first time he thought he had been ensorcelled. While still at school he had become ill. His father had had him cured by a *nganga*. His father did not pay the *nganga's* fees and when Gideon later became ill it was ascribed to the *nganga's* anger. Gideon's physical appearance was that of a man who was not well-balanced mentally and he had a rather rude manner of talking, which indicated that he was ill at ease, when he spoke to my wife. The trouble started on the second day of his employment. He had been told to teach a form which, apparently, was beyond his capacity as a teacher, since he appeared most ill at ease when asked to teach it. Furthermore my wife had, during the course of the day, cause to reprimand him for his behaviour. Trouble then arose over his accommodation. The school was chronically short of money and had no proper housing for teachers. While this was building Gideon had to share a hut with two other new teachers whom we will call Joseph and Emmanuel. There was one teacher who had been at the school the year before and he had built himself a very small brick cottage. This teacher, whom I will call Moses, had welcomed the new teachers; but, because his cottage was too small to share with anyone, had not offered to put any of the new teachers up. He was a Tumbuka by tribe from Zambia. All the others concerned were Zezuru. That afternoon Gideon was heard to complain in the store next door to us that Moses was 'proud' because he would not allow him to sleep in his hut. In the evening he complained that he had been informed that his salary would be a pound less a month than had been originally promised. There seems little doubt that he was dissatisfied with his conditions of service, uneasy about his ability to perform the task assigned to him and was in the mood to blame Moses for everything that went wrong. That night Joseph and Emmanuel were awakened by Gideon's screams. They tried to calm him and sought a light. Moses had come, being awakened by the screams, and was asked to fetch a lamp. He brought one. When Gideon saw Moses in the light he screamed again. Moses went away. Joseph attempted to calm Gideon and held his hand. Gideon then started screaming, 'Joseph, Joseph . . .'. This screaming awakened me and my wife. Gideon tried to exorcise the sorcerer by singing a hymn but this, apparently, did not work. He started screaming again and then ran away. Shortly thereafter there was a knock on my front door and Gideon burst in screaming that Moses and Joseph were killing him and were going to kill us. Needless to say, this reassuring news thoroughly alarmed my wife. I tried hard to find out what was the matter. He said that a white powder had fallen from the roof while he was sleeping and that this powder had been sent by Moses and Joseph. I have never seen a man as terrified as Gideon was. He stated that he was certain the powder was *chitsinga*. I tried to reason with him, but this proved useless; he insisted that he had 'proof' that Joseph and Moses were witches. He stated that Moses had a red tie on and that Moses had been squeezing the tie. Every time Moses squeezed he felt limp. I had not seen Moses with such a tie, but he is a nervous man and would, if worried, finger what he was wearing. Red is, of course, the colour of blood and associated with witchcraft and sorcery[1] and so significant in cases such as this. He added that Joseph had held his hand and that every time Joseph clasped his hand he, again, felt limp. All the time he was talking to me he was spitting on the floor attempting to rid himself of the *chitsinga*. I again tried to reason with him, telling him that this was all his imagination. To persuade me he adduced further 'proof' telling me that on the day before when he arrived on my property Moses had welcomed them and given them tea but Moses would not drink the tea himself telling them that he had just had some. I told Gideon, seeing that persuasion was useless, that he could sleep in the house; but he refused to be left alone even with the doors of the room locked. I had little desire to hold his hand until day-light. He asked then for water to wash the medicine out of his mouth. I went to the kitchen, which has an outside entrance, to get it. Moses and Joseph had, at this stage, come to see what was going on and seeing Joseph through the door Gideon started screaming 'Joseph' again, spitting the while. I decided it was necessary to remove Gideon from the house as my wife was showing signs of extreme agitation. As Gideon refused to leave and the more I tried to make him do so the more hysterical he became, it was necessary to tie him up and call for the police. When the police came he calmed and went with them willingly. While his conduct, particularly towards the end, resembled that of a lunatic I have no reason to think that Gideon was insane, although he had without doubt a personality which was highly excitable. His conduct was, I think, to be attributed to the effect of terror on an overwrought mind. The other persons involved in this episode seem to have considered Gideon a madman.

I am including the final case which I shall discuss in this section to illustrate the attitude of persons in authority when an unpopular person is charged with wizardry. The case of *R v Mison and Others* (101) involved as accused six compound policemen at the Triangle Sugar Estates. The cause of the allegation is not apparent

[1] A letter written in red ink would alarm the recipient as containing a threat.

although the person accused of wizardry was certainly a suspicious character, being both a cripple and a herbalist. Mison, the policeman in charge, believed that he was being 'bewitched' by Tarusiya and that his life was in danger. He sent the other five to arrest the supposed wizard. Although I refer to the accused as 'policemen' it will be appreciated that they were not members of the British South African Police but employees of the Estates. The following extract from Tarusiya's evidence describes the manner in which the persons concerned did their supposed duty. There is no reason to suppose that a person accused of theft would have been nearly so roughly handled. This is again a case where the persons concerned stood to lose their jobs had the matter been reported to the authorities as, indeed, it later was. Tarusiya said:

'I was in my hut at about 5.00 p.m. At this time accuseds Benson and Peter came to my hut and I was handcuffed by Alfred who said, "I am handcuffing you because you have medicine for killing people." After being handcuffed, I was assaulted. Alfred held me by the shirt and the back of my neck and Benson, Ranganayi, Michael and Peter began to punch me on the head. I fell down and was kicked by the accused. The punches and kicks were hard blows which hurt me. I was then taken to the huts where the compound police live and *en route* was again subjected to punching and kicking. I did not walk along, I was dragged along, and fell over five times on the journey. On arriving at the police compound huts Ranganayi said, "You are a bad old man, you have medicine for killing people." I was in the yard and from his hut Mison shouted to Benson and Peter to take me to the compound cells after receiving a report from them. Ranganayi then took me to the cells and put me inside. Having done so he poured two buckets of water into the cell and, locking it up, left me there. There was water up to my ankles and I spent the night there until next morning. I have a deformed leg and I sat and lay in the water all night. My leg was painful from the first assault. The following morning Mison, accompanied by all the other accused, came to my cell. They released me from the cell and Mison questioned me saying, "You have medicine?" I was asked if I was a herbalist and if I had medicine. When I was released from the cells I was punched on the head. I was then taken to the office and on arrival Ranganayi said, "You, old man, you want to kill the Sergeant." By this he meant Mison. I was also accused of having taken medicine to kill people by Ranganayi. I was then taken to my hut by Mison and another man. On getting to my hut Michael went inside and searched my hut and found some medicine in a small bag. Michael said, "I have found some medicine, where does it come from?" I told him this medicine was used for my sore foot. Michael said this was the medicine I used to kill people and to prove him wrong I ate some of this medicine in his presence. Michael then took me back to the office where all six accused were present. I again demonstrated the harmless properties of my medicine by eating some. I was left alone at the office until lunch time. When the accuseds had gone I saw the compound manager and made a report to him and then went to the British South Africa Police.'

CHAPTER XI

DIVINATION IN GENERAL

It seems to me that divination techniques can be roughly divided into three classes which, for want of better terms, I name:

(a) psychic
(b) psychological
(c) casual

By psychic divination I mean those forms of divination where the diviner purports to divine by relying entirely on his psychic power or, as the Rhodesian African would express it, by means solely of the spirit which possesses him. Examples of diviners who use such methods are the *shave* doctors, those who divine by looking into mirrors and horns, and the prophets of the Apostolic Churches. If one excludes the possibility of extra-sensory perception such diviners must rely entirely on their knowledge of the society in which their clients live. One is sometimes astonished at the knowledge of such diviners concerning matters of the neighbourhood. Should little more than the relationship between parties be known to the diviner then it is still open for him to make use of social stereotypes of conflict, such as the sexual rivalry between co-wives, to produce a divination acceptable to his clients. Sometimes, but I think seldom, he may guess. Thus in the case of *R v Kateya* (29) the *nganga* accused a certain Cecilia of having caused a woman's barrenness. As chance would have it there was no woman called Cecilia living in the neighbourhood. Generally, however, so great is the belief of his clients in the diviner that even where the diviner has erred they are unwilling to admit the error. Thus in the case of *R v Brown* (33) an Ndebele *inyanga* indicated as a 'witch' an old Kalanga woman. In actual fact there was no Kalanga woman in the village indicated, only an old Ndebele woman, but the client's attitude was as follows:

'Mavoluntiya and I came to the conclusion that both our troubles came from the same source. That is to say from an old woman—Kalanga—who lives at Mafohla's kraal. The only thing that did not fit the description was that the old woman in Mafohla's kraal is Ndebele. I could not be certain of that though as I was not present at the birth of the old woman.'

In the case of *R v Paradza* (37) a woman called Regina was accused by a prophet of 'eating' her daughter's child. Regina had no daughter with a child, nevertheless the people of her village accepted the fact that she was a witch. If a diviner is completely at a loss there are always comparatively safe verdicts, such as laying the blame for misfortune on an angry ancestral spirit.

By psychological divination I mean those forms of divination where the purpose of the divinatory technique is to extract the information which the diviner requires from his clients. Perhaps the best example of such a technique is the *ukuvumisa* ceremony as practised by the Ndebele *isangoma,* for there is little doubt that the manner in which his clients give the standard response, 'We agree' to the diviner's questions enables the *isangoma* to ascertain where the points of friction lie and who is suspected. The accounts of the *ukuvumisa* ceremony which follow are somewhat abbreviated, but the ceremony resembles that of the other Nguni peoples and the account given by Monica Hunter (1961, p. 337) of a Pondo divination gives a good idea of the manner in which a divination proceeds.

A further form of psychological divination, which might be

termed auto-suggestive divination, is a form of divination in which the diviner gets his clients into a highly suggestible state by means of various devices. In this state a person may, for example, be unable to pick up the *mutundu* (basket) of the Shona diviner or may be induced to see faces in the diviner's horn as in the case of *R v Kukubula* (87).

The third form of divination, casual divination, is divination based entirely, or largely, on chance. To this class, I believe, subject to what will be said about avoiding an unfavourable verdict, certain of Shona divination by means of the carved *hakata* belongs. So, too, I think do most forms of the ordeal.

Any particular diviner may, of course, make use of all three forms of divination. The mirror gazer may attempt to extract information from his clients. The *hakata* thrower may make use of his local knowledge. Thus, the outward form of the divination does not mean that it can be readily classified in the manner suggested.

Both psychic and psychological methods of divination are completely under the control of the diviner and if he has, or can obtain, sufficient information he should be able to produce a popular verdict. His success must, however, depend on his knowledge of psychology. Undoubtedly some diviners have a flair in this direction. The casual methods of divination, on the other hand, make few demands on the intelligence of the diviner—indeed in the past most Shona headmen could probably throw the *hakata*. For these reasons, one would expect the diviner using psychic or psychological methods to have a higher status than the diviner using casual methods. This is certainly true amongst the Ndebele where the *isangoma* has definitely a higher status than the *inyanga* who throws the bones. This probably accounts for the popularity of the Tsonga diviners, who usually use psychological methods, among the Shona. Psychological methods of divination depend on creating an atmosphere of awe, therefore, one would expect the equipment of such diviners to be more elaborate than other diviners. Unfortunately I have not sufficient information to prove this, but it is undoubtedly true that the dress of the *isangoma* is far more elaborate than the *inyanga* or the ordinary Shona *hakata* throwing *nganga* whose dress is unimpressive (see illustrations in Gelfand, 1956) and who, indeed, may have no distinguishing features in his costume at all.

A question of interest is whether a diviner varies his methods according to his knowledge of his clients and their affairs. Both Ester Ncube, an *isangoma*, and Kukubula, the Zambian diviner who used a head sliding on string to divine, possessed sets of *hakata*. There is no doubt that diviners do not always rely on the same method of divination. The selection of divinatory technique may, on further investigation, be found in some instances to be part of the process of divination.

The classification of diviners which has been attempted by me would not be accepted by the Shona or Ndebele who regard all diviners as being possessed by their ancestral or other spirits during the divination and to divine by virtue of this possession.

It is recognized that diviners often fail to divine correctly. This in no way affects belief in the powers of diviners generally. The diviner who fails is simply considered a charlatan. One unusually sceptical informant whose home was the Seke Reserve near Salisbury stated that all the hundreds of diviners in Salisbury were frauds, but he knew of one genuine diviner who lived at Inyanga. Clearly distance lends credence to belief. Another almost equally sceptical informant who lived in Salisbury said he knew of a genuine diviner in Marandellas. It is of interest that this latter diviner was not the ordinary *hakata* thrower but belonged to the type of psychic or psychological diviner comparatively rare amongst the Shona who was able to tell clients why they had come and what their symptons were. The more distant a diviner is, the more he is frequently trusted. Thus people go to the Plumtree area from Bulawayo and elsewhere to consult Kalanga diviners; but the people of the Plumtree district go to Bechuanaland, at least in serious cases. In many cases among the Korekore and in the Eastern districts evidence was given of journeys to Moçambique to consult diviners there.

CHAPTER XII

TRADITIONAL DIVINERS AND DIVINATION METHODS

DESPITE the enormous popularity of the Prophets of the various Pentecostal faiths, the Table in Appendix I shows the continuing importance of diviners of traditional type. While various methods of divination are common to all tribal groups in Southern Rhodesia certain methods would seem to have a definite prestige amongst individual groups. For example, the *isangoma* is the most respected of the various diviners of witches amongst the Ndebele while among the various Shona groups the Table will show the overwhelming importance of the diviner who throws the 'bones' (*hakata*). A description of divination methods must, therefore, take into account the various ethnic groupings. In the following pages I have, however, limited my description to the Eastern Shona, Ndebele and Kalanga. The accounts of the various witnesses unfortunately do not, generally, describe divination techniques in great detail since they are more interested in the more personal side of things—who was named and what the various persons' reactions to the diviner's pronouncement were. Although, therefore, there is a tendency to give rather a bald and brief description of the actual divination, the witnesses' accounts convey rather more of the atmosphere than a detailed examination of divination techniques by a scientific observer might do.

THE NDEBELE AND KALANGA

In view of the reciprocal cultural borrowings between the Ndebele and the Kalanga and the nature of the material available to me, it is necessary to consider these groups together.

The structure of Ndebele society is a hierarchical one and, as one might expect in such a society, diviners and doctors are also arranged in a hierarchy. The following description of the various types of diviners and doctors is taken from the evidence of Chief Gambo in the case of *R v Gwayi* (71) and explains the difference between the various practitioners:

> 'I understand that the *isangoma* is a type of witch-doctor who finds out the causes of troubles. He takes the people and groups them together, dresses himself in the clothes of his profession, uses an ox or a wildebeeste or a horse tail and sometimes sprays water with it. He first asks questions, and then the people tell him why they have come and he then tells them what has caused the trouble. This is known as the *ukuvumisa* ceremony. He does perform other ceremonies. The *isangoma* is the same as the *isanusi*. An *inyanga* is a doctor who throws the bones and is also a herbalist. An *umelapi* is a healer. The *isangoma* may indicate ancestral spirits or a person as causing the trouble.'

To this description it may be added that the *isangoma* does not, himself, treat his patients once he has diagnosed the cause of their trouble but refers them to a herbalist. He divines by virtue of possession by his ancestral spirits (*amadhlozi*) and apparently cannot become possessed if not correctly dressed. Dress is often elaborate. Gwayi, for example, was dressed in a skin hat, skins around the waist, snake skins round his shoulders and necklaces of bones around his neck. The ceremony he performs is known as *ukuvumisa* (to cause to agree) because of the form the divination takes—the diviner making various statements and his audience replying, 'We agree'. Needless to say, such a form of divination supplies ample opportunities to the skilled psychologist by listening to the manner in which this response is given to bring in a verdict that is popular with his audience. It is perhaps, because of their ability to produce a popular verdict that the reputation of the *isangoma* stands so high. It is said, for example, that the reputation of the Kalanga diviner Ester Ncube, had spread as far as Salisbury.

The following account of a divination by an *isangoma* is of interest because of the number of people involved, being reminiscent of divinations in the old days of the Ndebele kings. These days divinations ordinarily take place in the privacy of a hut. A further point to notice is that the narrator is an Afrikaner (i.e.

European) farmer and that he took more than a merely passive part in the proceedings. Belief in wizardry is not confined to the African population. In particular, belief in the witch's familiar, the *tokoloshe,* is relatively widespread amongst Europeans of Afrikaner origin. However, the farmer's action can also be accounted for by a desire simply to keep his 'boys' happy. The extract is taken from the case of *R v Mandebele* (45):

'At the time of this case I was on Fairfield farm. At the end of August this year my employee Velemu came and made a request to me. As a result I finally gave him permission to bring a person onto the farm who would tell me the reason for illness among my employees. By this I understood he would indicate the trouble through the spirits. On the second of December, 1956, there was a gathering on my farm. I attended with a neighbour, Mr. Lourens. All my natives and their families were present. At the gathering accused (the *isangoma*) made the natives sit in groups. He came up and danced before the individual groups. When I arrived he was dressed in old worn clothes. Before he started dancing he changed into skins, I think he had a skin cap. Before accused did anything at the gathering Velemu came and indicated accused to me as the person he had brought. I gave Velemu nothing at that time. The groups accused put my natives into their family groups. Accused went in front of one group and danced, talking and waving his ox tail. I understood accused, he continually said in Sindebele "You must admit" (*Vumani berganu* [sic]). The groups replied "*Si a vuma*". Accused would tell one group to leave and another took its place. Accused performed before each group. Accused then told all the natives to sit together. Accused then started dancing again. Accused then addressed the gathering demanding £3 in all. £1 from one group and 10s. from each of the other groups. Velemu came and made a report to me and I gave him £3. He placed the money behind accused with a piece of earth on it. Accused danced in a circle of the people gathered there. Accused then pointed out the old woman saying, "You are the person who killed the people. You are the person who caused the trouble." The crowd became excited and some assaulted the old woman. I went up to this woman and asked her if she admitted what accused had said. She replied "No". Mr. Lourens and I managed to prevent further assaults on the old woman. Had we not intervened it appeared to me she may have been killed.'

Usually, however, the divination is on a smaller scale and the following account by a witness of the manner of divination of the Kalanga *isangoma,* Ester Ncube (74), is rather more typical. The principal narrator, David Makwali had lost five children. His last surviving child was ill and he suspected witchcraft. He, therefore, decided to consult the accused:

'On Tuesday the seventh of November, 1961, I left my kraal and went to the accused's kraal. My child was sick and I wanted to learn the cause of my child's sickness. My child is Tshiwuke and is aged about nine years. She had been sick for one day before I went to the accused. I went to accused because the child was seriously ill. I went with Bukutu, Dingole and Bikiri (they spent a night on the road). At accused's kraal Dingole was sent because the custom does not allow that everyone should enter the kraal at the same time. We waited outside her kraal from about 2.00 p.m. to 5.00 p.m. Accused then came outside. She came dressed in the clothes she is now dressed in (i.e. ordinary everyday dress). In our presence she tied a skin (exhibit, the skin of a small animal) as an apron on her body and placed the white cloth (exhibit) around her shoulders. Accused was carrying that piece of stick (a stick with a tail attached) when she came. On her arrival she had a pin stuck in her dress over her chest. She said it was her permit to forsee what the cause of the trouble or disease which my child had. Accused is an *isangoma* (witchfinder). The pin badge was the badge which proclaimed her to be a witchdoctor.'

It is perhaps at this stage that the following took place, according to Bikiri:

'Accused spoke to Makwali when she arrived. While she was speaking she was sort of dancing in one place waving the tail. She said, "You have come here because of a child who is sick. The child is suffering from stomach trouble, the child is attending school." '

To continue the story in David Makwali's words:

'After she had shown me the pin she told us that if she should throw bones [sic] she probably used the word "divine") for a person who is sick, we had to pay £2 15s. She said if she did it for a person who was dead it was £3 10s. as the fine was high. I did not tell her what we wanted as she always knows. I gave her £3 and she gave me 5s. change. After I had given her the money she took the stick with the tail. She started swinging it around saying *"Vumani! Vumani!"* and we replied, *"Siyavuma, siyavuma,"* which translated means she said "Agree!

Agree!" and we replied "We are agreeing, we are agreeing". She was walking up and down and dancing while she was doing this. The accused said, "The wife of your kraal head, the wife of your kraal head, your niece, your niece, your niece knows what the cause of death is. Take out your money." I produce some money, that was the first payment I made. She started saying these things before I paid the money. She then said, "The fowl eats its eggs". She made us pay the money because she had told us the reasons. She did not say anything else apart from saying, "Your niece has not given the child the medicine with her own hand but has used an *mkoba* (familiar) which has made the child eat medicine in its sleep". An *mkoba* is an animal known to witchdoctors. She described the medicine as being poison from the parts of my children who had died. Five of my children had died and this was the sixth child. When I left my kraal this child was still alive. I know only one niece, she stays at my kraal. Her name is Tshivuma Madimgwili. Her kraal is next to mine. After the accused had said these words we left and returned to my kraal. My child was dead when we returned to my kraal.'

Ester's defence was that she had not indicated anyone as a witch but that the child's illness had been caused through failure to propitiate the ancestral spirits. When she was charged in 1956, with a very similar offence, a set of 'bones' was found on her; but unfortunately I have been unable to ascertain whether she practised, or had at one time practised, as an *inyanga*.

The traditional *isangoma* of the Nguni peoples was, as well as a diviner of the cause of sickness, a 'rainmaker' divining the cause of drought and prescribing the remedy. When, however, Vaughan-Williams (1946, p. 125) visited Lobengula in 1889 he noted that the rainmakers were the priests of the *Mlimo* cult, the Kalanga cult of the Matopos. According to him there were three classes of 'witch doctors'. The 'least harmful' who threw the bones (i.e., the *inyanga*), then the 'smellers out' of witches (i.e., the *isangoma*) and then the 'highest grade' were those originally associated with the great *Mlimo* of the Matopos. As might be expected in the light of the above the Kalanga, while adopting the *isangoma*, do not regard the *isangoma* as a rainmaker. As explained by a witness in the case of *R v Pange and Matini* (sentenced at the High Court, Bulawayo, 25.9.61), when there is a drought 'we go to *Hosana,* that is the rain goddess, and appeal to *Hosana* for rain. The *Hosana* may go and give people instructions to go and organize people to come and dance. They may appeal to higher authorities where we cannot appeal to for rain, and come back and tell us why we have had no rain.' Bullock (1928, p. 122) says that the *izihosana* are nominally the wives of *Mwari* (the *Mlimo*). The *hosana* referred to in the case is either one of these people or some offshoot of the cult of the *Mlimo*. In Vaughan-Williams's time, however, the *Mlimo* cult had not entirely supplanted the original rain magic of the Ndebele, for Carnegie's account (1894, Chap. III) of Ndebele rainmaking is very much in the authentic Nguni tradition.

It is clear that in matters of importance the *isangoma* is regarded as more trustworthy than the *inyanga*. Amongst the cases examined there was only one description of an *inyanga* indicating a 'witch' by throwing the 'bones' (*matambo*), the case of *R v Mbizeni and Isaac* (67). The following is an account of what took place. The witness's son was ill and people on the farm where she lived suggested that she go twenty miles to see the accused. She travelled with her husband:

'When we arrived at the kraal of the accused, Mamoyo (the *inyanga's* assistant) came out to see us. We did not enter the kraal. I told her that I wished to see the witch doctor. Mamoyo took us to the place behind the kraal. There was a large tree there and the ground beneath it had been cleared. There was nobody at this spot but the accused arrived just after us. We sat down. The accused had trousers and a shirt on. He sat in front of us and Mamoyo sat at his side. The accused took some "bones" (actually shells) from his pocket and threw them on the ground. He looked at the bones and said, "Your child has stomach trouble". I had not told him or Mamoyo this fact. He threw the bones a second time and then said that the child had been bewitched by the wife of the child's uncle. I thought that he referred to my brother's wife at Solus Mission Plumtree. The accused threw the bones again and I asked the accused to treat my son and he agreed. He asked me to enter the kraal with him and I did so. The accused and Mamoyo came with some medicine for which I paid five shillings. I only paid five shillings when the accused said that my son had been bewitched by the wife of the child's uncle and I believed him. I am the mother of the child but his father was an alien native who did not pay any *lobolo* (bride price) for me. The child, therefore, belongs to my guardian who is the brother I have referred to. My father is dead.'

The method of this *inyana*, as far as one can ascertain, was similar to many Shona *nganga*. It would be of interest to discover to what extent the Kalanga *nganga* of the past has become the Ndebele *inyanga* of today. An interesting feature of the above divination is that the *inyanga* appeared to have quite considerable knowledge of events some twenty miles away and managed to lay his finger on what was, quite clearly, a sore spot, the question of the guardianship of the sick child.

The above accounts are the ordinary methods of divination used by the Ndebele. The following account is illustrative of another method.[1] In *R v Maria Mdhlawuzo* (16) evidence was led that the wife of a certain Phillimon had become ill and he went with his wife's mother to consult accused:

'On arrival at accused's house accused told us to take a path leading into the veld. We took a path to a big tree where we all sat down. We had addressed her as *"Mahlangu"*, the words mean, "One who helps others". We had not asked her to help us, we went to her house, when I said *"Mahlangu"* she told us to take the path and go to a tree. I went ahead with my wife Tombana and her mother and when the accused arrived she found us sitting there.

When she arrived she had two sticks in her left hand. In her right hand she had a leaf of a tree. The accused swung the leaf up and down towards the ground (in the manner of tolling a bell), and asked, "Who wakes up at night at eleven o'clock?" I did not know what she meant at first. Then I thought she meant me because I got up at eleven o'clock to do the milking. Before I could ask her if she meant me she said, "Who is the witch?" I replied, "I do not know, that is what I have come to find out." The accused then said to me, "You are a bad man, you went and collected a spear, you put it into your house and today this spear is the thing which is destroying your house." I asked accused what she meant by the word "spear". I asked

---

[1] This method of divination is probably of Zulu origin. Bruwer (1963, p. 144) remarks 'Onder die Ngunivolke is 'n ingewikkelde divinasietegniek nie baie algemeen nie. Die oorspronklike divinasievoorwerpe wat deur hierdie volke gebruik is, bestaan hoofsaaklik uit waarsêstokke wat op magiese wyse sou rondspring in antwoord op vrae.'

her if she meant it was my relative. The accused asked me what type of man I was. She said, "By the word spear I mean that young woman you have brought into your house." She did not mention her name, she merely said, "Your young wife." She said, "Your young wife is the only bad person in your house because she puts bad things into food ... she is a witch and bewitches people." I understood accused to be referring to Margaret. All this time the accused was holding the sticks (one was three feet in length and the other slightly longer) in her left hand parallel to the ground and waving the leaf in her right hand up and down. Accused said, "If you feel the pain of what I have told you about your wife, you go and ask your wife if she is going to be worried about what you are going to tell her, she can go and report the matter to the police. I will tell her what she is in front of the police.' (The accused then asked for and received ten shillings.)

In the divination also, the accused clearly had a considerable knowledge of events in the vicinity and it is probable that she named Margaret as a 'witch' because of the friction known to exist between her and Tombana.

THE SHONA

While various methods of divination are described by writers on the Shona (see, for example, Gelfand, 1956, p. 115) an examination of the Table in Appendix I shows the overwhelming importance of the use of the divining dice (*hakata*) usually referred to in court records as the 'bones'. Except among the Korekore where the *hakata* usually consist of the split seeds of the *mungomo* tree, the *hakata* are four carved wooden dice each with a name—*chitokwadzima, kwame, nokwara* and *chirume*. Tracey (1934, p. 23) has published excellent illustrations of these. While designs differ, and where a diviner throws several sets together they must differ, there is sufficient uniformity both in this respect and in the readings of different diviners for persons who are not professional diviners to acquire some knowledge of the way in which the fall of the *hakata* is read. Descriptions of the manner in which the *hakata* may be read are given by Gelfand (1956, Chap. X), Hunt (1950, p. 40, 1954, p. 16, 1962, p. 14) and Tracey (1963,

p. 108). The dice, of course, can fall either face upwards or face downwards. Whether or not the throw is a fortunate or unfortunate one is determined by the nature of the dice which fall face upwards. Each 'throw' has its own name and significance. On the whole the two 'male dice, *chitokwadzima* and *chirume* and the combinations in which they predominate are unfortunate throws and the two 'female' dice, *kwame* and *nokwara,* and the combinations in which they predominate, are fortunate. Essentially the process of divination consists of putting questions to the dice which they answer on a 'fortunate' or 'unfortunate' or a 'yes', 'no' basis.

The Shona diviner or *nganga,* unlike the Ndebele *isangoma,* is not usually expected to inform his clients as to the reason why they have come to consult him. He may, indeed, say, 'I see you have come because you are troubled' or something similar; but then one is hardly likely to go to a diviner unless something is wrong. The few diviners who are reputed to be able to inform their clients of the reasons for their visit without having been told the reasons have great reputations. Because the diviner usually makes no pretence of omniscience, it is necessary for his clients to tell him why they have come. The *nganga* may well question his clients at some length as to the reason for their visit. If the *nganga* is consulted privately concerning a misfortune which, it is believed, has been caused by witchcraft, the names of the suspect or suspects will often be given to the *nganga.* If the *nganga* is to be consulted publicly—which takes place where the matter is one of public concern and, in particular, where the matter is of sufficient importance to concern the chief or headman—then the party collected to go to the diviner will contain, or be representative of all persons who might be suspected of wizardry. I can find little evidence in the cases examined of audience participation at the time of the throwing of the *hakata.* An informant, in giving an account of a divination which he attended, stated definitely that there was none on that occasion. Successive casts of the *hakata* often follow one another very quickly leaving no time for discussion between throws. It would seem that the vital part of a

Shona divination by means of the *hakata* often takes place prior to the actual throwing of the *hakata* and that the function of the *hakata* is largely, in those cases where wizardry is suspected, to say 'yes' or 'no' when a particular name is mentioned or when a particular person throws them. They thus resemble, in some ways, the poison oracle of the Azande (Evans-Pritchard, 1937, Chap. II) except that the *hakata* are rather more subtle an instrument than the poison and leave greater scope to the diviner to interpret the meaning of the oracle. If the *nganga's* clients do not know what caused the misfortune they cannot assist him in his divination. In such a case a verdict that the misfortune was caused by the *vadzimu* would probably be accepted.

Some diviners undoubtedly operate by throwing the *hakata* and by asking the clients to interpret or comment on the throws. Shona divination by means of the *hakata* is certainly not entirely casual. Nevertheless, divination by means of the *hakata* is a far more mechanical process than is, say, the divination of an Ndebele *isangoma*.

Because of the difficulty of manipulating the *hakata*, which is particularly obvious when they are thrown not by the diviner but by those suspected of wizardry, and because of the widespread knowledge of the readings of the more important combinations of *hakata*, it would seem that often the Shona diviner, when the stage of throwing the *hakata* is reached, must confine his attention not so much to ascertaining the frictions and tensions in the community in the manner of the *isangoma* or the Hlengwe *bula* thrower, but to avoiding an unpopular verdict. This is, I think, to some extent an unconscious process. I have been impressed with a diviner's obvious sincerity and belief in his craft. The easiest way of avoiding an unpopular verdict is simply not to throw the *hakata* for a person who is powerful in the community. Posselt (1935, p. 55) states that 'every member of the tribe, with the exception of the chief, is open to such an accusation (of witchcraft)'. Very noticeable among the cases examined by me was the fact that in no case were persons in authority, whether chiefs or village heads, involved. If the *hakata* are thrown for a person or

Traditional Diviners and Divination Methods

by him or his representative and clearly reveal wizardry, then it is open to the diviner to state that not he, but a member of his family, was involved. The case of *R v Gwatipedza and Amos* (23) from the Chibi district will serve to illustrate both the method of divination used and how a *nganga* may avoid an unpopular verdict.

The case arose as a result of the death of the brother of accused Amos. Gwatipedza's statement at the end of the Preparatory Examination is self-explanatory:

'I saw death in my kraal. I went to the kraal where he died and I buried him, then I returned to my hut. After a few days accused Amos came to me. He asked me to go to a witchdoctor to divine the cause of his brother's death I said everyone present would have to contribute money I should call all my people together and go together with them. I called all the people to meet where that man died. We met there. I told them all that Amos wanted to go to a witchdoctor to ascertain the cause of his brother's death. I said everyone present would have to contribute money to Amos. (Amos produced ten shillings). I gave sixpence so everyone there paid sixpence. I asked Amos to which witchdoctor we should go. Accused Amos said we should go to Gororo. We arrived (at the doctor's kraal), and Amos said, "I have come to find out what caused the death of my brother." The doctor agreed to throw the bones. He threw them and then asked for money. Amos gave him the money we had collected. Then Amos began to go round his spirits and when he had finished he came to his kraal. I agreed and he began with my kraal and the doctor said, "Yes, the person died in your kraal." I asked if he meant that I was responsible. The doctor replied that he meant one of my people in my kraal. I said. I wanted to know this evil person in my kraal. The doctor asked for more money. I told him I had no money. Amos produced four shillings. The doctor asked me to say the name of each person in my kraal. The doctor threw the bones and tested me and said I was innocent. We went on to one elder brother, we found him innocent, and so on until we came to Sungayi when the doctor said we had better stop as this person is bad. I asked him to repeat his throw to find out how bad. The doctor threw again and the result was the same. The doctor asked if there were more to be tested. The doctor asked me to tell him the names of one person and I told him it was Sungayi. I asked if it was Sungayi himself who was a witch. The doctor replied, "No, it is Sungayi's wife who has spoiled your kraal." I asked the doctor if he was telling lies. I said, "she is a small person and could not find medicine (or magic) to kill a person." The doctor replied he was certain and told us to approach another of his kind. So I was satisfied and ordered my people to go back home. When we got home I asked my people how we should approach the person, and they said I had better go and tell him. I went to my kraal, I gathered all the people and told them to meet where that person had died. When everyone was present I said, "Don't fight over the death in our kraal. The doctor to whom we have been says the wife of Sungayi was the cause of the death. Nothing happened there." '

It will be noticed that although the *nganga* avoided naming Sungayi he named a person who clearly no one would have suspected of being a 'witch'. However, as she was a 'small person' the verdict was accepted, although this does not seem to have led to the spontaneous outbreak of hatred against the witch which frequently happens where the verdict is popular. It is meant by 'Amos began to go round his spirits' that Amos named to the *nganga* the various *vadzima* that could have caused the death and that, only after their activities had been excluded, did the diviner start investigating the possibility of wizardry.

Wizardry is, of course, a crime in customary law and, indeed, one of the few crimes known to customary law which may not be compounded by the payment of compensation (Posselt, 1935, p. 55). Divination in such cases is really a method of trial and the political authorities are, therefore, closely associated with it. It is they who are responsible for gathering together the party that is to visit the diviner, and when the party returns with the verdict, it is they who gather the people together to hear the news and who, in the past, would have determined the punishment. Despite the fact that participation in this manner would, nowadays, lead to loss of office if the European authorities heard of it, chiefs and headmen still participate actively in these divinations. An attempt was made by me to ascertain from the cases examined the frequency of participation in the divination by chiefs and headmen but, unfortunately, most cases did not supply sufficient evidence on this point although it was clearly by no means uncommon.

The composition of the parties that are gathered to consult the diviner is of interest. Should the diviner live close at hand then all suspects, or at least the family heads of all the suspects, will form part of the party. These persons are drawn from the immediate neighbourhood of the place where the victim lives or lived and, again, illustrates that wizardry allegations are believed to take place only within a kin or neighbourhood group. Refusal to participate in such a party would be tantamount to an admission of wizardry. Where the diviner lives at a distance, as is often the case, since to obtain the verdict of a diviner who is free of any suspicion of using his knowledge of the neighbourhood for his own ends people will often travel long distances, then the party must of necessity be smaller and the members of the party will carry with them the tokens of those who are unable to go.

The use of tokens is widespread in all branches of Shona law and religion. The payment of sixpence by all kraal members to the headman in *Gwatipedza's* case was of the nature of a token handed over to indicate that persons' participation in the matter. Holleman (1952, p. 134) discusses the role of the token in legal matters; but tokens are used outside the realm of the law, for example, in *shave* rituals where persons become possessed, each person present produces a token, be it only a button. When a diviner 'catches' a 'witch' he returns the token to her. Other methods of indicating a 'witch' are to cut her hair or to tie bark round her neck. In the Zaka district evidence was led in the case of *R v Pargwavuya* (97) that when the 'witch' was named, mealie meal was sprinkled on the heads of all present except on the head of the husband of the 'witch'. The 'witch' herself was not present at the divination. Everyone except the husband was given mealie meal to sprinkle on their wives. The husband of the 'witch' was given a very small amount of mealie meal for his *vadzimu*. A rather similar custom exists amongst the Hlengwe of the same district.

Although the verdict of the diviner is usually accepted, it is always open to his clients to consult another *nganga*. Very frequently the diviner's verdict is only accepted after he gets angry or tells them that if they do not believe him they can consult someone else. Amongst the cases examined the only divinations which were not eventually accepted were two cases both involving diviners who divined, not by means of the *hakata,* but through possession by their *shave* spirits.

I close my account of divinations amongst the Shona with an account of a divination in which the suspects themselves threw the *hakata,* a method which seems as common as those cases where the diviner throws them for the various suspects. The extract is taken from the case of *R v Machuchu* (92). The son of a certain Makufa had been bitten by a snake and died. Makufa organized a party which travelled from Makufa's village in the Maranke Reserve, to the accused's in the Zimunya Reserve. The story in Makufa's own words is as follows:

'We were six altogether in this party. Mwaringeseni was with us (my sister). When we left we did not know what we would see—we were going to look for a witchdoctor. I made inquiries in Zimunya Reserve and then went to the Rimite area. We found the accused there at the kraal in a hut. There was an enclosure around the hut. We went inside the enclosure. I spoke to the accused. Before I spoke to accused he said, "I know you have come here because your child has been bitten by a snake." I did not know how accused knew that, but then I was quite convinced that he was a witchdoctor because he knew this. We clapped our hands as a gesture of respect to the accused. The accused brought his *hakata* from his hut. He had them in a cloth bag. He came from his hut with them when we first arrived. Accused threw the bones first and he handed them to me to throw. He said, "Pick up the bones and hold them." I did so and I threw them. Accused then said, "You have finished your part, you have done nothing wrong." He looked at the bones before he said this. I then moved away and sat down. All six of us went through the same procedure. Mwaringeseni was the last one to throw the bones. The others that followed after me were each told to go as they had done nothing wrong. Mwaringeseni threw the bones for the first time. She was then told to throw the bones again a second time and again a third time. She was then told to throw the bones again for the fourth time. He examined them each time. On the fourth occasion accused said she was to blame for the child's death. His actual words were, "You have been arrested, you are responsible for the snake biting the child and causing his death." Mwaringeseni said the accused had lied against her. She was very upset. I paid the accused. He told us we could go away then. The accused said he wanted £1 6s. for his services.

Traditional Diviners and Divination Methods

I paid him that. He spoke to me after he had accused Mwaringeseni. He said there was a spirit at the kraal which was working through Mwaringeseni and that we should go and make some beer and brew the beer for the spirit. I do not know about witchcraft. Sometimes you can believe it, sometimes you cannot.'

When a suspect is 'caught' the *hakata* will ordinarily be thrown a number of times to confirm the first verdict. But, in Machuchu's case, it will be seen that the witch was the last person for whom the *hakata* were thrown and one cannot help suspecting that, having cleared the other persons of complicity, the diviner was consciously or unconsciously determined to indicate Mwaringeseni and instructed her to continue throwing until a verdict was obtained. Whether this is so or not, the *hakata* can in theory be manipulated in this way if the first throw is inconclusive. I have been impressed with the speed at which successive throws can be made by a diviner. The speed would assist this sort of manipulation.

The witness's statement that sometimes you can believe in 'witchcraft' and sometimes you cannot must not be interpreted to mean that sometimes the witness is sceptical of all wizardry beliefs. All that the witness intends to express is probably the usual scepticism in regard to the claims of particular diviners. As often as not when 'witchcraft' is referred to in court records the art of the diviner is meant.

FOREIGN DIVINERS

In a country where so much migrant labour is employed it is to be expected that amongst the cases examined should have been found a number relating to foreign diviners. Surprisingly enough, in view of the numbers from Malawi in Rhodesia, only one of these diviners came from there; but there were two cases in which diviners from Zambia were involved. One of these diviners, the accused in the case of *R v Kukubula alias Bernard* (87), is of exceptional interest as he is a type of diviner I have not described elsewhere in this work. He was a 'high powered' witchfinder of modern type operating with a modern car and paid clerks to look after the financial side of his business. Had his activities not been brought to a sudden stop by the authorities there is little doubt that he would have started one of those wizardry scares of which there are a number of African examples such as that described by Richards (1935) and to which the activities of Mathew Hopkins in England form a parallel. Kukubula was tried on eight counts, mainly under the Witchcraft Suppression Act, at Tjolotjo. His clients were mainly Ndebele. The fact that Kukubula was a foreigner seems, if anything, to have enhanced his reputation. The equipment seized from him was most elaborate. Fortunately I have been able to obtain some photographs of it taken at the time of the trial. The list is as follows:

A carved model of a human head with bead decoration. There was a hole passing lengthwise through the middle. The hole was not straight but designed so that if a string were passed along it and the string tightened, the 'dummy' stuck in one place, while it slid freely when the string was slack. (Frontispiece.)
Two horns mounted in a wooden stand (Plate I).
A wooden elephant with a hollow tube mounted on its back and decorated with beads (Plate I).
A rattle consisting of two small gourds on a piece of wood (Plate I).
A solid model of an animal with a skin covering and six holes running along the back, each containing a decorated horn (Plate II).
A leather bag containing 'witchdoctor's bones'.
Two animal tails with decorated handles.
A staff with a carving of a woman as a handle, decorated with beads.
A similar model about nine inches high.
Two antelope horns.
A small animal tail with a bead decorated handle.
A decorated 'tomahawk type' axe.
A snake skin headband decorated with beads.
A piece of decorated wood with two gourds attached.
A quantity of 'European' medical equipment including an enema, syringes and parts of a stethoscope.

The following extract is taken from the evidence of Amos and relates to the first count. Amos's father committed suicide as a

I. Diviner's equipment: horns, gourd rattle, wooden elephant and head

II. Diviner's equipment: animal with skin covering and horns inserted in holes running along the back

Traditional Diviners and Divination Methods

result of being named as a wizard. I shall later (p. 246) give an extract of the suicide note he left behind him. Amos's evidence reads:

'I knew deceased Manjini in his lifetime, he was my father. He lived in the same line (i.e. line of villages) as I do. Deceased and I were moved from the Filabusi district to the Ndawana line in 1954. A native, Mahlambi, who also came from the Filabusi district, arrived the day after we did. I did not know him before this. Mahlambi disappeared for three weeks and was then found on the other side of the Manzanyama River. He was then brought back to the line, stayed for a short while, and then died. At the time of his death there was no suspicion of witchcraft.

I remember Sunday the nineteenth of February, 1956. Our line head, Masoja, called us together for a meeting. We were informed by him of Kukubula who had come with the sanction of the Government (sic) and anyone who wished to go and see him could do so. All of us, that is the members of Ndawana line, decided to consult accused to try to ascertain the cause of the death of Mahlambi. Mahlambi's widow, Jayina, then went and paid the line head the sum of two pounds sterling.

In our language the word *bulala* has two meanings, to kill and to bewitch. If Mahlambi had died of violence we would not have gone to consult the accused.

On Monday the twentieth of February we all went to Mkuazaan line. There were about twenty of us. When we arrived Masoja, our line head, took some money out of his pocket and entered a hut. Masoja came carrying a small piece of paper (a receipt for the money paid). We were told to return to our line and on Tuesday we returned to Mkauzaan line. We were again told to return to our line. On Wednesday the other members of our line went to Mkauzaan line and I followed them later. About 3.00 p.m. we all entered a hut where we saw accused. Accused instructed us men to sit in a line on one side of the hut and the women in a line on the opposite side. I see the dummy [Frontispiece], it was hanging from the centre of the hut by the string and the dummy was covered (one of the tails was lying outside the kraal on the footpath, the rest of the paraphernalia was arrayed in front of the accused except for the snake skin head band which was around his head).

Accused then took the rattle and shook it near his right ear and peered into one of the horns of the animal [illustrated in Plate II] having first removed a piece of cloth from the opening of the horn and put it in another horn. Having peered into the horn, he called Jayina, Mahlambi's widow. Accused then smeared some black ointment taken from one of the horns mounted on the wooden stand on Jayina's forehead a little above and to the side of her eyes. He then asked her to look into the horn mounted on the animal. Accused asked her what she had seen and she replied she had seen the picture of a man. Accused told her not to tell anyone who the picture was of and that we were to return home. We refused saying we wanted to know who had killed Mahlambi. We had heard about the dummy and asked him to use it to indicate the wizard. Accused then spoke to the dummy which he had uncovered. He then told us that each of us in turn was to say to the dummy *"Uma kuyini engabulala Mahlambi, bamba, si bone"* which means "If I am the person who has killed Mahlambi, hold, let us see." Accused then told my mother Tula to ask the question. As she asked accused projected the dummy up the string and it came down again. Accused then went from woman to woman, each one asking the same question, and the dummy behaved in the same way. Accused then started on the men and I was the first man asked. The dummy behaved in the same way with each man until it was my father's turn. He asked the question, the dummy was projected up the string and on its way up the string, it stopped. Accused then told my father to ask, *"Uma kuyini engabulala Mahlambi, iyethla, si bone"* which means, "If I killed Mahlambi, come down, let us see." Having asked this question the dummy came down the string. Accused then asked my father to go through the whole ceremony again—with the same result. My father was at the end of the men's line and accused then started coming back down the line calling to each man to ask *"Uma ugambulala Mahlambi yilo Manjini, bamba, si bone"* which means "If I killed Mahlambi with Manjini, hold, let us see." The question had to be asked as the dummy was travelling up the string. Masoja, sitting next to my father, was the first to ask this question and the dummy stuck at the top of the string. He was then told to ask *"Uma ugambulala Mahlambi yilo Manjini, iyehla, si bone"* which means, "If I killed Mahlambi with Manjini, come down, let us see." The dummy then came down indicating that Masoja had assisted my father Manjini to kill Mahlambi. Each of us men was then told to ask the first question and the dummy just went up and down the string. Accused did not tell the women to ask this question and did not project the dummy up the string with them. I was the last man asked. When the dummy stopped when my father Manjini asked the question I thought that he had been indicated as a wizard. When the dummy stopped for Masoja, I thought he was a wizard as well.

After the ceremony accused told us to return home and that he would come to our line with chief Siposo. He said he would come and get the "medicine" that had killed Mahlambi. Chief Siposo was present and saw and heard everything. I returned to our line with Manjini and he seemed to be sad. When we had arrived at the line Manjini went to his kraal and I went to mine. Later that evening my father came and borrowed a light from me to write some letters to my brother in Bulawayo. He then left me. The following morning, Thursday, the twenty-second of February, I saw Manjini and spoke to him. His voice appeared to me to be normal and he then left me. I did not see him alive again.

Later that morning accused and Chief Siposo arrived at our line. They were informed Manjini had disappeared. On receipt of the report accused took the rattle and shook it near his ear and peered down the tube on the elephant [Plate I]. Accused then said Manjini was going to a certain place but was still alive. He told us to go and look for Manjini and if we didn't find him we were to come back and report to him. I searched for Manjini, couldn't find him and went back and told accused. I was then given three of the accused's assistants and told to go and look again. We did not find Manjini. I searched again the next day without success. On Saturday, as a result of a message received, I went to see accused at Mkauzaan line. When I arrived accused told me that my father was going towards Bulawayo, that he was alive and that I must not be afraid. I then left accused and later that day was taken by Nkolone with Chief Siposo and line head Masoja to a spot in some thick bush. In this spot I saw my father Manjini hanging by his neck from the branch of a tree. There was a piece of cloth tied around his eyes. Manjini was hanging by a piece of bark rope. I also noticed that deceased's coat and hat were hanging from another branch.'

Jayina, the deceased Mahlambi's wife, it will be recalled, was referred to by Amos in his evidence. She also gave evidence. The following is an excerpt concerning her looking into the horn:

'When we were seated I was ordered to sit in front of the other women with my son Johane. I sat with my back to the women and facing accused. Accused then called me to come closer to him. Accused then took some black ointment out of one of the two horns mounted on a wooden stand and smeared it on my closed eyes. Before this he had taken the rattle, shaken it and patted two of the horns on the animal. He asked me what I saw. I replied that I saw a person inside. Accused asked me what sort of person and I said "a man". I actually saw a person in the horn, it was a picture of a man with a beard. The picture appeared to be of our line head Masoja. Having looked into the horn

I was told to sit down with the women again. Accused then called my daughter out, smeared her eyes with the black ointment, and told her to look into the horn. Having done this she then came and sat down with us.'

Kulubula was probably from Barotseland. Turner's description of 'rattle divination' amongst the Ndembu (1961, p. 81) is very similar to Kukubula's use of the 'dummy'. Turner's account is very brief but it would appear that the rattle, which runs on string, is used in the same manner as the 'dummy'—the point at which the rattle sticks marking a 'point of divination' at which a definite answer is given to a question. This method is stated to be of Lunda origin. Gelfand (1956, p. 115) describes a method of divination similar to the Ndembu sliding rattle amongst the Shona, so perhaps the method of divination may not have been totally unfamiliar to Kukubula's Ndebele clients. Turner mentions several methods of divination using medicated horns, but does not mention divination simply by looking into the horn. Melland (1932, p. 225) however, does give an account of a somewhat similar method of divination amongst the Kaonde and Lunda. Whilst this form of divination is found in Rhodesia, and also the allied mirror divination, the elaborate apparatus used, the carved animals, etc., is totally foreign to the local diviner. Jayina's evidence that she saw a person in the horn she looked into is somewhat surprising but it seems without question that some diviners can bring their clients into a highly suggestible state. Thus, among the Shona, the method of divination by means of the *nganga's* basket (*mutundu*) depends on the ability, or otherwise, of the suspect to pick up the basket used by the *nganga* for his paraphernalia. There is no doubt that persons do fail to pick up this extremely light basket.

THE EFFECT OF MODERN SOCIAL CONDITIONS ON THE TRADITIONAL DIVINER

It would seem that modern social conditions have not lessened the number of diviners, although the profession of a diviner has not become as commercialized in Rhodesia as it has in South Africa. In contrast to Pretoria and other South African towns where large quantities of divining equipment are made by Europeans and sold to diviners, the commerce in divining equipment in Southern Rhodesia is comparatively small, although markets such as that in Salisbury's Harare township supply some of the equipment a diviner needs. Diviners in the Salisbury African townships probably number hundreds but not thousands. There does not seem to be more than a handful of diviners in each of the Reserves in the Salisbury district.

In a country where most of the more responsible positions in commerce and industry are held by Europeans, the occupation of a doctor-diviner enables a man to achieve a higher status without coming into competition with European enterprise. The motives that induce a man to become a diviner are probably very similar to the motives that induce a man to become a prophet in the Pentecostal Churches, unless the man comes from a family of diviners.

The fees charged by diviners show that in the case of many diviners it is not so much pecuniary advantage that is sought but status in society. Most charges—as the Table in Appendix I shows—are not excessive bearing in mind the fees that some diviners are able to extort. *Kukubula's case* shows what sums people are willing to pay to diviners as also does a case such as *R v Sineki* (p. 220) while large sums will be readily paid for charms of various kinds. In one case evidence was given that businessmen had paid up to £15 or £20 for medicine to increase their turnover. While it is true that the fees charged by the Ndebele *isangoma* are high —as befits his status—the ordinary diviner could probably charge much more than he does. There are unscrupulous diviners in towns, some of whom probably become quite rich, but the ordinary country *nganga* is not a rich man. Many diviners believe in their powers and genuinely desire to assist their clients in their troubles. With one exception, all the fees charged in the cases examined were stipulated for in money although, on occasion, the debt was settled in kind.

The challenge of Christianity and, in particular, of the prophets of the Pentecostal Churches, as also the increasing secularization of society and the attitude of the authorities, threatens the existence of the doctor-diviner. So also does the large number of practitioners who, from any point of view, including that of the African, are mere 'quacks'. These threats have led the doctor-diviners of Rhodesia and, in particular, the so called 'herbalists' who practise in the large towns, to form themselves into a professional organization. In Appendix III I have given at length the constitution of this body and would draw particular attention to clause 7 (d) which stresses the importance of spirit possession or guidance. Under the circumstances, the fact that the body has been afforded a measure of recognition by the Salisbury City Council is, perhaps, to be wondered at.

Apart, however, from the growth of such organizations, there has arisen a class of diviner who has adopted the methods of divination of the prophets of the Pentecostal Churches from whom, however, they may be distinguished, whether because they call themselves *nganga* (Shona), or *inyanga* (Ndebele) or because they charge fees for their services. The distinction between prophet and 'witchdoctor' is, however, not always easy to make in the cases studied, as an uninformed witness may refer to a prophet as an *nganga* and persons who call themselves 'prophet', if they have to travel a distance when called upon to prophesy, ask to be reimbursed for the costs of transport—in one case the cost of hiring a bus for themselves and their followers. The following is an account of a practitioner who must, I think, be regarded as a *nganga* and not a prophet. The extract is taken from the case of *R v Mpabanga* (9), which comes from the Belingwe district:

'Accused is a "shaver". He is so called because he shaves people he finds to be witches. In July 1957, I was called to Ntubaidze's kraal. We were told to go to accused to find out what had caused the deaths of Machikwa's children. Next day we went to the accused's kraal in Chief Mudabanu's area with Pikira, Togarepi and Tandiwe, a woman. When we arrived the accused was absent. We waited and accused returned in

Traditional Diviners and Divination Methods

the evening. I went to accused and told him we wanted to find out about the death of Machikwa's child. He asked if I had any money and I replied "yes". I offered accused £3 and he said he wanted £5, so I gave him £5. I had been given the money by Machikwa. Machikwa had contributed £2 and Tandiwe had contributed £3. I gave the money to accused to divine (*shopera*) what had caused the death. Accused then dressed up in a red robe and pulling on a rope tied to his hut he prayed saying "God help me"; (another witness stated that he jumped about as he prayed). This is a Zionist practice and I did not associate it with witchcraft. He was a prophet. After praying accused said, "You have come to find out about a death". I said, "Yes". He said "A female child died". Accused's wife then took Tandiwe outside. Before this, while accused was praying, he told Tandiwe that she had some medicine. She denied this. After going out Tandiwe returned and she was shaved by the accused. Accused said to her "You witch." Accused sent us away the same night. He told us to go back to Ntobaidze and tell him that Tandiwe, who had been shaved, was a witch.'

An interesting feature of this case is that, according to Tandiwe, when the accused's wife took her outside she asked her where she kept her medicines. Tandiwe denied possessing any but had she admitted to their possession, there is little doubt that Mpabanga would have made use of this knowledge to impress his clients. Mpabanga claimed, in his defence, to be a real prophet and produced a 'Preacher's certificate', but it is difficult to regard Mpabanga as anything other than an *nganga*.

Apart from the influence of the churches, modern ways of life have produced new methods of divination. Perhaps mirror gazing can be regarded as merely an extension of the old method of divining by looking into the *gona* (the *nganga's* 'horn'—usually a gourd). One Tsonga diviner I knew used to make considerable use of a pamphlet on fortune telling which had been printed in England. The following extract was taken from the case of *R v Chemere alias Mahondoro* (15) from the Buhera district, and is an account of a diviner making use of a book. The witness's child had died and in the party which went to consult the *nganga* was Chiramwiwa, the wife of the witness's father's younger brother:

'Accused was outside the hut when I first saw him and I spoke to him. We then went into the veld. Accused produced a book and opened it. He said first that a beast was wanted for the mother of my wife (i.e. the *mudzimu* of the deceased mother). He alleged there was an evil spirit in the kraal. This spirit wanted a beast to be killed. Accused then said Chiramwiwa was the cause of the death. He pointed to Chiramwiwa and said, "You, grandmother, are a witch." He said then, "You have a portion of the head of the child and have eaten a bit of it. You have a snake at your kraal. You have evil spirits which strike your husband." Accused asked me then whether I had a pain in my side. I said, "Yes, I have a pain." Accused then said Chiramwiwa had taken urine from me and cooked it in a pan. Then the meeting broke up.'

As explained previously, belief that a *mudzimu* had caused death is not incompatible with belief that a witch was responsible. A *mudzimu* may possess a witch or an angry *mudzimu* may permit a witch to gain entry to the village. However, it would seem that Chemere named the *mudzimu* first in the hope that it would content his clients, for naming a witch can lead to a prosecution, and only named Chiramwiwa as a witch when it was obvious that his clients would not accept this verdict. In a number of cases where the *hakata* were used the ancestral spirits were thrown for first, presumably in the hope that the safer verdict would be returned. In many cases, however, where the death of a person was being investigated the *nganga* seems to have assumed that a wizard was responsible.

In most cases examined diviners, whether operating in the Tribal Trust Areas or outside, divined within the context of the traditional norms of village and family life. A case illustrating a diviner operating outside these norms and in terms of a different social context is *R v Aaron Hodza* (82). In this case evidence was led that a certain Braimu had entered into a contract with a European farmer in the Shamva district to build tobacco barns. Braimu employed his own labour to do this. One of these labourers, named Abel, appeared to go mad. Braimu decided to consult the accused who was a Shona diviner living in the Madziwa Reserve nearby. He went to the accused accompanied by one, Wilmot. They found the accused whose divining apparatus consisted of a mirror, bottle and basket lid. He produced these articles. Braimu's evidence then reads:

'I had at no time prior to the accused producing these articles said anything. While we were sitting down at the table the accused started speaking saying he knew why we had come. "It is your brother who is sick. This sickness has come from the farm. It is not a natural sickness. He was going to go mad but he will not now go mad. This sickness was caused by a certain man on the farm." Accused carried on to say "Before you came to the farm there were certain builders on the farm. One of these builders' brothers fell onto a fire and this was caused by a certain person on the farm. After he was burnt the European Master of the farm took him to Hospital. While this person was receiving treatment another labourer on the farm fell down and started going mad. Before the work had been finished these builders took their labourers and went off the farm." We were then told that all this had happened before we had come to the farm and that we had come to complete the work uncompleted by the previous builders. Accused went on to say that these builders had left because of one other builder on the farm. We were told that this builder was jealous of us as well and that he did not want us on the farm. Accused continued "That builder is a very bad person and is paid per ticket and that is why he caused the labourers to go sick. He did this so you would have difficulty in finding labourers". Accused was referring to the farm on which I worked. There is another builder working on the farm who is paid by ticket. There are no other builders on the farm. There is myself, a contract builder, and this other builder who is paid by ticket. I know this builder referred to but I do not know his name. I know him slightly only. If this ticket builder could make my labourers ill he would benefit by this because he would take over my work if I failed to complete my contract. The little mirror in the basket was placed face up. While looking into the mirror the accused took and shook the bottle and placed it on the table and started talking. This was done three times. On the second shaking of the bottle the accused told me that when I reached scaffold height on the building that I was doing a crack would appear in the wall and one of my labourers would fall down and break his leg. This would be caused by the ticket builder as he was bad. I paid five shillings for the services rendered. I returned to the farm and decided not to continue working as I thought if I continued working I would lose my life. I have five labourers under me. We were on contract to build barns and I stood to receive £200 for the entire contract.'

One can only say that one is astonished at the knowledge of the diviner and at the unerring way he diagnosed wizardry in terms of the rivalry between two builders working for the same employer. By a 'ticket' reference is intended to the usual method of employing labour on Rhodesian farms in which workers are employed to work a 'ticket' of so many days, each day worked being marked on a ticket. When the number of days agreed upon has been worked, the labourer is paid. A ticket labourer is thus in the position of a servant, while a contract labourer is a free agent provided he carries out his contract. There are not a large number of farms in the Shamva district, which is not a prosperous farming area; so, after repudiating the contract, Braimu may well have had difficulty in finding another. That in the circumstances he was willing to repudiate means that he could have had no doubts that the diviner was speaking the truth. £200 in a rural district is a very large sum of money.

Shona and Ndebele society is changing rapidly and these changes and the feelings of insecurity so produced have, if anything, led to an increasing fear of wizardry. So long as this fear remains the diviner is unlikely to lack employment.

CHAPTER XIII

THE SUPERNATURAL INDICATION OF A WIZARD

WIZARDS can be indicated supernaturally, according to the Shona, in a number of ways. Perhaps the most important of these is by means of dreams and through the intervention of the *ngozi* of the deceased. Strictly speaking, it is only by intervention of the supernatural that a wizard can be proved to be a wizard. I am not here, however, discussing supernatural revelation in those cases where a diviner makes use of his supernatural powers, but with supernatural revelation to persons who are not diviners.

There can be few people in the world who do not believe that

The Supernatural Indication of a Wizard

the nature of events can be revealed by dreams. Evans-Pritchard (1937, p. 374) classifies dreams among the forms of oracles known to the Azande. The same may be said of the people of Rhodesia. According to a Shona informant, some people have a reputation for dreaming true dreams; but the ordinary person can only tell if a dream has revealed the truth after the event foretold has taken place or if he consults a diviner. For example, if a person dreams of an ancestor he will consult a diviner to find out if, indeed, it was the *mudzimu* of his ancestor he saw and, if so, what it wants and how it is to be propitiated. However, dreams of wizardry are said to be in a rather different category since, if one dreams of wizardry and wakes up feeling weak and exhausted, there can be little doubt that one has, indeed, been wizarded. Some diviners claim to divine by means of dreams. In the case of *R v Mubiwa* (81) evidence was led that a Korekore diviner had lent his ceremonial axe (*gano*) to a client telling him that the axe would tell him things in his sleep.

Dreams, of course, reflect the anxieties and fears of the dreamer. Accusations which result from dreams reflect the social tensions and conflicts of the community in the same manner as any other sort of accusation.

We have seen how, in the case of *R v Kani* (p. 166), a dream played a part in the accusation of wizardry and a further illustration of the manner in which a dream can give rise to an accusation is the case of *R v Tachinson* (committed for trial at Machaba, 6.3.61). Tachinson was a farmer in a Native Purchase Area in the Mashaba district and thus the owner of a comparatively large farm. His dreams clearly reflect his anxieties over dispossession. This was not an altogether imaginary fear for, though Purchase Area land is not communally owned but held under individual tenure it can, while still under agreement to purchase (as is still usually the case), be forfeited for a number of reasons *inter alia* because it is not being properly farmed. In such a case the land would be given to some applicant who had the money to pay for the improvements and who, preferably, possessed a Master Farmer's certificate. Tachinson's statement at the summary trial gives the facts of the case and there is little doubt that he was endeavouring to tell the truth:

'The case did not start on the twenty-sixth, it started in 1958. I dreamt of a spirit coming to me saying to me, "I have been sent by Muneri to kill you." This happened four times. The spirit said that Muneri wanted to do this because he wanted to take over my farm. I told no one but Muneri came to me and said, "What do you see when you are sleeping?" I told him about my dreams. I went with Muneri to the church. We asked preacher Lazero to look for a prophet who would explain the dreams. The prophet said it was Muneri's father who wanted to kill me. Muneri was staying with me when he took his Master Farmer's certificate. We went to chief Banga. I explained to chief Banga about my dreams and asked to have an agreement written down in case I should die. I said, "If I die and Muneri stays on my farm it would be that he killed me because that is what the spirit said." I wrote this in the chief's book. Muneri also wrote and chief Banga signed it. There was a letter from the Member-in-Charge, British South Africa Police, Selukwe, that chief Banga should let these people make their agreement. We finished at the chief. On the twenty-sixth of February, 1961, I went to Mashe's and asked Muneri to write the agreement at Mashaba because we were no longer under Selukwe. Muneri refused. I said, "The reason why I am doing this is because the spirit of your father is still sucking my blood and I have no blood left in my body." Muneri said, "I cannot take your farm when I am a foreigner." I said, "Kenard (a Zionist leader) was staying with you and when he died you took his wife. Was he your relative?" He left for the fields and Elisha said, "This case is now finished, let us go home." '

That Muneri had a *mudzimu* which acted as a witch was a clear indication that Muneri, himself, was a witch for only a witch could possess such a *mudzimu*.

The manner in which the *ngozi* may indicate a wizard is shown in the case of *R v Garayi* (52). The accused was an Ndau chief in the Melsetter area. Before giving an extract from the complainant's evidence a short account of Shona belief in the matter is necessary. It is believed that when a man dies with a grudge, either because his relatives have not shown him proper respect or because he has been wronged in some way, his spirit may not leave the body on death, but may become *ngozi* and appear as a shadow denser than the natural shadow of the corpse. This shadow is said normally to appear only after *rigor mortis* has set in as it is only at this stage that the deceased is considered truly dead. It is at this stage that all the friends and relatives of the dead man are called together to offer their condolences. Failure to appear on such an occasion might well give rise to a suspicion that the defaulter was the wizard responsible for the man's death. In order to expel the *ngozi* it is necessary for a doctor-diviner to burn a medicine called *mbanda* which is a mixture of roots and aromatic gum, the exact composition of which is known only to witches and great *ngangas*. This belief would seem to be unrelated to the belief that a man may lose his shadow, a widespread belief found also among the Shona, who state that a *nganga* may take a man's shadow away from him and so cause him to become mad. With this background Biri's evidence becomes intelligible:

'I heard that George (Simon's son) had died. I went to Simon's house. When I arrived at the hut in which the body was lying I entered the hut. Inside the hut, in addition to the corpse, Simon's mother was there, named Tambudzeni. Anisi and Simon were also there and Chisekesa. There was a light burning in the hut. It was a small tin with a wick. The light was on the ground. It was near the child's side. The other people in the hut were sitting down. I stayed inside the hut for about two hours. Then I got up and went and sat down with the mourners outside. While sitting down outside the house Simon came out of the hut and made a statement saying "The child now has a shadow." I got up and entered the house and I saw the shadow. The shadow was coming from the child. As it was dark I could not see properly if it was moving. I did not ask for the lamp to be moved. I do not know what the shadow meant to me. According to our custom it means there is a very bad person (i.e. a witch) in the room where the shadow is. Simon said, "I am going to tell chief Ngorima (the accused)." Later Simon came back and he told me, "We shall see tomorrow." ("We shall see" is a threat). The following morning was a Sunday in February, 1959. After we buried the child chief Makora said, "Thank you very much my people, you have buried the child. You take these two chickens, go and use them as relish for your food. I have a word to say with Biri (myself). Let him come in front of me." I went in front of the accused and he said, *"Biri u ri muroyi"* (Biri you are a witch). He spat, "You, you are a witch." He then kicked me on the head and continued, "You are the one who killed my child." This means when he said "my child" that accused and Simon are relatives. He spat and kicked me on the top of my head. He was wearing shoes. It was a hard kick. He stamped on me. Chief, the accused, was sitting on a stool and I was sitting on the ground near accused. Accused stood up and kicked me. I got up and went away.'

As soon as the light was lit it must have cast a shadow. It is surprising that this should only have been noticed when Biri entered the room. It seems probable that someone in the room must have suspected Biri of wizardry and kept watch while he was in the room. The reason for this hostility appears elsewhere in Biri's statement. Some time prior to his being indicated as a witch Biri had forced open a box containing the money of a person who was absent in order, so he said, to look after it. Whether in fact he had a right to do this is not clear but trouble was caused either because his act was wrongful or by those who considered they had a better right to the money. In consequence, Biri was unpopular at the time of the accusation of wizardry.

CHAPTER XIV

SHONA NAMES

ONE way in which a Shona may make an allegation of wizardry is in giving a name to a child or, even, to a dog. Apart from the *mutupo* and *chidawo,* the clan and sub-clan names which a Shona inherits from his father, he has a name by which he is ordinarily known and which is normally given him when he is born. He may, if he chooses, rename himself in later life. On occasion, the name used in later life may have originated as a nickname. This may replace entirely any previous name. These days, of course, many names are of European, usually Biblical, origin. The *mutupo* and *chidawo* are, unlike the *isibongo* of the Ndebele, never used as surnames when dealing with Europeans, the name chosen by the Shona as a surname usually being their father's or grandfather's given name. This is, of course, a new phenomenon and nothing really equivalent to the surname was known in the past.

When a Shona woman names a child or dog she frequently chooses a name which draws attention to her unsatisfactory condition. Thus, if her husband has driven her away she may call her child *Mutizwa,* the outcast, or if she has been given in marriage against her will, perhaps in settlement of a debt, then the name given may be *Mashambadzwa,* which means 'you are bartered'. One of the great advantages of a name of this sort is that the person bestowing the name can publicize her condition with impunity every time she calls the child or the dog.

Names are frequently given with the intention of making an allegation of wizardry. The intention of the person bestowing the name is, however, not merely to complain of wizardry but, by publicizing her 'knowledge' that wizards are active in the village, to deter those wizards from attacking her child. It is obvious that, their deeds being recognized for what they are, wizards must behave themselves if they wish to avoid trouble. Names of this sort include:

Muroyiwa	—	the bewitched one;
Hanatswi	—	you cannot please (a wizard);
Nyamadzawo	—	their (i.e. the witches') meat;
Rusinahama	—	without relations (because all the rest have been killed by wizards);
Pedzeni	—	finish me (you have killed all the others).
Kufakunesu	—	death is with us;
Tasara	—	we remain (the others have been killed by wizards);
Karikoga	—	left alone (the others have been killed by wizards);
Garikayi	—	be satisfied (because you have killed the others).

Notwithstanding the wide use of names of European origin, names of the sort described above are still very common.

CHAPTER XV

THE ORDEAL

In the past the ordeal, and particularly the poison ordeal, played an important part in the life of the people of Rhodesia. It has been argued that, at least in the case of certain African peoples, the ordeal is crucial for the understanding of present day attitudes, for its abolition deprived the society concerned of a technique for resolving social tensions which were expressed in the idiom of wizardry. Various social phenomena can be explained as an attempt to fill the gap left by the abolition of the ordeal. It will be necessary later to see if this hypothesis has any relevance to the situation in Rhodesia. At this stage it is necessary to appreciate that, before the European occupation, the poison ordeal provided the only method of divination which was regarded as infallible and, hence, which was accepted in ordinary circumstances by everyone. A finding of the oracle resolved once and for all the question of whether a person was a wizard. The ordeal thus provided a way of resolving social tensions when they became intolerable. As a result, it might be sought not only by persons who suspected another of wizardry, but by the suspect herself. Neither the verdicts of diviners of the past, nor of the modern diviners of traditional type could or can provide this degree of certainty and, as a result, cannot as satisfactorily resolve social tensions in this manner. It will be suggested that the popularity of some of the Pentecostal Churches results, in part, from a striving to achieve that certainty in divination which the ordeal provided, but which traditional diviners do not provide.

Although there is every now and again a prosecution against persons administering the poison ordeal, the ordeal in its traditional forms seems to have practically died out except in the north of the country. Three sorts of ordeal were the subject of prosecutions in the cases examined; the two traditional forms of ordeal (*muteyo*)—the poison ordeal—the boiling water ordeal, and a new form of ordeal involving the use of the medicine *muchapi*. Other forms of ordeal existed in the past; for example, Kandamankumbo (1938, p. 70) mentions the licking of red hot hoes. The lifting of the diviner's *mutundu* (basket for holding his equipment) should, perhaps, also be regarded as a form of ordeal. Apart from the forms of ordeal described here, other new forms have been introduced by the Pentecostal Churches such as the fire walking ordeal of John Maranke's Church (p. 233). Any form of divination is, in a sense, an ordeal.

THE POISON ORDEAL

Where the poison ordeal survives it is normally administered to persons suspected of witchcraft. In the past, at least in parts of Manicaland, it is said that poison was partaken of regularly by all the inhabitants of a village to ensure that no witches could continue to exist in it. This may, however, be merely a legend of the 'good old days' designed to show how African chiefs and headmen, when they were allowed to do so, were able to protect their people against witchcraft.

Four records of cases in which the poison ordeal was administered were examined by me. One originated from the Korekore of the Kandeya Reserve and the other three from Chimanda.

A fairly full account of the poison ordeal amongst the Korekore is given by Howman (1935, p. 2) and it is evident that considerable ritual is involved in the preparation of the poison (*kapande*). Howman, however, states that the person administering the ordeal is the ordinary diviner (*nganga*). This is, apparently, not the case in Chimanda Reserve where a poison specialist called the *Kapuka* is involved.

In all four cases the ordeal was undertaken by women. In two the suspected witch herself sought the ordeal; the one because her children died; the other because of the death of her daughter and sickness in the village. In the other two cases the ordeal was probably subsequent to a divination by a diviner who threw the *hakata*. If a person to whom the poison is administered vomits the poison she is innocent, while if she retains it she is a witch.

The following is an account taken from the case of *R v Manyepa* (committed for trial at Mount Darwin 28.2.58) of a woman who, herself, demanded to undergo the ordeal. It is very similar to the other case of this nature. The woman's evidence was as follows:

'I live in the Chimanda Reserve. I am married to Bvumbgwe and have two children alive. I recall last dry season I lost a child and I was very grieved and thought of returning to my "father". I wanted to tell my "father" that I wished to drink *muteyo* (the ordeal) as I had lost so many children. I wanted to find out if I was a witch and was bewitching my children. I went to my brother Mubvumbi who is my guardian and told him of my wishes. I asked him to find me a diviner. The first day he refused but I persisted and next day he sent Fini to find a diviner. He returned without a diviner. Then, next day he went again and returned with Manyepa. He is a Kapuka (i.e. he prepares the *muteyo* but does not throw the bones). Manyepa said to my brother, "Is there not trouble? Who has sent this woman to come and call on me?" My brother replied saying, "No, she has asked for this herself". I told Manyepa that this was in actual fact correct. Manyepa then said we should go outside the kraal where he would administer the mixture. I complied and was accompanied by Mubvumbi and Fini and my husband Bvumbgwe. Outside the kraal I found where he and my husband had made a fire. I gave accused my pot and he poured water therein and placed it on the fire. Some medicine was put in the water. The mixture was then put into the dish with some cold water and, after cooling, I was given the contents to drink. Accused held the dish while I drank the contents. I took two plates of *muteyo* and then vomited. I did not have any diarrhoea. We then returned home after accused had said that, as I had vomited, it was clear that I was not a witch. I did not know it was wrong. I wanted to satisfy myself. Accused was not given any consideration for this service. I gave him food and killed a fowl for relish. Accused is a recognized *kapuka* and is called so by others.'

The next extract, which is taken from the case of *R v Muramwiwa and Others* (55), is taken from one of the cases in which, I believe, the ordeal was administered to confirm the findings of a diviner. The evidence of the person who underwent the ordeal is as follows:

The Ordeal

'I live in the Kandeya Reserve and am the wife of Mushori. About September last year Barangwe had a child. This was in the same kraal as ours. Mushori at this time was working in the Rusambo Reserve. About three months after the death of the child Barangwe said I had caused the death of the child by bewitching it. My husband was away at this time. As a result of this allegation I ran away to my father's kraal to report the matter. I stayed with my father for one month. I was too frightened to return to my kraal. I finally returned when my husband returned. Upon my return Barangwe continued to accuse me of witchcraft and he suggested that I undergo the *mtego* (*muteyo*) test to see if I was a witch. At first I refused this test; but Barangwe said that in this case I must be a witch because I was refusing. Therefore, in the end, I agreed to undergo the test. It was not of my own free will. *Mtego* is a medicine or concoction which when taken either makes one sick or it makes one purge oneself. If one is sick one is not a witch, if one purges oneself it proves one is a witch. I went to Kagwambu's kraal to take this *mtego*. Wajakache is kraal head of that kraal. At this ceremony were myself, my husband and others. Barangwe told me to drink *mtego*. I was in the bush. When I was called Muramwiwa, who by reputation is a witchdoctor, had the *mtego*. He gave the *mtego* to my father who passed it to Wajakache. When I drank this *mtego* Wajakache was holding the mixture. Before I drank this Barangwe said that if I was proved not to be a witch he would give me an ox. If, however, I was a witch I would get nothing. There were some eggs there, two of them, they were brought by Barangwe. They were put on the ground. Barangwe said that these were the eggs with which I had bewitched people. I drank this *mtego*—eight small dishes of it. Having drunk it Wajakache told me to sit down. I did so. As I sat down I got severe diarrhoea. I could not help passing this. It was a short time after I had sat down. All the people there could see what happened. This showed that I was a witch. I also went to my kraal. I have been called a witch since. I am worried about this because I know nothing about it.'

A case from the Chimanda Reserve is very similar to the above case except that there the witch was indicated by a diviner in Portuguese East Africa and the person indicated as a witch, instead of expressing reluctance to undergo the ordeal, wished to undergo it in order to clear her name. This, in fact, she did do.

The reason why as many as eight dishes of poison were administered in *Muramwiwa's case* was probably because the woman showed signs of vomiting. According to Howman (1935, p. 25) every endeavour is made to assist the accused to clear herself. Further doses are given if she shows signs of being able to vomit.

Although the ordeal is largely a thing of the past, it is said in Central Mashonaland that, until very recently—and perhaps even today—persons in the Seke Reserve, which is near Salisbury, and from elsewhere, would travel to the Mrewa district where poison specialists could, or can, be found.

In two of the cases read the person accused was found to be a witch. In the other two she was found to be innocent. Clearly the belief of persons in the efficacy of the poison ordeal is largely because of its apparent ability to discriminate between persons. Azande poison, which is administered to chickens, shows the same sort of unpredictable reaction as, indeed, must any type of ordeal.

THE BOILING WATER ORDEAL

I found four examples of the boiling water ordeal amongst the court records. Only one of these—in which labourers from Moçambique were involved—was a case of its use to prove or disprove an allegation of wizardry, the other three being cases in which a man tested his wife's fidelity. This form of ordeal does not, in fact, ordinarily seem to have been used in cases of wizardry. One of the cases not concerned with wizardry involved persons of the Budjga tribe, another Zezuru, and the third Nyasa labourers. It is clear from the cases in which Shona-speaking persons underwent the ordeal that the manner of administering the ordeal as described in the case of *R v Sandonda* (13)—the case where the ordeal was used to prove or disprove an allegation of wizardry—is similar to the manner in which the ordeal is administered amongst the Shona. A professional diviner was not employed in any of the cases where the boiling water ordeal was administered. This accords with Bullock's observation (1950, p. 170, note 49) that in such cases 'the *nganga* could hardly interfere'. In this respect the boiling water ordeal forms a marked contrast with the poison ordeal where the diviner prepares the ordeal with considerable attention to ritual. In the boiling water ordeal the accused person is normally instructed to remove an object from a pot of boiling water. If no injuries result the person under suspicion is innocent. Curiously enough, it is possible for a person's hand to emerge unscathed and this, indeed, happened in the case of *R v Hunda* (committed for trial at Mtoko on 17.2.56), a case where the husband accused his wife of adultery. A variant of the boiling water ordeal is described by Garbutt (1910, p. 76) in which the feet of a fowl were first placed in the boiling water and then—but only if the feet of the fowl were scalded—the suspect was required to put his hands into the water. The following extract from the evidence of the complainant, Shandodoma, in *Sandonda's case* will serve to illustrate the manner of administering this ordeal:

'Accused . . . is my brother-in-law. He lives in the same compound as I do on Uronga farm. About three months ago a female child called Matare died in the Uronga compound. She was the daughter of the accused. After the burial of Matare accused came to me and called me a wizard. Accused told me that I was the one who had caused the death of his child, Matare. On Thursday, 15th November, 1951, in the evening, accused and I were sitting outside my hut in Uronga compound. The fire was not burning at our sitting place. Musindi was present when accused spoke to me. He said, 'You are a wizard and caused the death of my child. I want you to undergo the boiling water test ordeal." Accused then said to me. "If you do not submit to this test I will poison you and you will die." In view of this threat I agreed to undergo the test of boiling water. Accused then lit a fire in the fireplace and obtained a pot of water. He placed the pot of water over the fire. In due course the water came to the boil. Accused then told me to put my hands into the pot of boiling water and that after that he would know if I had caused the death of his child. I was afraid of the accused who again threatened me with death if I did not undergo the boiling water test. I then dipped both my hands into boiling water. My hands were submerged half way up the palm of my hands. I was badly burned on both hands and cried out in pain. Accused got up and went into his hut. I then went to Bindura hospital where I received treatment. My hands were severely burnt.'

While in Sandonda's case the person undergoing the ordeal merely put his hands into the water, in the other boiling water ordeal cases the accused had to remove an object from the water. As in the cases relating to the poison ordeal there are cases where the suspect himself or herself asked to undergo the ordeal. In the case of *R v Hunda* the husband refused to accept the verdict of the ordeal and performed the ordeal again and again until a favourable verdict was obtained. This was an unconscious determination on his part for, unless he had believed in the efficacy of the ordeal, it is difficult to see why he should have directed his wife to undergo it.

THE MUCHAPI ORDEAL

Some elements of the practices of the modern movement of 'witchfinders' known in Zambia and Malawi as the *Bamucapi*, and which is described in its area of origin by Richards (1935, p. 448), extend into Rhodesia. It is said that the medicine, *muchapi*, was introduced into Rhodesia from Malawi about 1935 (*Nada*, 1935, p. 17). It had an immediate success. Whereas some of the persons who administer *muchapi* are migrant labourers, the accused in the Sipolilo case of *R v Sineki alias Nicholas* (committed for trial 13.5.58) was Shona-speaking. An extract from this case illustrates the manner in which *muchapi* is administered. The extract is taken from the evidence of the witness Murungayi Hosiah and, although he does not specifically name the medicine used in the ordeal, it is clear from the evidence of other witnesses in the case that the medicine was *muchapi*:

'During recent years a number of people have died at our kraal and, though the deaths have appeared to be normal, I believe they may have been caused by witchcraft. I therefore decided to visit this witchdoctor (the accused) and was introduced to accused by kraal head Kunatsa. I told him about the deaths at my kraal and he asked for £7. I had £6 with me, which I gave to Kunatsa who gave the money to accused. Accused said he would come to my kraal on his return from Mazoe. Some days later we gathered in my daughter's hut with Nyanhete, Kandenyi, my wife Erica and the women Gwambara and Raudzi. When we were all seated accused produced a bottle containing a liquid and put it on the ground. He said that if any of us were witches we should not drink the liquid or we should die. I asked if any of us was a witch and everyone made denial. Accused then gave each of us some of the liquid in a spoon and nobody died. My spoonful of liquid tasted like water and I suffered no ill effects. Accused then asked for £8 which I gave to Kandenyi who handed it to accused. Accused then examined the roofs of all the huts in my kraal for something which had caused the deaths but did not find anything. All he found was medicine we use for headaches. Accused said that it was his practice to burn medicine found in such circumstances and demanded £1 for this service. I paid him this £1, Kandenyi again acting as intermediary. Accused then instructed all people except my wife and I to leave the hut. We were left alone with the accused. He asked me for two bottles which I brought. In one bottle he put some of the liquid we had drunk earlier and from a calabash he took some powder and told us to put it in the children's bath water so they would be cured of illness. He said the liquid in the other bottle should be given to the children to cure them when they were ill. Accused then left. The total amount paid to him was £15.'

In demanding the surrender of medicines and the use of protective magic Sineki's manner of procedure resembles the Zambian *bamucapi*. However, there does not seem to have been any sort of preliminary sermon or other religious accompaniment. On the whole it would seem that the use of the medicine *muchapi* is, at least today, the main feature of the cult which has been borrowed by Rhodesian diviners, other features largely disappearing. In the dislike and public burning of medicines the approach of the *muchapi* specialists resemble the prophets of the Pentecostal churches.

CHAPTER XVI

DIVINATION IN THE PENTECOSTAL CHURCHES

THE court records show clearly the very great importance of the prophets of the Pentecostal churches in divining the cause of disease and indicating wizards. Forty-six per cent of all divinations of wizardry among the Eastern Shona subsequent to 1956 were found to involve such prophets and came from all groups except the Ndau. Nearly thirty-seven per cent of such Ndebele-Kalanga divinations were also conducted by prophets of the Pentecostal churches. Only a few divinations originated from groups such as the Hlengwe, Venda, Valley Tonga and foreign migrants and all these divinations were conducted by diviners of traditional type. While, then, the influence of the Pentecostal churches would seem not to be widespread in the peripheral areas of Rhodesia, they are largely supplanting diviners of traditional type amongst the more central tribes. Many Africans are, however, sceptical of the claims of the prophets, although they express no such general scepticism of the powers of the traditional type of diviner, while admitting that many are impostors, and it is unlikely that such prophets will succeed in entirely supplanting the traditional diviners.

The total membership of the Pentecostal churches is probably not great as compared with the more orthodox churches. As in South Africa, members of the Pentecostal churches tend to abandon their beliefs as they rise in the social hierarchy.

'Pentecostal', which is the word used by Pauw (1960, p. 44) to describe these churches, is probably in Rhodesia a better word than the word 'Zionist' used by Sundkler (1961, p. 53). Although the word 'Zion' is frequently used in the names of these churches, the word 'Apostolic' seems more common in Rhodesia. Members of these churches are usually referred to as 'Apostles' (*Aposteri* or *Mapostori*). Rather than use a term such as 'Zionist' or 'Apostolic' a more general term is obviously preferable.

The Pentecostal churches include both 'missionary' churches and independent churches. The dividing line between the two is not sharply drawn because church discipline is often lax. The beliefs of the Apostolic Faith Mission of Oregon are probably typical of the missionary churches and form what one might term the 'point of departure' for the beliefs of the independent churches. These beliefs are summarized by the church as follows:

1. *The divine trinity*—The Godhead consists of three persons in one.
2. *Repentance* towards God—Godly sorrow for sin.

3. *Restitution*—making past wrongs right, paying back debts, restoring stolen property, confessing wrongs.
4. *Justification*—an act of God's grace by which we receive remission of sins.
5. *Sanctification*—a second definite work of grace by which we are made holy.
6. *The Baptism of the Holy Ghost*—the gift of power upon the sanctified life with the Biblical evidence of speaking in other tongues as the Spirit gives utterance.
7. *Healing the Body*—provided as well as the salvation of the soul, as in atonement.
8. *The second coming of Jesus*—as literal as His ascension into Heaven.
9. *The Tribulation*—a time of great trouble upon earth.
10. *Christ's Millennial Reign*—a literal reign of Jesus upon earth, with His Saints for a thousand years.
11. *The Great White Throne Judgement*—God will judge the quick and dead according to their works.
12. *New Heaven and New Earth*—this earth, polluted by sin, will pass away and God will make a new heaven and a new earth in which righteousness shall dwell.
13. *Eternal Heaven and eternal Hell*—Hell as eternal as heaven, a literal place of punishment for the wicked.
14. *No divorce*—under the law of Christ there is but one cause for separation—fornication; and no right to remarry while the first companion lives.
15. *The Ordinances*—Water Baptism by immersion (in the name of the Father, Son and Holy Ghost); the Lord's Supper; washing of the discples' feet.

Only the 'saved' can partake of the communion and there are prohibitions on attending a secret society or attending places of sinful, worldly amusement.

For the present purposes the articles of faith which are the most important are the speaking in tongues, the healing of the body and the triune immersion at baptism.

According to Sundkler (1961, p. 48) the Pentecostal churches of Southern Africa are of American origin, missionary activity commencing in the Witwatersrand early in this century. The various Pentecostal churches of today in South Africa originated partly by schism from the original Pentecostal churches, which were European led, and partly by schism from the various African separatist churches of Ethiopian type—the practice of the sect frequently becoming more and more Pentecostal in character the further the sect was removed from the parent church. The spread of these churches to Rhodesia was accomplished partly by missionary activity on behalf of the 'European' Pentecostal churches; by migrant labourers returning from the Rand and elsewhere who brought their faith with them; also partly from schisms from the other churches in the manner so well described by Sundkler. The churches of Pentecostal type in Rhodesia closely resemble their South African contemporaries; but there are differences in emphasis brought about by differing social conditions. The colour bar is still strong in Rhodesia, but the country possesses a group of very vocal African politicians and, although they consider that the Government unfairly hampers their activities, there was, during the period studied, no need for the would-be politician or trade unionist to enter the churches—as happens in South Africa. Again, although the major grievances of the African concern land, over half the land in Rhodesia is now in African hands and land, even if considered inadequate, is generally available. Churches, therefore, are not important as landowning groups. The political aspects of the separatist movement are less noticeable in Rhodesia than South Africa although they certainly exist. In Rhodesia, unlike South Africa, Tribal Trust Land exists near all the main centres of population—reserves such as Seke becoming almost dormitory suburbs of Salisbury. At least as far as the indigenous peoples of Rhodesia are concerned, the separatist churches are not, therefore, of so great importance in helping persons from the country to adjust themselves to city life, as in South Africa. In a rapidly changing society, however, these churches do play a very real part in helping people in both town and country to adjust to the changes, substituting church for tribal loyalties and providing a much needed emotional outlet.

Pentecostal churches in the Salisbury district include mission churches such as the Apostolic Faith Churches of South Africa, of Great Britain and of Oregon and also separatist churches such as the Apostolic Church (John Maranke's), the Sabbath Apostolic Church, the Catholic Zionist Church and Mai Chaza's *Guta ra Jehova* (City of Jehova). In the separatist churches there is, of course, nothing to prevent those filled with the Holy Spirit from prophesying wizardry in the midst of the congregation; but it is somewhat surprising to find such prophesies amongst the mission churches, as one does. An African member of the Apostolic Faith Church of South Africa tells me that such divination is common although severely disapproved of by the European members of the Church; in view of the biblical authority to the contrary he found the attitude of his European co-religionists difficult to understand. The *Guta ra Jehova* sect did not prophesy wizardry while Mai Chaza was alive; but now that she is dead such divinations are taking place. Church discipline in churches of Pentecostal type is clearly weak and explains both the fact that wizardry divinations take place even in the mission churches and also the schisms from them.

From the cases examined it is clear that, although prophets may go to considerable trouble to impress church members with their prophetic ability, fees were not accepted. The dominant motive for a person wishing to become a prophet is almost certainly not wealth but social prestige.

Whatever the formal hierarchy of authority in any particular church it seems convenient to make a distinction, sometimes made by members of these churches, between 'Prophets', who possess the ability to 'prophesy', and 'Apostles' who do not. Sometimes the church is controlled by various elders—prophets and apostles —others are controlled by a single 'prophet'. Sundkler (1961, pp. 106-109) divides church leaders into two classes, the chief type and the prophet type. Pauw (1960, p. 71) found it difficult to make such a distinction amongst the Tswana and I must confess to a similar difficulty as far as the Shona are concerned. However, the tendency for a church to resemble a tribe in structure with its own courts and methods of trial is noticeable in Rhodesia. Thus, in the case of *Kodzani and Others v Regina* (Bulawayo judgement No. 347 of 1962) a young girl of fourteen was instructed by her father, a church elder, to marry another member of the church, an elderly polygamist with three wives. Understandably, the girl ran away with a young man who was not a church member, thereby breaking the rule that church members should only marry church members. She was brought back by members of the church, tried, together with her mother, by the elders of the church and sentenced to a really savage beating. This no doubt is an extreme case, but illustrates the manner in which a church enforces compliance with its rules. Dress of apostles and prophets is usually elaborate. The dress of a prophet arrested in the Plumtree district, which was very similar to costume observable at the week-ends throughout the country, consisted of a blue smock with a white cross and stars sewn on it, a white smock with a blue cross on it, a red sash with white crosses sewn on, five plaited cords with white tassels, a blue skull cap with white crosses and a goat-skin belt. Outside the prophet's place of residence was a flag on a staff. The flag had a blue background with the words 'The cross of Jesus Baptist (cross) Apostle Church of S.A.'. The flag was perhaps to ward off lightning (see Sundkler, 1961, p. 257). The colours and type of vestments are all of religious significance.

Sundkler has stressed that Pentecostal churches serve as a 'bridge' back to paganism (1961, p. 297); but equally striking is the acceptance of the Pentecostal churches by pagans into the structure of traditional beliefs. Court records show, not only that the prophets are replacing the diviners of traditional type, but that the manner of consulting these prophets is similar to the manner in which the diviners of traditional type were consulted. In other words, whatever the attitude of church members, non-Christians treat the prophets as but another type of diviner.

Sundkler (1961, Appendix A) has shown the close similarity that exists between the Zulu Christian prophet and the Zulu *isangoma*.

The same is probably true of the Ndebele and Kalanga. Certainly the following excerpt from a witnesses' statement in the case of *R v Madubeko* (73) from Plumtree reads extraordinarily like an *isangoma's* smelling out:

> 'I am Dunu's wife. I lived with him until November 1958. I left Dunu's kraal because his son was sick (the son of his co-wife Mtswulani), and went to consult accused who is an *inyanga* (sic). I went with Dunu, Tshandita, Mtswulani and Siqutswana. On arrival at accused's kraal we were eventually taken into accused's hut where we sat on the floor. Accused was in the hut and wearing a blue robe and carrying a blue flag. He danced and sang. He was pointing the flag at us as we were sitting down. After a while accused stopped singing and dancing. He spoke to Siqutswana first. He said to her "You are the one who is killing your husband". After speaking to her he spoke to me and said "You gave poison to the one who is sick". I did not understand what he meant by that. He said that it was an arrangement between me and Mtswulani. He said we were working together to cause my son's illness. Accused said that Siqutswana obtained some medicine and gave it to Masandhle which caused the trouble to come up. Accused said I rode an ant-bear together with Mtswulani. He said that the ant-bear was Tshandita and we turned her into an ant-bear and rode at night.'

The use of the word *'inyanga'* by this witness is most interesting. Prophets claim to be able to heal the contrite; but in this case, as is usual when a pagan employs a prophet to divine, no attempt at curative treatment was made. The accused in this case was the owner of the equipment described previously.

Among the Shona on the other hand, the closest parallel to the prophet in traditional belief is the *svikiro* of the *mhondoro* spirits, or even the mediums of those possessed by the *mashave*. Shona religion is still viable and, indeed, the greatest of the prophets is probably the *svikiro* of the *mhondoro* Chaminuka. The Chaminuka legend is of importance in understanding the attitude of the Shona to the Christian prophets for it explains, firstly, why the prophets are so readily believed in and, secondly, why the pagan Shona regard them far more as they would a *svikiro* or a *nganga* than as the leader of a religious sect. Chaminuka, unlike the spirits of other *mhondoro,* is a well attested historical figure, his death in the hands of the Matabele being described by Selous (1893, p. 113). The account of his death has now grown into the legend narrated by Gelfand (1959, p. 30ff) and Chaminuka has taken on the aspect of a folk hero, his praises being sung, according to the local press, at political rallies—no doubt as a reaction to Ndebele dominance in the leadership of the nationalist parties, which are predominantly Shona in membership. In the death of Chaminuka and in his reincarnation in the mouths of successive mediums (*masvikiro*) there is a parallel to the death and resurrection of certain Pentecostal prophets. Another reason for the popularity of the Chaminuka cult among the nationalists is because he is a 'prophet' entirely of pagan origin and thus free of European taint. That a believer in the traditional beliefs of the Shona should regard the *svikiro* of the *mhondoro* and the Christian prophet as differing only in the spirits that possess them is understandable. Paulos who has inherited the *Guta ra Jehova* from Mai Chaza is possessed, not by the spirit of God, but by the spirit of Mai Chaza. The parallel here to the *svikiro* of the *mhondoro* is very close. Even the form of all night services popular with the Pentecostal sects is similar to the night long dances of the pagans, where the *shave* or *mhondoro* spirit makes its appearance in the small hours of the morning.

The Pentecostal sects accept the reality of the various forms of spirit possession, whether the spirit concerned is an ordinary *shave*, or a witchcraft spirit; but the techniques used to deal with these forms of possession differ from the traditional. The churches offer hope to the witch because they claim to be able to cure the truly contrite and to drive 'the devils' from the afflicted by the laying on of hands or some other technique. Medicine is regarded as not the cure of disease, but the cause of demoniacal possession; hence the importance of producing the medicine of a witch at divinations (Sundkler, 1961, p. 226). Confession by a witch of her sin is also important as only if she confesses can she be cured. In addition confession enhances the reputation of the prophet. This desire to obtain a confession is well illustrated in the case of *R v Kiwanyana* (50) from Kezi. In this case an Eurafrican farm owner

Divination in the Pentecostal Churches

requested the accused to visit his farm in the hope of stopping beer drinking. Kiwanyana arrived with ten apostles, male and female. Kiwanyana commenced praying and divining and summoned to him Zikamani, the wife of another Eurafrican. He accused Zikamani of witchcraft. As the wife of an Eurafrican (who seems to have been some sort of overseer), Zikamani was probably unpopular, racial prejudice being what it is. As with so many diviners, Kiwanyana seems to have been aware of local frictions and jealousies. The story as told by Zikamani is as follows:

'I received a message from my daughter Annie, and as a result of this I went to Mjaji's kraal where I saw accused. There were a number of accused's followers present. I saw accused throw up his metal walking stick. It descended and stuck in the ground near me. Accused then came to me and took ash from a brown paper and smeared it on my face. Accused said he was prophesying. He did not say he was going to pray for me. I did not want any of his praying so I left the hut. Next morning on Sunday, my husband, my daughter and I were sitting in our kitchen when I heard a party of Zionists arrive in our yard. They were singing and throwing ash on the hut roofs and into the huts. They entered the hut. I was sitting in the middle of the hut and they danced around me. There was a fire in the fireplace—they removed the burning coals leaving the glowing embers. Accused then arrived, he danced round and round, then he climbed on top of my shoulders. He then took me by the ears and threw me to the ground. He then caught me by the throat and choked me. Accused then picked me up and put me in the fireplace. He put grass around me and when this grass did not ignite he lit it with a match. He repeatedly asked me if I *loya'd* (bewitched). Accused held me in the fire. I tried to break away but he forced me back. He kept saying that I was a witch. After I had been badly burnt I admitted being a witch but I am not a witch. Accused then took me outside and said "Go and fetch your ant-bear". I said "Fetch it yourself, since you know it". We went outside the kraal and a follower came behind us, he was carrying grass. Accused said, "If you do not show me the ant-bear I'll burn you again". I collapsed outside the kraal. After they left me I rose and tottered back to my hut. When I got back to the kraal accused said, "You witch, you have an ancestral spirit (*idlozi*) which bewitches". I denied this. Accused then struck me on the head with a rattle. He then demanded my *idhlozi* clothes. I produced two pieces of cloth but accused did not burn them. They left. As he went away accused said "Stay a witch. We have burnt you, now how will you ride your ant-bear?" . . . There are people who keep these spirit clothes. When your child has a spirit you keep it for him. There was nothing unusual in having these clothes. I would have admitted anything in order to get out of the fire.'

Zikamani was not only the wife of an Eurafrican but two of her children had died. She had been suspected of killing them by witchcraft.

The use of ashes in purification rites as occurred in *Kiwanyana's case* is described by Sundkler (1961, p. 212) amongst the Zulu and by Pauw (1960, p. 189) amongst the Tswana. Religious dances are described by both writers.

Although no fee is ordinarily charged by prophets for divining, transport costs may be asked for. These may be quite considerable if the prophet travels with his followers and brings them in a bus.

An important element of the beliefs in the Pentecostal churches is the importance of various ritual taboos. I shall give accounts of divinations where the possession of medicine was regarded as proof that a person was a wizard. Other taboos mentioned in the texts read by me include prohibitions on the use of tobacco, strong drink and the committing of adultery. In *R v Pfacha* (41) a child's illness was ascribed by the prophet to eating 'dirty foods' which included white ants—usually considered a delicacy—and the meat of animals which had died from natural causes. I have been told that children born in adultery may be put to death by members of these churches. I do not know if this is, in fact, true.

All divinations take the form of a religious service; but for convenience I propose to divide them into divinations during the course of a service and divinations on the request of a person.

DIVINATION DURING THE COURSE OF A RELIGIOUS SERVICE: BAPTISM

Sundkler (1961, p. 208) has drawn attention to the central role of baptism in 'Zionist syncretism' and has also mentioned the hearing of confessions previous to baptism which may take the form of the 'crossing of Jordan'. Baptism is here a rite which cleanses from magical and other pollution. Baptism must be in a river, at any rate where a river is available, and is by total immersion. Pauw (1960, p. 147) in defining his use of the word magic states that 'When the rite of baptism is in itself nothing more than a symbolic representation of inner cleansing, the rite is nonmagical. But when the performance of the rite in itself is believed necessary to have beneficial influence, whether of a spiritual or physical nature, it bears a magical character.' Adopting this approach, baptism in the African Pentecostal church can only be regarded as bearing a magical character, the cleansing from pollution effected by baptism being essential, or at least a necessary prerequisite, for the salvation of the person who is baptized. Sundkler (1961, p. 201) links baptism amongst the Zulu with traditional Zulu ritual practices in streams and pools and a similar link no doubt exists among the Ndebele. There are traces of a *dziva* (pool) cult amongst the Shona, sanctity attaching to certain pools. But it is difficut to see any very close links between Pentecostal practice and traditional ritual and belief. However, the generally magical character of the rite of baptism is undoubtedly one of the reasons for its popularity.

For the baptismal rite to be effective confession must be full and complete. To ensure that it is so, prophets may prophesy the sins of those about to be baptized. If the person seeking baptism admits to these sins and is truly contrite then, if no curative treatment is required, baptism can take place. If the person is possessed by a witchcraft spirit, this spirit must be cast out before baptism can take place, and, at least in certain churches, the person concerned is expected to become possessed by the spirit in the process. If the person possessed by such a spirit refuses to confess, as happened in the case of *Joshua v Taruwodzera* (38), an extract from the evidence of which is given below, then no baptism is possible. The extract is taken from the evidence of a woman, Serayi, who lived in the Gutu district and who was one of the persons indicated as a 'witch':

'Accused is a prophet of the Apostolic Faith. He prophesies the sins of people about to be baptized. (She then gave evidence that her husband's brother's child had died and she and various other persons related to deceased decided to consult the accused to discover the cause of death.) We arrived at Ndimba kraal about noon and found the accused there. Mondiwa (the dead child's father) spoke to accused and asked him to "fix us for the things we have come for". Accused spoke and said, "Do you want to be baptized?" Mondiwa replied and said he was already baptized; but he wanted his wife to be baptized. Accused then started to prophesy and told Mondiwa that since his baptism he had smoked and drunk and committed adultery. Mondiwa replied that he had not drank or committed adultery but had smoked. Mondiwa was asked to produce his tobacco, which he did. The tobacco was burnt by the accused. The wife of Mondiwa was asked by accused if she kept some medicine. She replied she had some which she had used for curing the child when it was sick. She produced the medicine and it was burnt together with the tobacco produced by Mondiwa. The accused then said, "Let us go to the river", which he called "Jordan". We all went to the river with the accused. At the river accused began to demand more medicine from Tinhai, wife of Mondiwa. She denied having any more. He then said to Tinhai, "Your child's death was caused by this woman (meaning me) because of a quarrel about some fowls". The accused did not explain this but I understood it to imply that I had caused the death of the child by non-natural means, by witchcraft. All this time accused was standing facing East and praying. He was talking to himself. I could not understand. He did all this before he made the pronouncement that I had caused the child's death. He stood with his back to us. He was dressed normally, not as a prophet. After he said I was responsible for the death of the child I said to him, "Do you mean me?" he replied, "Yes". The accused then said to the people, "The work of baptizing people in the Jordan has failed, you must all go away.'

Perhaps the most interesting thing in this case is the attitude of of the people wishing to be baptized—the ceremony was regarded by them as merely a device to extract information from the prophet. It seems that the prophet was relying to some extent on his knowledge of the family. This and other cases show quite definitely that prophets, in common with other types of 'psychic' diviners, rely heavily on local knowledge where possible. The same prophet, *Taruwodzera alias Joshua,* came before the court on a similar charge some time after the previous case (11) and the evidence of Rambgwi in this case serves further to illustrate the methods of this prophet:

'As a result of the death (of my daughter) I decided to send for Joshua the accused. Accused first prayed and we all prayed, accused said we must pray. Accused then said we must all go to the river Jordan. Accused said after our arrival at the Jordan, "The one who is unable to cross the Jordan is the one who has killed your daughter Maiti". A number of people including myself waded through the river Jordan. Siriya started wading across the river when accused told her to come back. After we had waded across the river Jordan we all sat down and accused was there. Siriya crossed the river above the pool through which we waded. She came over to us and it was then that accused said to her, "It is you who caused the death of Maiti". He used the words: "You are a *muroyi,* you caused the death of Maiti by putting medicine in her beer". There were a lot of people at the river, I do not know how many prophets there were at the river Jordan. There were other prophets in the water. They belong to the Bikita district. There were other people who were not baptized in the river. They were called back and had various articles taken from them. These articles, beads, medicines, charms, bottles of vaseline and so forth, all these articles were burnt'.

From the evidence of other witnesses it would appear that those who were permitted to receive baptism passed through the river to the other side while those who were refused baptism were turned back and, eventually, crossed the river higher up.

THE PROPHET ON THE MOUNTAIN OF GOD

One of the more prominent Pentecostal type churches in the Salisbury district is John Maranke's Apostolic Church. As one would expect from the name of the church, it is a church which consciously or unconsciously has made an attempt to Africanize itself. It is a separatist church with no connection with any European dominated body. There has been an almost complete abandonment of the forms of worship found in the recognized churches and, in their place, is substituted forms of worship based, to some extent, on Old Testament parallels. The Church has no buildings of any sort whether temporary or permanent. Its services are held on hills. Before the service persons go and prepare a large fire and, when this is made, members of the church congregate at this spot. The place where the service is held has to be approached barefoot, shoes being removed. As usual in Pentecostal churches the ceremony which follows falls into two parts, the congregation first singing the hymns of the church and thereafter the prophets becoming filled with the holy spirit. The prophets announce who has sinned, including who has been guilty of witchcraft and sorcery, and will also give instructions to the believers: for example saying who is to marry whom. In addition, the prophets will pray for the sick and prophesy the causes of sickness. Again, this may involve the indication of witches. If an evil spirit is indicated the person concerned may become possessed by that spirit. At the conclusion of the service the congregation moves across the fire. If anyone's clothes catch fire as a result it is known that that person has sinned. In so far as it is a purification rite the passing through the fire is clearly analogous to similar rites found in the other Pentecostal churches, the passing through the river Jordan and through the gate of heaven; but the introduction of an ordeal is an interesting feature and again emphasizes the close links between these churches and traditional ways of thought. This church at one time enjoyed a great popularity in the Salisbury district but its importance has since declined.

THE PROPHET AT THE GATE OF HEAVEN

Just as only the pure may enter the church through baptism by crossing the river Jordan, so only the pure may—in certain sects—attend the services of the church. To ensure this, worshippers may pass through a gate by which a prophet is stationed, as he is at the waters of the Jordan. The significance of gates in the thinking of Zulu Zionist churches has been explained by Sundkler (1961, p. 289) and the actual construction of such a gate during the course of a service is a development of these ideas. The gate is the gate of Heaven through which the faithful pass on their death and it is guarded, not by Saint Peter, but by the prophet who is the leader of the church. Thus the Zulu prophet Shembe is described as 'The Holder of the Keys'. This belief is given concrete expression during the course of some services, where the prophet stands in the entrance of the gate made by the worshippers and prophesies their sins. Evidence as to this belief was given in the case of *R v Matiyo* (43), the witness being a certain Mandawa who, together with his second wife Dzanisayi, were members of the 'Apostolic Faith'. His statement reads:

'At the beginning of 1958 I decided to marry a third wife and announced my intention to my first and second wives. Dzanisayi objected and an argument resulted which continued until the time of her death. The argument was known to neighbouring people. I went on with the arrangements to take this third wife and I paid *lobolo* (bridewealth), £11 in cash and two head of cattle. This third wife came from nearby. Her name is Rayina. I received Rayina into my kraal early in 1958 as my third wife. After she came my second wife Dzanisayi left, I did not know where. Shortly after that I attended a church meeting with Rayina on accused's plot. Other people were present. We were gathered at the usual meeting place. Accused was there in his robes and rose to start the service. It is customary for people attending the service to march through a "gate" of worshippers, at the entrance of which the accused stands and tells people what God has told him to say to them. I went through the gate with my third wife Rayina. As I passed accused he said "Dzanisayi has got some medicine" (*a no muti*). He said "She has gone away to get *muti* to kill Rayina". I understood from this that Dzanisayi had gone to get magic medicine and that she was a witch with magic means at her disposal. At the end of this service we went home, I on bicycle and Rayina walking. I went ahead and she was out of sight. Nearing my kraal I came across Dzanisayi for the first time since she had gone away. I was surprised as I had just received the warning from accused. I accused her of being a witch and said I knew what was in her mind. Dzanisayi became very angry.'

Dzanisayi thereafter created such a fuss that her husband was forced to return Rayina to her parents and ask for the bridewealth to be refunded. However Dzanisayi left again. Thereafter one of Dzanisayi's children died. Remembering the allegation of wizardry and thinking Dzanisayi had caused its death, Mandawa asked her to return. Then Dzanisayi became more and more morose, lived apart and, eventually, hanged herself.

As in the case of pagan diviners Matiyo, the prophet, showed great knowledge of affairs in his neighbourhood and, in the same way as his pagan colleagues, divined in terms of this knowledge and the social stereotypes of the people: the belief that a jealous co-wife—and there can be no doubt as to Dzanisayi's jealousy—will make use of magical means or of witchcraft to destroy her rival.

DIVINATION DURING THE COURSE OF A SERVICE FOR THE SICK

As in South Africa, so in Rhodesia, prayer for the sick is one of the most important features of Pentecostal services. The pattern of these services follows the usual pattern in such churches: firstly prayer and singing, secondly speaking with tongues. Sundkler (1961, p. 229) gives an account of a woman confessing to possessing an *indiki* demon at such a meeting. In Rhodesia not only may such confessions be made but the 'demon' concerned may actually possess its victim. Extraordinary as the evidence led in the case of *R v Mapfumo* (3) may seem, I am told that such possession is quite an ordinary occurrence and, indeed, even essential if a cure is to be effected. In view of the part that spirit possession plays in the religion of the people of Rhodesia and, more especially the Shona, this aspect of religious belief in the Pentecostal church is not, perhaps, entirely unexpected. The extract is from the evidence of a woman, Kavatonde. The case originates from Beit Bridge:

'There was a Zionist Church meeting at my kraal. Amos was in charge of the meeting. Matodzi and Ruvengo (both women) were sick and the meeting was because of their illness and they were praying for these sick people. Ruvengo was suffering from headache and Matodzi was suffering from pains in the head and body. Accused was present at this meeting, he arrived during the service. The service continued after accused's arrival. I did not see accused speak to Matodzi. I heard him speaking to Kulumeni, saying, "Yes, you are the one who bewitched Matodzi, you put something into her body called *tuli* which is something which witches put into people's bodies, it is like a spirit. Before accused said this to Kulumeni he stood up and told the people to be quiet. He called Matodzi and Kulumeni to come to him. He was standing in the centre of the people. There were many people there. Matodzi and Kulumeni went to accused and sat down. Matodzi then said to Kulumeni, "Kulumeni you are my mother". This was the spirit of *tuli* talking through Matodzi. The *tuli* then said through Matodzi,

"We want to kill Matodzi because we have already killed her son". Then accused said to Kulumeni "You are the one who put *tuli* into Matodzi's body". Accused then said "This *tuli* is the one that also killed Matodzi's child". Accused then said that Matodzi's child had died through the *tuli* working when the child suckled at its mother's breast. The *tuli* left the mother, Matodzi, and entered the child when she suckled it. Kulumeni denied that she had put *tuli* into Matodzi's child. The service then broke up and everyone went away. This service took place at about mid-day.

'In the evening, after sunset, there was another meeting at my kraal. It was called by my husband to pray for the illness of Matodzi and Ruvengo. Accused was present and also Matodzi, Musekwa, Kulumeni and Ruvengo. We all prayed. Kulumeni was not by herself, she was part of the gathering. We prayed to God to make these people well. Then Matodzi was possessed with this *tuli* and she ran to Kulumeni saying, "I want to suck your breast, I want to suck your breast". Kulumeni ran away. Matodzi appeared as a person who was mad. This meeting took place outside my hut. Kulumeni was saying as she ran, "What can I do, I agree I am the one who put *tuli* into Matodzi; but I am unable to get it out." Matodzi later quietened down. Kulumeni moved her kraal because of this allegation. She is a widow living with her son.'

One further example will serve to illustrate this aspect of divination. In it we come across the liturgical dance which forms such an important part of Zionist ritual in South Africa, as is also the use of cords or ropes. The extract is from the case of *R v Mapfumo Mufongonyedza* (4) and the witness speaking is the widow Mutsindo:

'On Sunday during August 1957, I heard people shouting at Sikulumanis' kraal and saw a crowd of people there. The crowd was dispersed in a circle. I saw the accused in the middle of the circle. The accused was dancing a religious dance. They were singing prophet songs. The songs were those of the Zions. There were other people I know as well. Dondona was the only other person I knew there. During this time while I was there the accused put a rope around my neck and pulled until I fell. By this act, the accused indicated that I was a witch. The accused also said, "At night you go and sit on a dead person's tomb." I replied to the accused that there was no grave nearby so how could I go to it? The grave we were talking about was that of Makati. Before this accused said, "You are a witch". The accused only said, "You are a witch and always sit on the grave of Makati at night". That cord which the accused put around my neck shows that one is a witch. I know it means this because I have seen it used before by religious people. According to what they told us they are God's messengers. No other religious denomination does this. When the accused called me a witch I do not know whether the people believed him. I have lost some of my friends. Matsiko was the other woman who was called a witch. I was at the meeting for about four hours.'

DIVINATIONS ON REQUEST

Whereas a prophet who prophesies during the course of an ordinary religious service does so, apparently, mainly to impress his audience and—since mistakes are easily avoided, there being no necessity to divine if he does not wish to do so—he is only likely to divine if he has personal knowledge of the case or is certain his statement is unlikely to be challenged, a prophet who is consulted to ascertain the cause of illness or death is very much in the position of the traditional diviner. Such a diviner is not able to use what I have termed casual methods; if personal knowledge is lacking and psychic methods are, therefore, too dangerous he is likely to follow very much the methods of the ordinary psychological diviner and seek to make his audience talk. A good account of such a diviner of traditional type is Ashton's somewhat satirized account of a Basuto diviner (1952, p. 297). The following account of a divination by a Ndebele prophet, Aaron Ndhlovu (88)—although somewhat sketchy—describes a prophet divining in very much the same way. The witness is Mkulunyelwa:

'I went (with others) to Marumo's kraal. We went to the prophet there to find out what had caused the death of Konzapi's child. On arrival at Marumo's kraal we found many people there, they had all come to see the prophet. On arrival we were told that the prophet was still asleep and that his time had not yet arrived. We waited until 7.00 p.m. when we started singing with the children who are the prophet's followers. When he finished praying he stood up and sang (according to another witness there were "School songs"—apparently "Jesu Christu" repeated again and again. He was singing all the time). We followed this by clapping our hands. We then all stood up, his followers in one line and we stood in the other line behind him. He then went down the line of his followers touching each of them on the stomach, chest and forehead. He did the same to us. He speaks in a very queer language and was saying something I could not understand. He then asked all those who had troubles to come forward into another line. We all sat down and the prophet told each of them their troubles. We were taken into a hut eventually. My group was then told by the accused to sit down. He said to Konzapi, "What's your trouble Konzapi?" Konzapi said, "We have our troubles". He then said, "A man died at your kraal." He then changed, "No—it was a baby boy." He then looked at another man and said, "What does this old woman want here." Mapeli replied, "I have come to see what caused the death of the child." Accused replied, "You, old woman, you are the one that killed Konzapi's child. You killed this child by your spirits. There is another old woman who gave you the medicines to kill the child." Mapeli said, "I know nothing about what you are saying. I also do not know this old woman you are talking about." Accused then said, "If you argue, old woman, I will keep you here and then take you to your kraal.'

They then went home except Mapeli who was ordered to remain behind.

The rather high-handed action of the prophet when the person indicated questioned the divination is reminiscent of similar high-handed action by traditional diviners if their divination is questioned. The *isangoma* pattern seems to be discernible in this case. In cases from Mashonaland there are statements that the diviner 'shook his head' and otherwise behaved in the way persons do traditionally when possessed by a spirit.

Sometimes divinations require considerable preparation, medicines or horns being concealed beforehand and produced at the psychological moment. I have already remarked on the preoccupation of these churches with medicine, a preoccupation that, on occasion, would seem to amount almost to an obsession. While diviners of traditional type do, on occasion, produce the horns in which the medicine of sorcery is said, by them, to be kept, few diviners make a regular practice of this. Such production only occurred in one or two of the court cases involving traditional diviners. The position is otherwise with the Pentecostal prophets. Divinations in which medicine is produced are numerous and, in many cases, the production almost seems to form the major purpose and the consummation of the ceremony. Perhaps the fullest account of such a divination is given in the case of *R v Mutambo Sayikondi and Musokwe* (84) from the Sipolilo Reserve. The extract is taken from the evidence of Chinewako, who explained that he and other members of his sect had been called to a farm by the bossboy to 'sort out the trouble of death at Chikonyora Compound'. The witness was the principal preacher but not a prophet, several of whom came, together with a great many apostles. After explaining this Chinewako's evidence continued:

'We started our meeting in the veld on the farm near the farm school. This was Saturday evening. During the course of praying and singing Mutambo announced "There is a horn here" and went off a little way in the bush to where the women were cooking by the fire. Then near the base of a bush in the soil, Mutambo, having removed the soil, exposed a horn and picked it up. He gave the horn to me (a calabash handle filled with D.D.T. or something similar with the end closed by a bit of cloth). We all returned to the meeting place. Here I held the "horn" for all to see. I heard a voice from the back say, "This horn belongs to you apostles". I recognized the voice as that of Manjoro the tailor. We spent the rest of the night praying and singing. Sunday morning, Chirmomo, Muchenge and Gideon went away. They came back and made a report to me (the gathering then went to the hut of the "bossboy" Sayikondi and Sayikondi asked them to indicate who was causing death at the farm). We replied we would not do anything without first starting by prayer. We started praying. After prayer Mutambo stood up and announced, "There is a bag containing some medicine, there is a horn that stays in the river". So the bossboy searched Mutambo to see if he had anything in his pockets. I asked him to do this. Then we all began to search. The leaders of the search were myself, Mutambo and Sayikondi. All the others followed behind. We found a khaki bag. Mutambo indicated by his stick the bag in an ant-heap near the river and I picked up the bag. It was on top of the ground in some tall grass (the bag contained a round bit of wood, a piece of blue and white material knotted to form a bag and containing a white substance, a snail shell with a mixture of soot and earth in it and two chicken bones, one with cotton wrapped round the end). We then searched the Shinje River. Here Mutambo went into the river and the spirit in Mutambo led him to walk up stream. As he walked up stream I saw a horn in the river bank about two yards from me. I did not see it placed there. I picked it up and showed it to everyone holding it up (a piece of wood about nine inches long tapered like a cattle horn with beads and feathers decorating it). The horns (the first and third objects found) are the horns sent by a person to kill that person. The owner of the horn would send it and would not be a child or a woman but a man, but that man would be a wizard, only a wizard would send horns. We all went back to Sayikondi's hut where we continued the service and preaching. Sayikondi asked the assembly to indicate the owner of the things found. Then Mutambo stood up and said, "Sayikondi, are you allowing us to speak?" Petros continued, "Are all the employees on the farm present at this meeting?" Sayikondi replied that some were not present. Mutambo said, "Call the tailor to come here". Sayikondi went off to call the tailor. While Sayikondi was away the prayer meeting carried on. (The tailor then came.) Petros asked the tailor, Manjoro, to stand up. The "horns" were on the ground in the centre of the circle formed by the assembly. Mutambo indicated the "horns" to the tailor and said, "Do you know these things?" Manjoro said he knew "nothing about these things, if they are mine you must prophesy. Mutambo then said, "They are yours". We continued our meeting. While we were at the bossboy's hut after our return from the river I continued and said that the horn (the one found in the river) "moved about and sucked milk from the breasts of mothers with young children". By this I mean that the horn goes about poisoning the milk of the mother thereby killing the child. I was preaching and I said all this while I was preaching because I knew that the owner of the horn would send the horn to poison the mother's milk. We were all preaching. I knew that this "horn" goes about sucking and poisoning the breasts of women because Mutambo said so at the meeting. I repeated what Petros had said because, as leader, I wanted all the people to understand.'

The divination in this case is interesting. The naming of the sceptical tailor had the advantage both of silencing a critic, for thereafter everyone would consider his scepticism the malice of an evil man, and of naming a person who was, almost certainly, the subject of envy. The wages of tailors, who are employed by most European farmers at the farm store, are generally considerably in excess of the ordinary labourer. The divination was thus likely to be acceptable; the reaction of the crowd when the tailor was called for doubtless showed that this was so. I would call attention to the fact that the diviner was searched before he produced the 'horns', presumably to confound the sceptics. In the Salisbury district, and probably elsewhere, non-believers in the faith express considerable scepticism in regard to the claims of the prophets.

One more example of such a divination will suffice. The case is *R v Nyikadzino* (86) and is interesting in that the activities of the prophet are here seen through European eyes. It also illustrates, as did the case of *R v Kufa,* which I discussed earlier, the part that belief in wizardry can play in a village school. Accused was a primary school teacher. Ill feeling had arisen between himself and a Salvation Army Captain called Mangava, because Mangava would not let the accused marry his daughter. Probably as a result of Nyikadzino's machinations the children of the school and also, somewhat surprisingly, two of its teachers, became afflicted with a somewhat peculiar derangement which was described in the evidence of R. J. Paget, Member in Charge, British South Africa Police, Sipolilo. While the genuineness of the affliction may be doubtful, I do not think some form of mass hysteria can be entirely excluded. After the illness had arisen the accused charged Mangava with causing the illness and a prophet of the Apostolic Church was called in to divine the cause of the affliction, which commenced on the return of the school team from playing an away match at Mazoe. The following is Paget's evidence:

'Accused is a teacher at Chimbuma school. On the twenty-sixth of October, 1961, I went to this school and saw accused. There I saw twelve schoolchildren. Both accused and children gave the appearance of being mentally deranged. They named Captain Mangava, the Salvation Army evangelist, and one Chitsiga as being the cause of this. Inquiries were made and no reason was found for this condition or whether they were, in fact, mentally deranged. The following day I again went to Chimbuma school. I saw accused and the twelve children and they were in the same state. They were together and they said they could not be separated because, if they were, the one away from them would die. They spoke as one. I could not speak to one without them all replying. They stated that part of their bodies was painful. Accused, whilst I was there, said his arm was stiff and he could not bend it, and only after an attempt by the children could he bend it. Accused knew what was happening in that he was conscious of the difference between himself, the twelve children and normal people. Accused told me he would be unable to remember what had happened during his period of mental sickness when he recovered. Whilst I was there an Apostolic prophet arrived and there followed what I can only describe as a witch hunt, with prayers and singing. As a result certain articles were found in and around the school area. I took possession of these articles and produce them before the court—a cone shaped piece of wood hollowed out and filled with putty, a pin and embedded in the putty, human hair. This was found in a drinking utensil outside Mangava's hut. The second was a piece of wood covered with black putty, this was found in a pillow case under Mangava's bed. The third one is half a peach kernel, broken in half. This was found in a suitcase under Mangava's bed. The last one was a pin covered with black putty bound round with red wool—human hair on the end. This was found buried in the earth beneath the seat occupied by Mangava at school. After further singing and prayers the accused then became normal. When he did this I considered that he knew what had gone before. During November this year additional children became deranged. The children continue to become deranged."

Much of the remainder of the record in this case is concerned with an attack by Nyikadzino on Mangava's property, while in his 'deranged' state.

PART IV

THE CONSEQUENCES OF THE ALLEGATION OF WIZARDRY

CHAPTER XVII

BEHAVIOUR OF PERSONS INVOLVED

THE person most concerned in an allegation of wizardry is the person accused of being a wizard. In the following pages I shall —in so far as the material available to me permits—discuss both her behaviour and that of other persons concerned in the affair.

THE ATTITUDE OF THE WIZARD

In the court cases people indicated as being wizards frequently denied the charge. Almost as often, however, they admitted it. This, at first sight, is surprising, but becomes comprehensible in the light of the belief that a wizard can be a wizard without knowing it and in the feelings of guilt which oppress so many of us. In many of the cases the question was not put as to whether the person indicated as a wizard believed the accusation; but where it was, for example, in *Kukubula's case,* it was clear that many of the people indicated accepted that they were wizards. Sometimes the attitude of the person indicated as a wizard is one of bewilderment. Thus the *isangoma* Ester Ncube (*R v Ester Ncube* (69)) accused a woman called Mapundu of being a wizard and of killing her grandson. Her reaction to the accusation, in her own words, was as follows:

'I am a witch because I have been accused of being one. I do not practice witchcraft. I did not cause the death of the child. I do not know how (to bewitch). I was accused. It does not worry me to have these accusations made against me.'

Unless the person indicated can escape from the community in which she lives, either by death or by flight, she can do nothing very much about it, except, perhaps, to wait until the affair blows over or to accept the fact that she is a wizard and, maybe, sometimes to establish a reputation of being a witch and develop those fantasies such as are testified to in Dawu's and Mazwita's cases.

Where a young married woman is named as a wizard she can, willingly or unwillingly, return home. In many cases she can reintegrate with her parents' community, which may be willing to accept that the wizardry allegation made by her former husband's group was inspired by malice. She may well remarry. A young man can always go away and work for a European until the matter is forgotten. Elderly people have no such easy way of escape and it is, therefore, not surprising that the incidence of suicide was fairly high among this group in the cases examined. I do not wish to be understood as meaning that the sole cause of the suicide was the allegation of wizardry; but the allegation seems often to have been a precipitating factor in the case of a person who already had a feeling of estrangement from his community. The incidence of reported suicide in Rhodesia is fairly low, the steady increase in African suicides as reported in the Reports of the Secretary for Justice from 94 in 1941 to 202 in 1961, being mainly occasioned by the increase in population. My impression is, however, that many cases are not reported. I have read inquests and inquiries into African suicides and it is clear that the majority of people who take their own life are elderly men and women living in rural areas.[1] It is difficult to know what part wizardry allegations play in these suicides; but it would seem to be a not infrequent element.

It is possible to postulate at least two reasons why a person accused of wizardry should take his or her own life. Firstly, because of a sense of rejection by the community and a desire to escape from the community's hostility and, secondly, because of a feeling of guilt. African suicides seldom leave notes behind to

---

[1] There are, in addition, a number of young people who take their lives after an unhappy love affair.

explain their motives. However, in the case of *R v Kukubula* (87) the suicide note of Manjini, an Ndebele, was produced in evidence and from this it would seem that the predominant motive was guilt. It is clear that Manjini had a highly developed social conscience and he was the sort of man, by all appearances, who would have been badly upset at the thought that he had committed a crime against the community. His note, which almost takes the form of a will, reads as follows:

'I am sorry for my children because of starvation for if I was still on earth I would know what to do. What made me lose my life is that it was said that I was a witch, that I had learnt witching here in Tjolotjo. If I die for a sin I know it is very good. All people out of line (i.e. the line of villages) remain well or goodbye according to the reason said by Kukubula, if it is true that I came to learn bewitching by Mahlambi. As a chief how have I killed them or with what? If it is true even in heaven it is alright. I have died for my sin. I am writing this paper to my children to see me and forget. The mother of my children should not be worried about being questioned (by the police?); I left her being asleep only. My children do not be sorry for me, the world has hated me. Each and every one will die, there is one God. You, Mkene, look after the youngsters and mother with food and clothing. Pay *lobola* for Joyce. Keep cattle so as to educate these two. Amos, you should sell the black ox so as to get food for the children and clothing and cattle fees. You, Amos, should not go. I had no money. You should not worry your mother about money, money will come from cattle. You should go and take the one which is in Mate's kraal. Plough for all the children and educate them with those who will be born. My children do not bury me with two blankets, bury me with one blanket because I am dead. In the box you should not lose even one, because there are new things only. I felt very much worried that I learned to bewitch Mahlambi (then follow further dispositions of property, cattle and clothing).'

It has been suggested that among the Shona, suicide is sometimes committed by a person in order to revenge himself on another by turning his spirit into an *ngozi* to avenge the wrong. This may be so; but I have found no evidence to support this save, perhaps, in one or two cases where a young person has killed him or herself wearing the clothes of a faithless lover. This is almost certainly intended to indicate the reason for the suicide; but whether it is intended to go further and put fear of spirit revenge into the person whose clothes were worn, is difficult to say.

The case of *R v Shonayi Chipembere Juwere* (committed at Fort Victoria 30.6.64) is of interest from the point of view of the reaction of the person accused of wizardry. The accused was charged with three counts of indicating a 'witch'. Evidence was led on the first count that a woman accused by the diviner of bewitching her husband killed herself after her husband's elder brother had scolded her. On the second count the diviner accused a woman of being responsible for the loss of her child who was missing. This woman, Raina, had been married twice. Both of the children of her first marriage had died and so had two of the four children of her second marriage. She had put an end to her first marriage because her husband had not paid an adequate bride price. Raina was clearly the sort of person who is likely to be accused of witchcraft. After the diviner had told Raina she was a witch and possessed three *zwidoma* he continued:

'These three *zwidoma* are the things which took your child away. And you have got a snake and you have got a crocodile and you have got a hyena . . . You go back home and make a lot of *sadza* (thick porridge) and also take this *sadza* and milk. Put these things in the veld. Then leave these things in the veld and you will come back later. If you find this *sadza* and milk has been eaten by *zwidoma* you will find your missing child alive.'

Raina was asked what her reaction to all this was. Her remark was very much what one would expect in a society which believes a witch can be one without knowing it and, also, which treats diviners with a certain amount of scepticism. In her own words:

'Well, I said to myself, if what the accused told me was going to happen (did happen), I would then believe him.'

Raina prepared *sadza,* as suggested, and left it in the veld but nothing happened. Two months later the skeleton of the missing child was found in the veld. Although Raina seems to have treated the non-appearance of the *zwidoma* as establishing her innocence, at the time of the hearing of the case the people of the village were still 'bad against' her. The contrast between the reaction of the one woman who killed herself and Raina, who seems to have adopted a commonsense approach, indicates how much depends on the personality of the persons concerned and also, probably, on the reactions of the people among whom they are living. One of the features in which Raina's case differs from the other in which the woman hanged herself is that Raina seems not to have lost her husband's sysmpathy.

ATTITUDES OF OTHER PERSONS TO THE PERSON ACCUSED OF WIZARDRY

The reactions of other people when one of their number is accused of wizardry depend very much on whom is accused of wizardry and the circumstances in which such an accusation takes place. If a person is much loved and respected by people in her village they may refuse to accept that she is a wizard. Thus in the case of *R v Mahloro* (39) a witness stated, 'I am still friendly with Mandisa (the person idicated) as I am not certain if the diviner was correct in his allegation. Mandisa is still treated all right at the kraal. If the people had believed that Mandisa was a witch the kraal head would have driven her away.' Usually, however, at very least, the person indicated is avoided—at least until people forget about the affair. Such an allegation is unlikely to be entirely forgotten and may be remembered at a later date if trouble arises.

Quite often when a wizard is indicated the indignation of persons present is so great that she is severely assaulted. Such assaults may be regarded as a ritualized way of showing indignation and occur, not only in cases where a wizard is indicated, but in cases where a person is arrested for having committed a murder or rape. In the case of *R v Ester Mancube* (69) a witness was asked why he had taken part in such an assault and answered, 'I attacked Toliwe because I believed she caused the child's illness.' So much is a physical assault regarded as part of the act of indicating a wizard that it is possible for a person accused of indicating a wizard to make a statement to the police such as the accused did in the case of *R v Ndomene James* (78):

'I understand the charge. I did not say to her "you are a witch" . . . I only said to her that I was no more in use to female and that I had consulted from an African doctor who had informed me that your girlfriend had caused it. If I had accused her of being a witch why do I not assault her? What she is saying is untrue.'

Although these assaults are common enough, they are unlikely to be made after the first emotional reaction to the allegation has subsided, since wizards are feared.

Quite commonly if a 'wife' of the village is alleged to be a wizard the headman of the village will order her to return home. What happens if this order is ignored is illustrated by the evidence of Zvavamwe in the case of *R v Zwavanjanya* (31) which comes from the Sabi Reserve:

'The headman Madzimba told me then and there in front of other people that I must remove my kraal to another place. The diviner (a prophet) then left with the other people from Chikadzi kraal. I refused to move. From that time one of my huts was burnt down and my property destroyed. Stones have been thrown at my hut at night. People have spoken unkindly to me and have not behaved as nicely as they used to.'

Arson is a weapon commonly used against an alleged wizard. Not only does the destruction of her home provide one of the strongest possible inducements to a wizard to build her home elsewhere, but arson has the advantage of anonymity. To assault a wizard may result in the wizard bearing a grudge against you and wizarding you. Arson has the advantage that the wizard need not know who has attempted to harm her.

The consequences to the person named as a wizard are likely to vary very much in accordance with the degree of publicity which is accorded to her denunciation. Where a member of a wizard's family is told privately by a diviner that she is a wizard the family may well keep the secret. Indeed, it is not altogether a disadvantage to have a wizard in the family. An attempt was made to ascertain from the cases examined whether the treatment of a wizard depended to any extent on whether a diviner had 'proved' the allegation or not. The results are set out below:

TABLE IV. TREATMENT OF A WIZARD

Diviner involved

	Violence to persons or property	non-violent consequences	no consequences recorded	total no. of cases
Shona	14.3%	50%	35.7%	28
Ndebele	40%	15%	45%	20

No Diviner involved

Shona	42.2%	26.3%	31.5%	19
Ndebele	33.3%	50%	16.7%	6

By 'non-violent' consequences I mean divorce, ostracism and the general hostility of the community. Clearly the number of cases examined is too small to regard the figures given as entirely reliable; but two points would appear to emerge. Firstly, that in only a comparatively small number of the court cases no diviner was involved. It may be assumed that in Shona and Ndebele society far more allegations of wizardry arise spontaneously without the intervention of a diviner, than with. It is reasonably clear that only those cases where no diviner is involved which have led to serious consequences to the person named as a wizard are likely to be reported to the police. Such allegations are generally regarded as not serious and do not lead usually to serious assaults on the witch or damage to her property. The second point of interest is the large number of Ndebele divinations, as compared with those of the Shona, which resulted in violence. I am unable to offer a complete explanation of this difference; but there appears to be some sort of link between Ndebele divinations which result in violence and the method of divination used by the *izangoma*. This method of divination depends on the creation of an emotion-charged atmosphere. The emotions so created would appear to be relieved by an assault on the person indicated as a wizard. Divination by means of the *hakata* excites the emotions of the onlookers less and is less likely to result in an attack on the person indicated as a wizard. The Ndebele are traditionally a somewhat more aggressive society than the Shona.

On the whole I found it difficult to obtain details of the histories of people after they had been indicated as a wizard for the simple reason that, in time, most accusations are forgotten. An informant was able to give the names of certain women who must have been named as witches decades ago; but this is exceptional. However, an accusation of wizardry may not be entirely forgotten and may be remembered many years later when trouble again arises in the village of the wizard. The Shona realize that accusations are forgotten and that most persons indicated do eventually lead normal lives. This knowledge is harmonized with their other beliefs by giving as a reason for this the fact that some women have undergone the proper treatment to expel the spirit of witchcraft while other women, those still remembered as witches, have not. There is no reason to suppose that this belief has any foundation in fact; but the very existence of this belief assists in the rehabilitation of the person accused, for it will be assumed that if she succeeds in re-establishing herself then she must have been cured of her evil ways.

There are a few alleged wizards that are entirely rejected both by their husband's community and that of their parents. In the past these might have become complete outcasts but now other avenues are open. It is difficult to obtain reliable details as to what happens; but in two cases related to me the women left home and went to the towns. One of them succeeded in establishing herself as a prostitute.

While violence may break out spontaneously as a result of the feeling of indignation aroused when a wizard is indicated, action taken against a wizard subsequently is generally designed to force her, by one means or another, to leave the community where she resides, thereby, it is hoped, removing her evil influence. Such action consists of threats, often of arson, social ostracism and the like—followed, if this is unsuccessful, by arson or other physical measures, preferably collective or anonymous.

In the past a wizard would often have been put to death by the political authorities. However, references in folklore to settlements of outcast wizards and curative measures indicate that death was not inevitable. It is popularly supposed that very large numbers of persons were, in the past, put to death for wizardry. This was probably not so. Mzilikazi and Lobengula, the Ndebele kings, have a particularly evil reputation in this regard; but this reputation is only partially justified by the figures given. Carnegie (1894, p. 54) gives an average of nine or ten people put to death every month in Lobengula's time for wizardry and this is, really, not a large number bearing in mind the total population of Matabeleland, which must have amounted to some hundreds of thousands. It is clear from the various accounts of persons who were present at the time of these executions that many of them were undertaken for political reasons. While the Ndebele wizard is usually regarded as being a woman, the persons executed were mainly men. When a man was indicated as a wizard, his family was often put to death also, so the number of persons named as wizards and executed for their crime was probably not more than a few dozen a year. The month when thirty persons were executed (Carnegie, p. 35), was exceptional. Among the Shona there seem to have been few of the political executions of the type known amongst the Ndebele nor, I think, was a man's family destroyed because he had been named as a wizard. If the figures given for the Ndebele are any guide, and bearing in mind these factors, it is highly unlikely that executions for wizardry were frequent among the Shona. In Mashonaland places where wizards were killed are still pointed out. There is, for example, a cave in the Chinamora Reserve into which wizards were lowered down a cliff face and, since they could not escape, they starved to death. I can, however, find no evidence to lead me to suppose that a large number of people died in this way. No doubt, as in Europe, there were occasional waves of panic killings.

These days, for obvious reasons, the tribal authorities refuse to have any part in putting to death a person accused of wizardry. Where a wizard is killed, it is purely a matter of private vengeance or done from a desire to remove a source of danger. I have discussed previously one such case, *R v Aaron and Siliva Matshuma*. A few other cases of the premeditated murder of a wizard have come to my attention. The blood feud forms no part of the customary law of the Shona or Ndebele and acts of deliberate revenge for any reason are rare. Beer drink stabbings are common enough and grudges may well be worked off when in a state of drunkenness; but this cannot be regarded as a form of premeditated crime. Among the examples I know of in which a wizard was deliberately killed is the case of *R v Mathias and Kariba* (17). In this case it was proved that Mathias had hired Kariba to assist him in killing Mathias' father whom Mathias believed had killed his son by witchcraft. Mathias' father had, apparently, told Mathias that he was a witch and had said the child was going to die. The murdered man was a herbalist and would, therefore, have been credited with supernatural powers. The deceased's threats which included, apparently, 'If you are going to take this child with you you are going to bury the child in a grave and you are going to mourn the death of your child', played a large part in convincing Mathias that his father was a witch after the death of his son, but were, however, probably symptomatic of a long standing feud between father and son. The court believed that the deceased had made these threats and it was probably for this reason that the accused Mathias escaped the death penalty. A not entirely dissimilar case occurred fairly recently in the Bikita district.

Sometimes, however, even though it is not intended to kill the alleged wizard, the assaults inflicted on her are so severe that she dies. This happened in the case of *R v Jeka and Others* (102). The account of this case gives some idea of the emotions released by an accusation of wizardry. It differs only in degree from a number of other cases read by me. While the reason for the extremely strong feeling shown by the accused in this case towards the deceased, Reta, did not appear in the preparatory examination, at the trial evidence was given that Reta had had four husbands before she married Sakaniko, one of the accused. Each husband had rejected her in turn and *rovora* (bridewealth) had had to be refunded by her kin on each occasion. There had also been a dispute about the *mapakuro* (cow of the motherhood). As a result Reta was most unpopular—the repayment of the bridewealth by the various persons amongst whom it had been disbursed caused considerable unpleasantness amongst her kinsfolk. As often happens these social tensions were given concrete expression in the allegation that she was a witch. The story starts with the sickness of a child belonging to a certain Wunganai. A *dare* was held by the kraal head and a party formed there to consult the *nganga*. Reta confessed to the *dare* that she was a witch and implicated another woman, Murembu, as her accomplice. Murembu denied her guilt. Jeka was nominated by the kraal head to lead the party. Meso was nominated to accompany him. Sara, Sanyanya and Wanesi, all accused in the case, went also. The party travelled from the Zaka to the Bikita area and spent a night on the road. When they arrived, the *nganga* told them to return the next morning. Murembu's evidence then reads:

'The following morning we all gathered under a tree near Mera's kraal. Each of us had to pay a certain sum of money and throw the bones on the instructions of the witch-doctor. When my turn came to throw the bones the witch-doctor said I was innocent (this is probably a lie). Immediately after me came the deceased, Reta. As she was about to throw the bones Jeka said she was the one who had been responsible for the sickness. Reta agreed. The witch-doctor said nothing. Reta admitted responsibility but she said that I had caused her sickness. Accused Jeka then said that as we were witches we should have to have the hair in front of our heads cut. It was cut off with a razor blade. The money which Reta and I had paid was then refunded to us (a token of guilt) and the party then left the kraal. We spent the night in the bush. Everyone seemed happy and there were no incidents. The following morning, Saturday, we continued on our way to our own kraal, arriving at Mkwasine River at about noon. On arrival, Jeka said Reta and I were to be beaten. He then said that Reta and I were to be stripped and beaten while naked. I refused and offered them money if they would let me remain dressed. All the others, with the exception of Meso, refused. Jeka came and pulled my skirt off so that I was naked from the waist down. I retained my blouse as I had my baby on my back. Then everyone, excepting Meso, cut sticks from the side of the road. Reta was also naked at this time. She was completely naked. The whole party then commenced beating Reta and myself on the buttocks with the sticks. Jeka used two pieces of leather from his cycle which he had with him. Meso did not take part. They drove us along beating us in this fashion. Reta and I were carrying our own clothes and all the party's blankets on our heads and we were unable to protect ourselves. We were not beaten continuously. There were two breaks before we reached Chitiyo school. When we arrived at Chitiyo school we saw the wife of the headmaster. She asked us what was happening and when told she said it was wrong that we should be treated in this way. Reta and I then got dressed and passed through the school where the children were having sports. When only a short way past the school Jeka again forced us to undress and the beating was resumed. At this stage Wanesi took a piece of leather from Jeka and beat both Reta and me with it. In this manner we continued to Hove kraal. Twice between Chitiyo school and Hove kraal the deceased fell. On many occasions the sticks which accused were using broke from the force of the blows and new ones would be cut. Somewhere between Chityo and Hove we all stopped to eat. Deceased also ate. We ate mealie meal and drank water from the stream. When we reached Hove kraal we walked along the path passing through the huts. Eventually we came to Wanesi's huts. We were still naked and still being beaten. Wanesi took her blankets and put them in her hut before we continued. While at Wanesi's hut Tadios joined the party. He took a piece of leather from Wanesi and started to beat Reta and me with it. We eventually came to Majuru's hut where we saw Wunganai and Lydia, the parents of the sick child. We passed through Majuru's huts and some unoccupied ones and eventually arrived at Wunganai's huts. We were still being beaten by everyone including Tadios. Just before reaching Wunganai's huts Reta had fallen. I walked on and sat down amongst Wunganai's huts. I was too upset to take notice of Reta. While sitting in Wunganai's kraal, Lydia, his wife, came up and struck me with a stick. After she had beaten me I was allowed to put my skirt on. I went to my own kraal leaving the party at Wunganai's huts. I was too upset to notice what happened to Reta after she had fallen. The following day, early in the morning, I went to Wunganai's kraal and found Reta lying where she had fallen. She appeared to be dead.'

Wanganai, the father of the sick child, gave evidence that after Reta had collapsed on the ground her husband, Sakaniko, came up and beat her with a stick. Medical evidence showed that the deceased had sustained over two hundred and ninety seven blows.

ATTITUDE OF THE HUSBAND OF THE WITCH

Again, attitudes depend on the popularity of the person

indicated to be a witch and the circumstances of her accusation. It is not uncommon for husbands to stand by their wives when an accusation of witchcraft is made. In contrast, in *Jeka's case,* the woman's husband was one of the attackers. Commonly, husbands take the attitude that they cannot live with a witch. Thus in *R v Rosi* Hinani, Ngurirayi's husband, stated quite categorically, 'I cannot live with a witch.' Since marriage is virilocal amongst the Shona and Ndebele, divorce has the advantage of removing the alleged witch from her husband's community. Witchcraft is a well recognized ground of divorce, though seldom raised in the courts of the District Commissioner (Native Commissioner), and a husband is justified in repudiating his wife in such circumstances. However, difficulties arise over the return of the bridewealth if the wife's family is unwilling to believe the allegation. As Holleman (1952, p. 281) remarks, the dominant feature of dissolution proceedings amongst the Shona is usually an adroit manœuvring of the opposing parties to get into a favourable position with regard to the cattle involved. The same is probably true of the Ndebele. Rather than drive away a wife suspected or accused of witchcraft, a husband may prefer to render life intolerable for her in the hope that she will leave of her own accord. Since the father is the guardian of his children a woman must leave behind her older children when she goes, and, because of this, attempts to force her to leave may not be successful. Thus in *R v Gwayi* (71) a woman, Mtshado, was accused by the *isangoma* of witchcraft. Her family did not accept the divination and wanted another *isangoma* to be consulted; but her husband's family refused. Thereafter Mtshado's husband assaulted and illtreated her—although he also made her again pregnant. In the end Mtshado, instead of leaving, reported the matter to chief Gambo who, in turn, reported the case to the police. Generally, however, women do not display such courage.

LEGAL ACTION BY THE PERSON DEFAMED
Under section 3 of the Native Law and Courts Act (Chapter 73)

customary law is recognized and, indeed, where applicable, is the only law that can be applied in actions between natives. Customary law is administered by the courts of the various chiefs and sub-chiefs and by the courts of the District Commissioners (formerly Native Commissioners). Although this system is under review, the preceding statement remains true at the date of writing. Cases may come before the District Commissioner's court either through the exercise of its original jurisdiction or on appeal from the tribal courts. In the latter event the trial consists of a complete rehearing of the case. From the District Commissioner's courts appeal lies to the Native Appeal Court which, until 1958, was entirely composed of members of the Native Department, who had scant legal training; it now has a qualified lawyer as President. Cases involving customary law may come before the magistrates' courts or the High Court. These latter cases are rare and need not concern us now.

Little information is available as to the customary law of delict (tort) as the law of delict does not fall within the ambit of works such as Holleman's *Shona Customary Law*. While the Native Appeal Court has, on the whole, administered 'common sense' justice it has sometimes done so by misinterpreting both the common law and the customary law. Speaking generally it has, except where the quantum of damage is concerned, assumed that the customary law of delict, outside the scope of the action for seduction and adultery, was broadly similar to the common law Aquilian action, where pecuniary loss was occasioned, and the Actio Injuriarum in cases of insult. The communal aspect of these offences in customary law appears to have been overlooked and, except in the case of a woman (who must be assisted by her guardian) redress is granted to the person injured. Whether this is a correct interpretation of the customary law is doubtful; but certainty on this question is a matter which must wait until the customary law is properly studied. In customary law, delict cases where blood had been shed had to some extent a criminal aspect, a fine (*ropa* in Shona) being payable to the chief in addition to the compensation payable to the aggrieved party. Although chiefs can no longer legally levy *ropa* it is believed many still do so, and pressure is being brought by them on the Government to recognize this right.

It is defamatory in Shona and Ndebele customary law to call a person a wizard without adequate grounds for so doing, and damages are payable to the person defamed. The leading Native Appeal Court case in regard to defamation is *Marufu v Ehraim* (1938, S.R.N. 40) which was followed in *Quegele v Nawu* (1950, S.R.N. 253). In the words of the President, Mr. Charles Bullock, as reported in the earlier case:

> 'This Appeal Court has no doubt that an action for slander does lie in the Native law of Southern Rhodesia. The plaint used is "He must whiten my name." In stating this the Court would wish to reconcile this *dictum* with circumstances now obtaining in Native life by stating that words spoken lightly or in a heated quarrel and later withdrawn should not form the base of an action nor should common abuse. An indication of the type of words which can be classed as defamatory in native law is whether or not they would "alter the attitude of members of his social group towards the man maligned, and so endanger his tribal status and the harmony of his social life (*The Mashona*, p. 310).'

If the chief's courts gave adequate redress to persons accused of wizardry one would expect few cases to be brought to the attention of the police, since criminal proceedings do not really 'whiten' the name of the alleged wizard. It seems clear, however, that the tribal courts do not necessarily consider an allegation of wizardry wrongful, notwithstanding the attitude of the European authorities. In the case of *R v Mubiwa* (81) from the Madziwa Reserve damages were only awarded by the court after the diviner had admitted the accusation of wizardry was untrue. Extracts of this case were given previously and it will be remembered that Chutare, otherwise known as Hamadziripi, was one of the people accused of wizardry by the diviner, Mubiwa. Thereafter Nyamaparadza, the father of the children who had died, accused Hamadziripi to his face.

Hamadziripi insisted on the calling of a court (*dare*) to try the case and made Nyamaparadza call Mubiwa to the *dare*. On arrival Hamadziripi accused Mubiwa of defamation. Mubiwa was induced to confess—'there is a mistake which was made by my spirit'—and produced a shilling as a token that he had blackened Hamadziripi's name. This producing of a token is common in Mashona legal procedure (Holleman, 1952, p. 135). Mubiwa agreed to pay a cow in damages and took Hamadziripi to his cattle kraal and pointed one out to him. The other person named as a wizard at the same time did not obtain damages though he tried to do so; presumably he was a less forceful character and not able to brow-beat the diviner, and secure a confession. He later took the case to the police. Hamadziripi had a position of some authority in the tribal group. This case illustrates how such persons can bring pressure to bear on a diviner—which is no doubt the reason why they are seldom named as wizards.

CHAPTER XVIII

MAGICAL VENGEANCE AGAINST A WIZARD

THESE days it is dangerous to take physical action against a wizard and, because of this, many people are said to attempt to achieve their ends by the use of magic. There is, however, nothing to suggest that vengeance magic is of recent growth—there were probably always people too powerful to be attacked in any way other than by magical means. Where vengeance magic is directed against a particular person it must often, manifestly, fail and as a result, the Shona are distinctly sceptical about the effect of vengeance magic although, as is usual in such matters, this scepticism takes the form, not of denying the possibility of such magic, but of believing the particular doctor-diviner claiming to know the secret is a charlatan. According to Hughes (1955, p. 43) the Ndebele do not consider the use of vengeance magic an adequate substitute for physical retaliation and there is no doubt that this also reflects the Shona attitude. Frequently, however, such magic is regarded as directed against the wizard's family—this renders failure less obvious.

There are a number of types of vengeance magic amongst the Shona. One method, stated to be common, is by raising the spirit of the dead man so that it becomes *ngozi*. A *nganga* is employed by the family of the deceased to do this. One such ritual was described to me by an informant who had actually been present at such rituals. Firstly, the *nganga* must throw the *hakata* to ascertain the wishes of the *vadzimu* of the family and, if they are in agreement, he will then go to the grave of the deceased. From the head and the foot of the grave he will take a small quantity of earth. This earth will be mixed with medicine, and then salt will be added to make the spirit of the dead man 'bitter' (*vava*). Then the *nganga* addresses the *ngozi* telling it what is required of it. Thereafter the *ngozi* will materialize either as an incurable disease in the village of the wizard or in the form of lightning which will strike the inhabitants of the village. The *ngozi* will be accompanied on its way by its *vadzimu*. Another method of raising the *ngozi* involves the blowing of bone and reed whistles and the burning of a substance which produces a vile smelling smoke. Children and nursing mothers may not approach while the *ngozi* is being raised; but the ritual is not otherwise performed in secret. It is thought that the *ngozi* cannot, ordinarily, destroy the wizard herself, since the powers of the wizard must be greater than that of her victim. However, it was described to me how, in such a case, the *ngozi* must seek amongst the *vadizmu* a spirit which is, itself, a witch and accompanied by this *mudzimu* the witch can be overcome and destroyed. The affliction caused by the *ngozi* to the family of the wizard will continue until peace is made with the original victim's family, whether by offering a daughter or otherwise.

A method believed to be used by many *nganga* is to send *chikwambo* or *runhare*. Belief in the *chikwambo* is general amongst the Manyika and Eastern Zezuru; but informants from other areas knew only *runhare*. Bullock (1950, p. 170) and Gelfand (1959, p. 120) describe the manner in which *chikwambo* is sent,

Magical Vengeance against a Wizard

and little need be added to these descriptions here. It has the nature of a spirit and when sent to the village of its victim, may possess animals such as the baboon, tortoise, or frog and explain why it has come. If its demands are not complied with disaster will follow. Again, where *chikwambo* is used to avenge a person killed by wizardry, the *ngozi* of the deceased may be invoked to assist *chikwambo* on its way. *Runhare* appears to have rather more the aspect of a familiar, being a sort of creature owned by *nganga* and fed as the *zwidoma* are. Curiously enough the word *runhare* is now used to mean 'telephone', apparently because the sound travels in the manner in which this creature is supposed to travel.

The Shona court records did not describe an attempt to kill a wizard by the methods referred to above. There were, however, two cases where the ordinary methods of sorcery were used. A person who possesses medicines such as *chitsinga* and *chipotwa* for such a purpose is not, of course, a sorcerer, if vengeance is socially justifiable.

The case of *R v Mangwari* (28) illustrates the manner in which a diviner may be consulted for advice on how to destroy the wizard. The following extract is taken from the evidence of Mawela. The case comes from Chipinga:

'We had gone into Portuguese East Africa where we threw the bones. When I say we, I mean Muvecha, Sam and I. We went to Portuguese East Africa because in Garahwa's area (the witness's home), we do not know of a man who can throw the bones. My wife also came. We found a witch-doctor in Portuguese East Africa. As a result of what he told us we believed that the spirit of Muvecha's father was making the children sick. When we came back Muvecha brewed beer, called on the spirit and tried to appease the spirit in the traditional way, but he did not succeed because the children remained sick. Two of the children died after we saw Muvecha, the others remained sick and have been sick for five years. I decided to find some medicine to kill Muvecha. I believed that if he was killed my children would become well and also he would not call the spirit correctly. I got some medicine from the accused. I went to him because he is a witch-doctor—he is known as one. When I saw him I told him I wanted some medicine to kill Muvecha. He asked me why and I told him it was because Muvecha did not want to call his father's spirit. He agreed to give me some medicine. I said I had five shillings and gave it to him. Accused told me to put the medicine in the snuff—he knows Muvecha, they used to visit one another. The accused told me the medicine put into snuff would cause Muvecha to die. It was not ordinary medicine but bewitched. I gave it to my wife with instructions (to put the medicine in Muvecha's snuff). She was caught in the act.'

This case is interesting from a number of points: because medicine was used as a last resort in the hope that the children would recover and because the doctor-diviner was prepared to supply the medicine without ascertaining if Mawela's story was correct. However, Mangwari was Mawela's uncle. It was stated in evidence that Mangwari was not asked to divine the cause of the sickness of the children because Mawela wanted a doctor who 'did not know us.'

Another case where evidence was given of magical measures used against a wizard was *R v James* (46), a case from the Gwelo district. In this case the child of one of accused's wives died and accused blamed the wife of the farm 'bossboy'. Apparently on the advice of a diviner, he took the root—which, it was alleged, had killed the child—and, mixing it with donkey dung, he gave it to the alleged wizard to eat. She refused. Accused announced that if the root killed the woman he would claim ten head of cattle from the woman's husband. This case, incidentally, is the only case I know where a suggestion was made that the family of the wizard should pay compensation for the death of one of the wizard's victims.

O'Neil (1906, p. 226), in his account of the Ndebele-speaking Kalanga of the Mangwe district, describes how the *uzimu* avenging spirit of the man killed can be raised by a 'big *inyanga*' who goes to the grave of the deceased at night stripped naked and, to the accompaniment of spells, blows on a whistle made of a human radius and so raises the spirit. Thereafter, the spirit would appear to act in much the same manner as the Eastern Shona *ngozi* is supposed to act. A further method, described by O'Neil (p. 188), where a child has died is for the mother of the deceased to tie the dead child's apron round her neck. If she goes about like this the sorcerer will see the apron and die. The only example of Kalanga vengeance magic known to me is the case of *R v Aaron and Siliva* (see p. 96). In this case an unsuccessful attempt was made to kill the alleged witch by means of sorcery.

Vengeance magic was either mentioned or attempted in several of the Ndebele court cases. In the case of *R v Zaba* (committed for trial at Bulawayo on 16.2.56) a fairly full description as to the manner in which the *uzimu* may be raised amongst the Ndebele is given. The heavy fee demanded corroborates O'Neil's statement (op. cit. p. 225) that a heavy fee is usual in such cases. Even as long ago as 1906 the fee for raising the *uzimu* was from £2 to five head of cattle. In the record, evidence is given that the wife of a certain Joe had died and shortly after this the accused, Zaba, had arrived offering to help. He announced that the deceased had eaten certain vegetables with which medicine had been mixed. When everyone's interest was aroused he asked for 30s. to divine and, when he had received this he asked for £13. Joe had not this amount of money, so he handed Zaba his bicycle and three pounds. It was arranged that the ritual should take place on the following Sunday:

'On Sunday morning when we got up the accused demanded two goats which he said he wanted to kill at the kraal. Two goats were brought out from the kraal to the village and killed. After skinning the goats the accused came and disembowelled the animals. He took the blood of the goats and some of the undigested food from the inside of the animals. He placed the blood and this undigested food in one of the huts. While inside the hut the accused placed thin sticks of a *mtewa* tree inside the basin where the blood and undigested food were. We were then instructed by the accused to take the basins containing the blood and undigested food and the sticks and dig two holes by the gate leaving the kraal. The stuff inside the basins was buried in the two holes. Some of it was buried in the centre of the kraal. Then we were led by the accused into a small garden where the grave of the deceased is. Then we were instructed by the accused to dig a hole on the top of the deceased's grave and inside the hole the accused instructed us to place one of the dresses which the deceased left. Before the dress was covered with earth the accused took some medicine, powder and oil and made a cross over the dress of the deceased. He made this cross by smearing with his finger. Then the accused took some medicine which was powder mixed with some fat. After warming this medicine he placed it on top of the dress before it was covered. Then the accused struck a match and burned that medicine. Then it was covered with earth. We were then instructed to go back to the kraal. Some of the goat's meat was already cooked. We were then given instructions by the accused to eat the meat. Then the accused said to us as we were eating the meat "The person who caused the death of the deceased will soon be found. He is going to become mad, this is how you will find out the cause of the death of the deceased." We are still waiting to see this mad person. Up to now we have not seen one.'

An informant says that if an Ndebele family wishes to avenge the death of one of their number, they will consult an *isanusi*. The ritual to raise the *uzimu* includes the burning of medicines mixed with fat so as to produce a dense smoke and the calling up of the *uzimu* in order to take vengeance. As the smoke rises and disperses the onlookers must run away and the ritual is, thereby, completed.

Hughes (1955, p. 33) says that the Ndebele raise the *uzimu* by 'striking the grave' (*ukutsaya iliba*). The *uzimu* then takes the form of a hare which goes to the wizard's kraal and waits to be killed. Thereafter people die; but the *uzimu* cannot kill the wizard herself since the witch is protected by her medicines. If the doctor cannot 'close' the *uzimu*, the people who sent it must be approached and requested to take it away.

The chief social value of vengeance magic is that it enables people to act purposefully when someone dies through wizardry and that it is less harmful from the social point of view than physical violence. Further, it provides yet another sanction against wrong doing; for fear of vengeance magic is one of the various reasons why one village should remain on good terms with another. Vengeance magic is not confined to deaths by wizardry. For example, the *ngozi* may be raised amongst the Shona to avenge death by violence and *chikwambo* sent to punish a thief. The fear of vengeance magic, therefore, tends both to stay the hand of the would-be criminal and also to encourage the reconciliation of the family groups involved once the crime has taken place. Attempts at vengeance magic are probably sporadic. There is no reason to suppose that in Rhodesia vengeance magic serves a purpose in any way akin to its role amongst the Azande where vengeance magic has become a social duty (Evans-Pritchard, 1937, p. 540).

CHAPTER XIX

THE CURE OF THE WIZARD'S VICTIM

As is the case throughout the world, if a person becomes ill a cure is sought. Here again, I can only speak at any length about Shona beliefs and cures, insufficient material being available to me on the Ndebele. However, Shona belief in this regard would seem to me to be very similar to those of the other Rhodesian groups.

There are three ways in which it is believed that a person afflicted by wizardry can be cured. Firstly, by removing himself from the area of the wizard's activities; secondly, by getting the wizard to withdraw her wizardry; thirdly, by calling in a doctor and submitting to his care.

REMOVING ONESELF FROM THE AREA OF THE WIZARD'S ACTIVITIES

As reference to the Table in Appendix I will show, wizardry allegations usually take place within the kin or locality group. This seems to be recognized by Shona who, as a result, consider that a wizard may be powerless beyond these groups. Accordingly, it is considered that if a person removes himself to a place some distance away from the place where he was wizarded, he may go beyond the reach of the wizard and be cured. Evans-Pritchard has noted a similar belief among the Azande (1937,

p. 488). This belief was mentioned by a witness in the case of the inquiry into the death of *Bhuja Amos* (p. 116); but the best illustration of this belief is to be found in the case of *R v Mazwita and Others* where evidence was given that the wizarded Mukozho '*sengudza'd*, himself (pp. 50 and 53).

The dictionary translation of the verb *kusengudza* used by the witness, kraal head Dendere, is 'Remove (belongings); carry away.' (Hannan, 1959). The idea is that one can carry oneself away from the area of wizardry.

The same effect as removing oneself from the area of wizardry can be produced if the wizard is driven away from the village or neighbourhood of her victim or if she is killed.

The creation of new villages or the segmentation of old ones is often explained in terms of wizardry and the belief that one can escape it by moving; although the real cause of such removal or segmentation will usually lie in conflicts for land or power and suchlike communal friction. Sometimes, if many people die in a village, the whole community will move elsewhere. More common, perhaps, is the history of a certain village in the Domboshawa area, not far from Salisbury. A long time ago a man married and set up a small homestead of his own. He married a number of wives and had a large family. In time, when his sons married, the village grew very big and the founder of the village became recognized as the village head. No doubt the usual frictions between the various houses of the polygamous family developed; but these remained hidden during the lifetime of the old village head. After his death disputes about succession to his estate took place. This ill feeling was aggravated by the fact that the community—having grown—was short of accessible arable land. Eventually an heir to the position of village head and the property of the deceased was found but there was considerable resentment at the choice. The new village head did not find universal acceptance. Then a child died and a diviner indicated that the person causing the illness was 'someone with whom the parents of the child had quarrelled'. Identifying this man with the village head, the family of the dead child moved away from the village and set up a new village some way away from the old one. They were accompanied by other people from the old village.

Informants say that village histories of the sort described above are very common. This is confirmed by Kingsley Garbett's study (1960, p. 4ff). He found that wizardry allegations were, indeed, the 'prelude to village fission'.

GETTING A WIZARD TO WITHDRAW HER WIZARDRY

A wizard is believed to know the antidote to her magic or medicines and, as a result, considerable pressure may sometimes be brought to bear on the suspected wizard to make her cure her victim. An example is the case of *R v Mangisi* (8). The alleged wizard obviously could not do what was demanded of her. She avoided an impossible situation by killing herself. The following extract is taken from the evidence of her husband, Kufa:

'I remember Thursday, the 5th of September, 1957 when accused came and took my wife Wanzire to his kraal. At about 9.30 a.m. the accused returned with my wife Wanzire and said, "You, Wanzire, go and dig up some medicine to cure me as you have bewitched me." He then left saying he would return in the evening of that day. My wife Wanzire then cried, wondering where she was to find the medicine to cure the accused, her son. She was very upset about what the accused had said to her. At about sunset the accused returned to my kraal and we sat together discussing the case. There were three of us present; my wife Wanzire, the accused and I. On arrival the accused inquired if Wanzire had dug up the medicine and I replied she had not. He also said that if the medicine had not been dug up there would be no peace in the kraal at night. He said he wanted the medicine because Wanzire had caused him pain through witchcraft. In other words he had suffered physically through her witchcraft. He said that she had killed his child by witchcraft and by the same reason was himself ill. Wanzire then went out of the hut and committed suicide.'

Again, however, the best example of belief in this matter is to be found in *Mazwita's case*. In this case it will be remembered that because three witches had bewitched Mukhozho it was necessary for all three to administer the antidote. This is another illustration of the fact that the Shona believe that often medicine is only to be effective if administered by a particular person.

CALLING IN THE DOCTOR

In this context 'doctor' means usually the traditional *nganga* or *inyanga* as it is believed that wizardry or—as it is termed—'an illness of the soil' is resistant to European medicine. Methods of treatment used by doctors are diverse and Shona and Ndebele medicine is a field too vast to attempt to deal with at length here. All I can do is to give a few accounts of the manner in which a doctor or doctor-magician may operate. For further details Gelfand's works should be consulted. First, of course, it is usual to diagnose the cause of the illness. Once the cause of the affliction is diagnosed then it is possible to proceed to the cure of the illness. Perhaps the commonest method of cure is for the doctor to make cuts on his patient's body and to rub the medicine into them. The following account of such treatment from the record in the case of *R v Chemere alias Mahondoro* (15) from Buhera illustrates the manner in which the doctor proceeds, and is also a fine example of psychological medicine. Some days before the incident related Chemere had accused a woman, Chiramwiwa, of killing and bewitching people in Josiya's village. Josiya's child was one of the persons alleged to have been bewitched. After the divination accused was called in to treat the victim. The following is Josiya's account of this:

'Two days later I received money from Chiramwiwa (who did not believe she was a witch and wanted her village searched for evidence) which was to be handed to accused with a message. I next saw accused the following Sunday, after a week. On this occasion accused had come to the huts of Chiramwiwa and he went into all the huts making a search for a snake and the head of my son who had died (which he had, at the divination, accused Chiramwiwa of possessing). He found nothing. He dug and produced a bottle, he produced it from the ground. He kept the bottle. He put liquid from the bottle on cuts in Chikwaiwa's head. He made cuts on the child's forehead with a razor blade.

Accused said there was medicine in the bottle. Accused then went away. After this visit I saw the accused again. I said I wanted him to cleanse my hut with medicines. Accused agreed to do this. This happened a week after the visit to Chiramwiwa's kraal. Accused arrived at my kraal. He produced a horn from the grass roof of my hut. He just nodded at the roof and it fell down. I have never seen the horn before. This was in the hut where my son died. Accused said the horn had caused the sickness of my child. I then asked accused to treat my daughter who was sick. I wanted him to cure and protect her. Accused treated my daughter by making incisions on her forehead and another part of her body with a razor. He rubbed medicine on her forehead. He took this medicine from a small suitcase he had. This daughter is about four years old. After he treated my daughter he said he wanted £1 for finding the horn and £3 for completing the treatment. I gave accused the £4 as requested. Accused accepted the money and then left.'

When charged by the police Chemere's reply was what might have been expected from a man proud of his skill:

'I was given the money because I had done a good job for him (Josiya). If he was not satisfied he would not have given me any money. If he was not satisfied with the job I would have given him the money back. I wish to ask Josiya a question, "If I was not the one who had fixed your hut would it not be the position now that you would be afraid to sleep in the hut?"'

Another popular method of treatment amongst the Shona is the use of a medicated steam bath. The following account of such a treatment is by the *nganga* himself and is taken from his statement to the police in the case of *R v Njini* (committed for trial at Hartley 1.8.60):

'I was at Preshaw estate when I was approached by Dolika. She stated she was suffering from pains in the region of her arm, the left side of her body and left leg. I asked her to give me 2/6, after which I would throw the bones to find out what was wrong with her. She gave me 2/6. I threw the bones and then told her that I knew what was wrong with her and would come the following day to her. The following day, during the evening, I went to Preshaw estates and dug a small hole in the ground near Dolika's hut. In this hole I placed a lot of small stones. On top of these stones I placed some medicine after which I made a fire on top of this. I allowed the fire to burn for about two hours after which I removed the burning coals. I then instructed Dolika to take off all her clothes other than her petticoat and also to bring a blanket with her. I then took three mugs of water which I threw onto the warm stones in the hole. After having done this I placed three lengths of wood over the hole and instructed Dolika to kneel on top of this. After she had knelt down I covered her with a blanket. I then took another mug of water and, lifting the corner of the blanket, threw this water into the hole. Dolika did not scream when I did this, but only said it was very hot.'

In quite a number of the cases of alleged rape which I have read, evidence was adduced that the doctor had sexual intercourse with the patient on the excuse of attempting to cure her—usually of barrenness, an affliction often caused by wizardry. Until recently I have considered this type of case to be an act of lewdness, and not a recognized method of cure. However, Junod (1913, II, p. 435) states that he considers such acts of intercourse 'probably part of the treatment' among the Tsonga and I think that the case of *R v Kateya* (29) tends to show that it is part of the treatment amongst the Shona. In this case evidence was given that the doctor-diviner had stated that a woman's barrenness had been caused by the sorcery of another woman called 'Cecilia'. Kateya undertook to cure the affliction and took her into the veld to do so. After a considerable amount of 'mumbo-jumbo' the accused placed medicine on his penis and had intercourse with the complainant from the rear, standing. Under the circumstances it is a little difficult to see how he could have derived much sexual satisfaction from the act.

The medicines a wizard gives her victim may be transformed, in the body of her victim, into snakes and other objects. Hence, both amongst the Shona and Ndebele, there are doctors who cure by sucking the object out of the client. The following account from the case of *R v Gombwe* (committed for trial at Miami on 31.1.57 from the evidence of a woman, Maggie:

'I remember Sunday the 26th of January 1957. At 7.00 a.m. that day I went to a hut in the compound where the accused was. I went because I had pains in my body and accused was reputed to be a "doctor". I told accused I was ill. Accused said, "You have something invisible circulating in your body." I sat down opposite accused. He placed a cup containing water on the plate in front of me. He then stood up and stood behind me. He cut me twice with a razor blade above the right collar bone and then bit this spot and sucked the wound. A short while later accused produced a snake-like object and said that it was the cause of my illness. He later produced another object. Prior to accused cutting me he said he wanted five shillings for his cure. I paid him the five shillings he demanded. I then left the hut. Accused said that I would still feel the pains but if they had not dispersed within a fortnight he would repay the five shillings.'

As I remarked previously, when writing of the ordeal, the medicine *muchapi* has spread to this country from the northern territories. In the case of *Sineki alias Nicholas* (p. 220) the accused, a Shona, was prosecuted on a number of counts of administering *muchapi* to people to cure them of diseases caused by witchcraft in return for payments of up to £6. On one occasion as part of the ritual and after *muchapi* was administered, an egg was broken on the patient's head and blood taken from his arm by means of a cupping horn. Another cure used by this doctor was described by a man, Tewe, as follows:

'Accused said he was the son of Chiringa and a witchdoctor so I told him my wife suffered from heart trouble and asked him to treat her. He stated his charge would be 17s. and I actually gave him 15s. He commenced treatment by blowing into my wife's ear and then he shaved a small patch of my wife's hair from her head. He then put some bee's wax on the shaved patch and replaced the cut hair on the top of the wax. He then set light to the wax which only burned for a moment. Accused said there were two fish in my wife's chest causing the trouble but that he was treating my wife's head because that was his method.'

CHAPTER XX

THE CURE OF THE WITCH

MANY people take the attitude that 'once a witch, always a witch' and for this reason when a witch is 'caught' by a diviner the efforts of the community are usually aimed at removing her from the community. If, however, a woman is in this way driven from her husband's village she is, unless she is to become a wandering prostitute, obliged to return to her parents. Usually a woman's parents will offer her hospitality and—if they believe her to be a witch—they may take measures to have the spirit of witchcraft driven from her. A husband who is really fond of a woman who is believed to be a witch may also attempt to cure her. If such treatment is supposed to be successful then the former witch will be accepted by the community and live, again, a normal life. Perhaps more important, the belief that women may be cured of witchcraft means that if the erstwhile witch succeeds in reintegrating with the community, it may be believed she has undergone curative treatment even if she has not.

I have previously described how a Shona woman may refuse the spirit which wishes to possess her and make her a witch. Among the Zezuru it is said the lesser *nganga* will cure a woman in the way previously described, by sitting her on an animal and transferring her spirit—be it *shave* or *mudzimu*—to an animal. The greater *nganga* are said to adopt a different procedure which, however, except in introducing the universal cleansing agents, fire and water, is, in essentials, the same as the procedure used by the lesser *nganga* and involves the transfer of the spirit of witchcraft from the afflicted to some object. We will suppose that the witch is a much loved wife and her husband wishes to cure her of her affliction. They consult a great *nganga* who tells them what to do. A grass hut called a *dumba* is constructed on an island in a river which may be infested with crocodiles. The husband and wife then wade across to the island—the witch being naked except for a covering of black cloth. In the meantime the *nganga* hides himself in the vegetation of the river bank. Reaching the island the couple begin cooking. Into the porridge they cook they put roots, bark, skins and other medicines given them by the *nganga*. While this concoction is cooking the man holds one side of the pot while the woman holds the other side and stirs. Both have to hold the rim tight. The *nganga* then secretly emerges from

The Cure of the Witch

his hiding place while the man and woman are humming the correct magical formula and swims to the island. He sets fire to the *dumba*. The couple then break out of the hut and must recross the river, still holding the pot of porridge. While the river is being crossed the husband must duck his wife and while holding the witch's head under water must release the pot. The choking woman will also let go the pot which will sink to the bottom of the river carrying the spirit of witchcraft with it. The husband must then drag his wife out and the two of them must then run away as fast as they can without looking back. They must run a long way and will eventually meet the *nganga* who will administer further medicines. The unfortunate person who eats fish which has eaten the porridge in the pot will be a victim of the *ngozi* (assuming the spirit of witchcraft was a *mudzimu*) for the spirit that has been cast away will be angry at this treatment. Because of this belief people do not like to eat the mudfish because these fish are scavengers.

The running away without looking back indicates that the rite described above is essentially a rite of separation, the person cured being symbolically separated from her previous existence as a witch.

Apart from those cases involving diviners of the Pentecostal Churches, the only case examined by me in which a curative treatment was attempted was *R v Kukubula* (87). Kukubula, it will be recalled, was a Zambian diviner practising amongst the Ndebele of the Tjolotjo district. On one occasion he indicated two persons, Gagwini and Londhlela as having caused the death of two children. Thereafter he adopted what is clearly a curative treatment and which is described by a witness in the following passage:

'Accused then (i.e. after the divination) told us all to go out of the hut. He would produce a mirror in which we would see a witch. We went out and sat in a circle under a tree. Accused came out with a horn and drew a line on the ground around us. Accused jabbed a horn into the ground near myself, Gagwini and Londhlela. We were sitting together. After this we heard a roaring noise inside the hut we had just left. It sounded like a lighted primus stove. Accused then came out with some cups containing a substance that looked like watery porridge. We each had to drink from some of the cups. Londhlela asked what ours tasted like as hers was very sour. Ours were all tasteless and we told her so. Accused came with burning embers and put them into the horn he had jabbed into the ground. Accused told Londhlela and Gagwini to come near the horn out of which was coming smoke. They did so. They smelled the smoke on accused's instructions. It appeared to them to put them into a coma. I told accused I wanted to take these two women to hospital. Accused told me not to take them to hospital and they would not die. I left them there, reported to my chief, and returned to my kraal. They returned to the kraal late that evening. They could walk but not speak.'

It is not usual for a *mhondoro* spirit to be concerned with witchcraft; but the *svikiro* (spirit medium) of the rain spirit Kakumarara who lived at Chavaroyi near Domboshawa hill in the Chinamora Reserve used, I am told, to cure people of witchcraft. The name of the *svikiro* was Zimbiru and he only had the right to cut rice on Domboshawa or take honey from the well-known cave. Kakumarara was primarily a rain spirit and when rain failed to fall was propitiated with offerings of beer. The spirit seems to have been closely connected with Domboshawa hill, and there seems here to be a parallel to the spirit of *mlimo* in the Matopos which manifests itself in certain caves. The hill had the somewhat extraordinary power to cure witches of their witchcraft. Zimbiru was the person who was able to make use of the curative powers of the hill. Persons accused of witchcraft, after receiving certain medicines, had—so it is said—to go round the hill many times carrying a *katundu* (basket of medicines) on their heads. They were accompanied by people to ensure that they did not take a short cut. After performing this rite they were again doctored with medicines.

While I know of no other similar belief, evidence was led in a case from the Gwelo area that it is believed that there is a hill near Bulawayo which can indicate 'witches'.

Attempts to cure witches in Rhodesia appear to be haphazard and sporadic unlike, for example, a country such as Zambia where witches are, in places, regularly given emetics to cure them of their evil ways (White, 1947, p. 4).

One of the reasons for the power of the prophets of the Pentecostal Churches is that is is believed that a prophet can cure a witch of her witchcraft. While, however, this is firmly believed in by members of the faith it would seem that persons who ordinarily accept the prophets as diviners express considerable scepticism as to their healing powers and in most of the court records no action was taken to have the person pointed out as a witch cured by the prophet. Perhaps the commonest method, because it has Biblical authority, is the cure by the laying on of hands. The following is an extract from the case of *R v Ruka* (60) describing such an attempt. The extract is from the evidence of a man, Munhu, who first of all narrated how Chiromo was named as a witch and accused of killing her grandchild. Munhu arranged a further meeting for the following day:

'I saw the accused again the following morning, he was near my kraal in the veld. I met him there by prior arrangement. There were many apostles there as well. I went with my wife, my mother and my grandmother, Chiromo. When I first saw accused he asked where my grandmother was and told me to fetch her. I did and took her to the accused and the other apostles. Chiromo sat down. Accused said to her, "Grandmother you walk about carrying two pieces of human flesh with which you bewitch people." Accused then accused Chiromo of bewitching Janie and causing her stomach trouble. He explained to her that he would place his hands on her head in order to remove the evil from her. He placed his hands on her head but the evil spirit did not leave her and the old lady demanded to know where the spirit was. She then told accused that he had wrongly accused her of being a witch and he said, "I have done wrong." While all this was going on the accused's friends all ran away. When he placed his hands on her head they were singing. After this accused left. Accused did not ask for any reward for his work.'

When the accused placed his hands on Chiromo she should have become possessed by her spirit—the *shave* or *mudzimu* which gave her the psychic powers of a witch. She failed to become possessed and that is, I think, why the prophet admitted failure.

Various other methods of cure are recorded in the cases

examined. Thus, in the case of *R v Elias alias Elijah* (35) the prophet, after naming the witch, prayed and put stones on a fire to heat. He then placed these stones in water and made the witch wash in water. He then ordered the body of the witch to be smeared with vaseline. In the case of *R v Aaron Ndholvu* (88) Mapeli, the woman named as a witch, was left behind with the accused after her denunciation. She stayed in accused's village for a week and was made to drink salt water with four others who had similarly been indicated.

CHAPTER XXI

CONCLUSION

In the previous pages, views have been expressed on a number of occasions as to the nature of wizardry beliefs and wizardry allegations—in particular, among the Shona. Of necessity these remarks have been scattered throughout the text. I shall now try to gather the threads together and to discuss further one or two matters arising out of what has previously been said which are important for a proper understanding of Shona beliefs and behaviour. There is, in addition, one matter which has hardly been dealt with at all so far and that is the normative effect of wizardry beliefs.

It is clear that wizardry beliefs are still of importance for the proper understanding of present day Shona society. This is a society undergoing rapid changes which have already resulted in the transformation of a portion of the Shona community of subsistance farmers into an urban proletariat. It is probable that the general feeling of insecurity which rapid change and transition inevitably brings had, if anything, given wizardry beliefs a new importance by providing a comprehensible explanation in the malice of one's fellow men for the difficulties which economic factors and other matters beyond the understanding of the ordinary worker occasion. I would, however, hesitate to say that wizardry beliefs are more or less socially relevant now than in the past.

Conclusion

A person accused of wizardry had less to fear than used to be the case and there is also a group among the Shona, although I believe it to be small, which has adopted the sceptical attitudes characteristic of a section of the European population.

It is of interest that, notwithstanding the great changes that are taking place in Shona society, the vast majority of the cases which came before the courts in the period studied arose from areas where the traditional way of life is still strong and reflect the tensions and conflicts within communities of basically traditional type. One reason for this is almost certainly because serious allegations arise as often as not consequent on the death of a child or young person and, therefore, are more frequent in areas distant from the main hospitals and clinics. Another reason is probably the breakdown in the towns of the extended family of the past into the simple family of parents and children. This means that wizardry allegations arising from tensions between lineages or within the lineage, as so many do, are unlikely in these areas. Further, complaint to the police by the person accused is easy in the towns and the areas of denser European settlement. Although wizardry cases seldom come before the courts in urban areas there is no reason to suppose that belief in wizardry is less, and indeed, houses in towns are as carefully protected against wizardry by means of medicines as any village. Accusations of wizardry recur in situations of inter-personal rivalry or competition in schools, factories and elsewhere. It would seem, however, even although town dwellers still believe in wizardry, that the comparative scarcity of serious allegations in the towns means that beliefs in wizardry have not now the same emotional intensity as they have in the country.

It is difficult to know if any particular significance attaches to the decline in the 1950's of wizardry cases (p. 6) reported to the police and their increase in the 1960's. (The increase in the number of preparatory examinations in 1962 was continued in 1963.) The 1950's were, however, a period of general economic progress for the Rhodesias with full employment, by Rhodesian standards, and an expanding economy. This process became accelerated after

1953 with the creation of the Federation of Rhodesia and Nyasaland. The early 1960's, by contrast, were years of uncertainty in the political field and of economic recession. In addition, the rise of African nationalism encouraged widespread opposition to the Government and in some areas a breakdown of law and order. It is tempting to link the incidence of serious wizardry allegations with the economic and social state of the country and to see in the rise of wizardry allegations in 1962 a reflection of the disturbed state of the country. One might see a similar reflection in the high incidence of wizardry cases in the late 1940's after the return of Africans who had served in the armed forces overseas and who returned with new ideas. At this time too, large areas of land were opened up for European occupation and large numbers of European immigrants entered the country. Tempting though the drawing of this sort of inference may be, obviously the figures may be ambiguous and any conclusions drawn from them are likely to be suspect.

The most obvious symptom of social change in the material studied was the popularity of the prophets of the Pentecostal Churches. Although apparently of little or no importance in peripheral areas among the Hlengwe, Valley Tonga and certain other backward and remote groups, they were almost omnipresent throughout the Shona and Ndebele areas, both in town and country, in the European farming areas and the Tribal Trust Land. Their popularity suggests, in view of the role these churches play in assisting persons to adapt themselves to social change, that social problems created by a changing society are of very much the same order in both urban and rural areas.

Turning now to the question of the normative aspects of wizardry belief, a number of cases have been referred to where a breach of the social norms has been followed by an accusation of wizardry. In some cases it would seem that the breach has something to do with the accusation, in other cases after the allegation has been made the fact that the person accused has acted in an improper manner is seen as evidence confirming the truth of the accusation. On the face of it, if accusations follow breaches of the

Conclusion

social norms, the fear of an accusation might be expected to operate as a sanction against the breach of these norms. Obviously it is important to establish whether, in fact, the fear of an accusation is a sanction against anti-social behaviour. Many anthropologists assume that it must be such a sanction. While, however, it is usually easy enough to decide why people depart from the social norms of the community in which they live, it is less easy to establish the reasons why people conform to those norms, although it is easy enough to appreciate that a group of persons can hardly live together as a group unless they do conform to certain standards of conduct. A large part is notoriously played by informal sanctions such as public opinion, reciprocity and so forth. Of course formal sanctions are, on occasion, necessary. In our own society the thief no doubt ordinarily appreciates the anti-social effect of his conduct but the financial rewards of his crime are such as to render this sort of conduct attractive notwithstanding this. It is, for this reason, necessary to impose an institutionalized sanction in the form of criminal punishment. A formal sanction such as this is no less a sanction because the chances of punishment for any particular offence are small as they are, in our own society, in the case of certain driving offences. It is, therefore, not fatal to the theory that wizardry accusations serve as a social sanction, that an accusation by no means necessarily, or even usually, follows certain sorts of anti-social conduct. What does, however, create a measure of doubt is that the types of anti-social conduct in respect of which the allegation of wizardry is supposed to serve as a social sanction are, among the Shona, the types of conduct which Shona society has not singled out as being actionable wrongs. It is this very class of conduct which rural communities throughout the world control effectively whether or not they believe in wizardry. When I have discussed political or other matters with a Shona it is usually clear that public opinion or, as he would express it 'what the people say or think' is a matter which plays a considerable part, and often a conscious part, in the formation of his own views and attitudes. It is abundantly clear that, whether or not the fear of a wizardry allegation is, among the Shona, a sanction against social conduct, it is possible to explain the high degree of social conformity which exists among the Shona without invoking wizardry beliefs. Sorcery however is a sanction which can be of importance, particularly in the enforcement of a contract or in quasi-contractual relationships. If an employee, for example, finds a replacement while away on holiday, fear of sorcery may ensure that he regains his post on return.

While there may be a measure of doubt as to whether wizardry beliefs are an effective social sanction there can be no doubt that such beliefs can be used as a means of manipulating public opinion in much the same manner as allegations of heresy in mediaeval Europe or Communism in modern America and Southern Africa were, and are, used. Malice can be expressed as an allegation of wizardry and will find credence if the person against whom hostility is expressed is unpopular, particularly if he has also acted in an unusual manner. It is thus easy to marshal public opinion against the social non-conformist. The person manipulating public opinion in this manner need not do so consciously. If one person dislikes another he is likely to attribute to him evil ways. After all, everyone knows himself to be a reasonable person and he is hardly likely to dislike someone unless he merits this dislike! If the person has evil ways, one tends to define these in terms of one's social stereotype of an evil person, for most of us do our thinking in stereotypes. If one is a Shona, the stereotype is that of a wizard. When the suspect's behaviour is examined, it is found that he has acted suspiciously in disregarding social norms, and who of us always does everything he should do? This confirms one's views and, that being so, it is one's plain duty to tell one's friends of the danger in their midst. Whether or not one's friends will believe what they are told will depend in part on whether other people want to believe the accusation and whether reasonable grounds for suspicion exist. It is obviously easier to turn public opinion against an unpopular than a popular person. If the accusation is believed the accuser has successfully marshalled public opinion against the object of his dislike which is what he, consciously or unconsciously, set out to do. A person is most

Conclusion

likely to dislike persons who are sexually, economically or politically in competition with him and the accusation of wizardry affords a technique for marshalling public opinion against the rival in what is, essentially, a private quarrel. It is suggested that beliefs in wizardry are more important as a means of social manipulation than as a sanction against anti-social conduct. An allegation of wizardry by a diviner is, however, not necessarily such an attempt at social manipulation but—in common with other accusations of wizardry—I see it as an attempt to associate the community as a whole with an event. There can be no doubt that the effect of an allegation of wizardry by a diviner is to make the divination the concern of the community as a whole. If this is the effect, it is probable that this is also the end desired. In the case of a professional diviner, the motive for the allegation may, no doubt, be primarily to enhance his prestige. An allegation of wizardry is, therefore, an appeal to the moral feelings of the community in an attempt to involve the community emotionally in a certain state of affairs. The reasons for making the appeal depend on the person making it and the events of the moment.

It is frequently suggested that wizardry allegations have a 'cathartic effect' in resolving the social tensions of a community. A moment's thought will convince one that this cannot be entirely true. A mere accusation of wizardry can do nothing except worsen social relationships. Immediately, of course, it will worsen relationships between the accuser and the accused. If some believe the accusation and some do not, then the community is likely to be divided into opposing groups, normally no doubt, into groups reflecting a pre-existing segmentation or potential segmentation in the community. It is only 'proof' of an accusation—and, what is more, 'proof' of a nature which will convince everyone in the community or in a section of it—which can serve to resolve social tensions whether by the finding of a scapegoat, by the crystallization of the various interest groups or the exculpation of the suspect from all guilt. It is, therefore, vitally important to distinguish between the accusation of wizardry and the 'proof' of wizardry. Here, there can be no doubt that, in the past, the most convincing 'proof' of wizardry was, in the case of the Shona, the poison ordeal. Shona attitudes were very similar to those of a number of other African peoples. Douglas (in Middleton & Winter, p. 123) has a suggestion of some interest about the poison ordeal amongst groups in Central Africa north of the Zambesi and, in particular, about the Lele of the Kasai. She states that, in the past, the poison ordeal was the only sure way of indicating a sorcerer. If suspicion fell upon a young man he could move away from his village but the position was not the same with an old man who found it less easy to move and whose village became a closed community. If his quarrel built up cumulatively he could easily 'acquire the reputation of a fully committed sorcerer, responsible for every death in the village.' An ordinary oracle could not clear the name of such a person but the poison oracle could. In the absence of such an oracle he faces social extinction and, probably, social exile. In addition, if his name was not cleared his clansmen were faced with the payment of blood compensation. The ordeal provided a solution to the problem. If the person concerned survived the ordeal he could demand compensation and make a new start. If he did not survive and died, his kin and supporters had no option but to pay compensation and, when this was done, there could again be a new start. With the prohibition of the ordeal by the Colonial Administration there remained no way of resolving social tensions by recourse to the ordeal and no one could be certain who was, and who was not, a sorcerer. The situation became intolerable. A way out of the problem was found in the various anti-sorcery cults which spread through Lele country at various intervals from 1910 onwards. By initiation into the cult, of which the *Kabenga-Benga* is the most recent, a person was cleansed of sorcery. Should a person, once initiated, practise sorcery again it was believed he would die. The cults, therefore, enabled a person to be cleansed of suspicion and to re-integrate himself into the community and also removed the tensions and suspicions which were making community life increasingly intolerable. Inevitably these cults collapse in the end as the theory that only sorcerers who have been initiated die becomes inadequate to account for the deaths of, for example, small children. Each cult becomes, in turn, discredited.

Among the Shona, diviners have never been supposed to be infallible, although they may have considerable reputations. The only way a person could finally clear himself of suspicion of wizardry was by means of the poison ordeal. I have already shown how women, in areas where the ordeal still survived may, of their own volition, seek the ordeal as a means of freeing themselves from an intolerable situation. Now that the ordeal is prohibited recourse to it is, in most parts of the country, impossible. The Shona solution to the problem has not been, however, the development of cults on the lines of the *Kabenga-Benga* cult or of those described by Marwick (1950, p. 2) or Richards (1935, pp. 448-461) although the *muchapi* movement, when it first spread to Rhodesia before the last war, was probably very similar. *Muchapi* is still known and persons still administer it; but the movement has long ago spent its force. Instead, the role of the anti-sorcery movements among the Lele is, among the Shona, largely taken by the Pentecostal Churches. I have previously described the manner in which these churches cleanse initiates of wizardry and divine wizardry. Some churches have even developed new forms of the ordeal; here the manner in which the Churches have tried to make good the vacuum occasioned by the prohibition of the poison ordeal is particularly evident. If one accepts, as a believer must, that a Pentecostal prophet is speaking with the voice of God, his pronouncements are clearly infallible, unlike those of a doctor diviner. A prophet accepts no money for his services—at any rate directly—and that he has no obvious reason to tell lies is an added reason for credence. The prophet in his bright robes, with a mitre on his head and a crozier in his hand, is a much more impressive figure than the ordinary Shona diviner and his psychological impact on his congregation correspondingly greater. The Pentecostal Churches do not, of course, afford an entirely satisfactory alternative to the poison ordeal because many of them are comparatively small and not everyone belongs to them. Even if the church is large, the congregations are often widely scattered and their followers are seldom dominant in any particular community. Because of this, and because they cannot convince everyone of their power, the churches are probably less effective than the *Kabenga-Benga* cult or the poison ordeal in resolving social tensions. On the other hand, if a person becomes disillusioned with the church he can always transfer his allegiance to another. One does not, therefore, in Mashonaland get the widespread cycles of belief and disbelief which occur among the Lele, although there is undoubtedly a pattern of growth and decay among the individual Pentecostal Churches. From the point of view of the person suspected of wizardry the joining of a Pentecostal Church may not free him of suspicion as far as non-believers are concerned; but at least he is joining a group with whom normal social relationships can be established.

It should be stressed that the Pentecostal Churches are more than an anti-wizardry cult, for they manifestly have other social roles as well. Of these, perhaps the most important is their role in helping the Shona to adapt to the modern world and to provide an acceptable *tertium quid* between the beliefs of the past, the beliefs of the various European sponsored Christian Missions with their discipline, prohibition of polygamy and their European background. The Pentecostal Churches have often an advantage over the Mission Churches, merely because they are African.

The Shona have developed a reasonably coherent cosmology and wizardry beliefs are in accord with their general religious beliefs. The religious beliefs do not, however, appear to be essential for the existence or survival of wizardry beliefs. If the religious framework of Shona wizardry beliefs were an essential part of those beliefs one would expect wizardry beliefs in societies with religious beliefs differing from those of the Shona to take a very different form. This is not the case. Again, if the religious aspect of Shona wizardry beliefs were an essential part of these beliefs they would be abandoned on the acceptance of Christianity. This is not so—the various spirits which the Shona believe are associated with wizardry are simply transformed into Biblical devils. It is because wizardry, although explained in terms of Shona religious beliefs, is not dependent for survival upon those beliefs that it shows such remarkable resilience to social change. As long as children and young people continue to die it is unlikely that belief in wizardry will be abandoned. The main importance of Shona religious ideas today (as far as we are concerned with them in this book), at least in the case of persons who no longer find these beliefs adequate for their needs, is that—being essentially belief in various forms of spirit possession—they prepare a person seeking fresh religious experience for the reception of beliefs of Pentecostal type. Traditional Shona beliefs also ensure that, where a church of essentially non-Pentecostal type is joined, it will tend, if controlled to any extent by the Shona, to conform increasingly to the Pentecostal pattern. The life of most of the Shona is today rather drab and in the circumstances, and even without the background of traditional beliefs, the colour and excitement of ceremonies of Pentecostal character would undoubtedly prove attractive.

An element which Shona witchcraft beliefs share with the beliefs of many other societies is the ascribing to a witch of perverted conduct or conduct which is an inversion of that approved of by society. An example of perverted conduct is the Shona witch's predilection for human meat; a food strongly disliked by ordinary men. It has been suggested by Winter (in Middleton and Winter, p. 292) when discussing a similar situation among the Ambo that one of the reasons why it is believed that a witch can only harm persons within the village or neighbourhood is to be found in the fact that a witch's conduct is believed to be an inversion of socially acceptable conduct. The local community is a moral community where persons must conduct themselves in their relations with one another in an acceptable way and in accordance with the concepts of the society in regard to good neighbourliness. It is, therefore, unnatural for a person living in the community to seek to harm it. On the other hand, communities living outside the neighbourhood are, among the Ambo, essentially hostile and, therefore, there is nothing unnatural about an attempt to harm a member of these groups. No question of inverted conduct and no question of witchcraft arises.

However probable this theory may seem among the Ambo it gives rise to difficulties if one attempts to apply it to the Shona. In the past the moral community of the Shona embraced at least the tribe and it is probably wider now. One was expected to conduct oneself in a proper way with other tribesmen even if they were not members of the village. In fact, members of the same tribe usually regarded one another as kinsmen even if blood relationship could not be established. Witchcraft allegations, however, as among the Ambo, are confined to the village or neighbourhood. While I am not suggesting that Winter's theory is wrong, for society is complex and there is often no single cause for any observed pattern of conduct, I think that, at least among the Shona, the reason for the confining of witchcraft allegations to a comparatively small territorial area is best explained—not in terms of any 'moral' community—but in the fact commented upon by many social anthropologists that accusations are most likely in situations of intimate personal contact where the status of the persons concerned is more or less equal. In rural areas one only normally comes into intimate personal contact of this nature with persons living in the same locality. Wizardry allegations also occur in factories and rural schools which cannot be regarded as 'moral communities' save in a rather extended sense of the term. The concept of the 'moral community' does not, in any event, explain why accusations are made against certain members of the community and not against others. It is surely best to apply Occam's razor and find the explanation for both the pattern of accusations within the community and the limitation of accusations to a village or neighbourhood in inter-personal contact and rivalry rather than to find a different reason for each. Even if Winter's theory is unsatisfactory the concept of the moral community is not without relevance as far as the study of Shona wizardry allegations is concerned. There is, among the Shona, nothing improper in the use of sorcery or magic to destroy a member of a hostile group. The person who uses such means against an enemy is not a wizard, as would be the case if he turned his supernatural weapons against one of his own community. Indeed, the ability to fortify one's own group magically against the machinations of an enemy group is obviously a socially desirable ability. In the past, no army would have set out to attack another group without being adequately fortified by means of magic.

Shona wizardry beliefs throw light upon what the Shona conceive the 'moral community' to be; but I am a little doubtful if the concept of the 'moral community' has any great effect as far as the pattern of wizardry allegations are concerned.

There is no need to say much here about the distinction the Shona make—but do not well express—between witchcraft and sorcery. I believe, however, that I have shown that this distinction is vital for the understanding of the nature of witchcraft allegations. The importance of the distinction arises from the fact that witchcraft allegations are made against women and sorcery allegations, which are less serious, are made against men. In a patrilineal society with virilocal marriage this inevitably means that witchcraft allegations are, in the main, made against the wives and mothers of lineage members and that sorcery allegations are made against lineage members. In other words, the solidarity of the lineage is maintained at the expense of non-lineage members. It is essential for my argument in this respect to show that witchcraft allegations against women are socially of greater consequence and are more serious from the point of veiw of the person accused of witchcraft than is the case where a sorcery allegation is made against a man. The figures given previously show, with very little doubt, that allegations resulting in serious consequences to the person accused are more often made against a woman than a man. This, of course, does not establish my case as one might, for example, argue that this does not mean that allegations made against a woman are, in themselves, more serious than those made against a man; all that is shown is that women are in a position of inferiority in Shona society and are thus less capable of coping with the situation which arises. There may be something in this argument; but in the few court records where a witchcraft allegation, as opposed to a sorcery allegation was made against a man, the consequences to that man appear to have been as serious as is frequently the case in allegations made against women. In any event, even if an able-bodied Shona man can avoid the consequences of a believed allegation of witchcraft or sorcery by moving elsewhere, an old man, unless he is a chief or headman, is hardly in a better position to cope with his environment than a woman. In the result, therefore, the evidence in my opinion supports the view that the consequences of an allegation against a woman are more serious than against a man because the allegation against a woman is a more serious allegation, rather than the view that the differing consequences are merely the direct consequence of a difference in social status.

I have referred on a number of occasions to allegations of wizardry which I have stated have arisen from or been generated by social conflicts of various sorts. The question now arises as to whether this is an altogether accurate statement of the origin of the accusation of wizardry and also whether it is entirely correct to regard an accusation of wizardry as an expression of social conflict. Where co-wives are competing for the favours of their husband and accuse one another of wizardry, it is very difficut not to regard the accusation as being a reflection of social conflict—although it may be other things as well. In such circumstances is would appear to be not incorrect to state that the allegation arises from the conflict. Where, however, the diviner is consulted about the death of a child and divines the cause of the death to be wizardry, naming a particular person to be a wizard, it is clear that the allegation does not arise directly from any social conflict. The diviner may, of course, be acquainted with, or may discover, the social conflicts in the community from which his consultants come and may make use of this knowledge when indicating a wizard; but it is clearly not correct to regard the accusation as arising from any particular social conflict. In both the case of the accusation by a co-wife and the accusation by a diviner the accusation will reflect social conflict in the community; but in the first

Conclusion

case there is a direct causal link between the conflict and the accusation. In the second there is not. The diviner need not have divined the presence of wizardry at all and, if wizardry were divined, need not have named the person he did name as a wizard. A social conflict may have guided, but it did not determine, the diviner's choice. Although the two types of accusation have a different origin they both, as I suggested previously, are in essence an appeal to the community with the intention of involving the community as a whole emotionally in some particular occurrence.

Too much emphasis on the allegation of wizardry as being the reflection of social tension leads one into the error of supposing that an allegation is a mere symptom of social malaise and is not, in itself, a dynamic force in the community. There are, indeed, many social anthropologists who would appear to overlook the dynamic importance of wizardry allegations. An allegation of wizardry may originally reflect a state of enmity between two persons but, once made, a chain of events may be set in motion which can lead rapidly to the most unforeseen and often tragic consequences. There is no reason to suppose that any other form of expression of hostility would ordinarily result in the tragedies occasioned by an allegation of wizardry, nor is it easy to think, in the context of Shona society, of any other type of accusation which can so readily embitter social relations and increase social tension. One can no more regard wizardry allegations a mere expression of social conflict than the all too common beer drink stabbings among the Shona. The accusation, as in the case of the stabbing, reflects social conflict; but the deed itself may entirely alter the nature of the conflict and, in any event, adds to it an entirely new dimension.

If the allegation of wizardry is primarily a device for involving the community as a whole in some particular happening then the reason why some sorts of social conflict result in a wizardry allegation is—at least in part—explained. One would really only expect allegations to occur in situations where the marshalling of public opinion against an offender serves a useful purpose. If, for example, one's daughter is seduced, a Shona man's primary interest is in obtaining recompense. The marshalling of public opinion against the offender, particularly if he is a member of another community (for public opinion is most effective within the community) does not serve any very real purpose, as the only reasonable way to recover damages, if the seducer will not willingly pay them, is action in the chief's court. What is primarily required is not emotion, but a good case. Of course, if legal proceedings become frustrated, as we have seen, an appeal to public opinion made in the idiom of wizardry is not unlikely. I would also suggest one reason why a commoner would not normally make an allegation of wizardry against a chief, and that is that the marshalling of public opinion against a chief would not only serve no useful purpose, but would be distinctly dangerous.

If any reason is to be sought for the limitation of wizardry allegations to a village or neighbourhood other than that allegations result from intense inter-personal relationships, it lies in the nature of the wizardry allegation as a device for controlling public opinion. If a person is a stranger from outside one's community the marshalling of public opinion in one's own community against the man serves little purpose and, indeed, is probably unnecessary. The views of the members of one's own community about the conduct of the stranger will probably coincide with one's own.

The use of the allegation of wizardry as a device for directing public opinion against a person is particularly obvious in a struggle for political power within a community in which each contestant tries to involve as many persons as possible in the dispute and get them on his side. The weapon is, of course, a two-edged weapon and is as useful in securing the retention of power in the face of a challenge as in securing the advantage of a person seeking to challenge established power. The use by the Ndebele kings of wizardry allegations to remove those who were politically dangerous is notorious. It would seem that this device was not entirely unknown in the Shona chieftaincies also.

It does not follow that because, among the Shona, the allegation of wizardry is often an instrumental technique—although not

Conclusion

necessarily a technique consciously used by those concerned—it can never be merely a stereotyped response to misfortune. Obviously it may be, and there are indeed, among the Shona as elsewhere, certain superstitious individuals who tend to see in almost any misfortune the hand of a wizard. The response of such a person to misfortune is little more than an expression of that person's superstitions. It is not, however, wizardry allegations of this type that form the subject of this book.

As far as the consequences to a person accused of wizardry are concerned, it is necessary to appreciate that there are usually two views about a person's guilt—at any rate unless the person accused is extremely unpopular or has been proved to be a wizard irrefutably by means of the poison ordeal or some other generally accepted method. In particular, close relatives of the person accused are unlikely to believe the accusation. From the point of view of the person accused, however, the fact that not everyone believes the accusation is only relevant if the people who believe he or she is innocent are sufficiently close at hand to afford protection. This is not necessarily the case where a woman is accused. Her close relatives—or at least those of them who are able to assist her—unless she has adult children, do not normally live in her husband's village. So long as she remains in her husband's village she is virtually defenceless save in so far as her husband and his group may be induced to stay their hands either for personal reasons or because they are unwilling to forego the *rovoro* if a divorce is occasioned by their conduct. A man, on the other hand, living with others of his lineage, is not in the same position if accused of sorcery and in the event of an accusation is likely to find support from persons who belong to his own segment of the lineage. Clearly the identity and number of persons who are prepared to disbelieve an accusation of wizardry or sorcery made against a man are, amongst the Shona, of greater social and political significance than is the support which a woman may muster amongst her own kin. It is for this reason that in the process of village and lineage segmentation accusations of sorcery against men play such an important part.

There remains the question as to the extent to which wizardry beliefs affect the everyday behaviour of the Shona. Here it must be realized that to single out a particular aspect of Shona culture as I have done in this book tends to give that aspect a status and importance which it may not necessarily deserve. The Shona no more spends his ordinary waking hours thinking about wizardry than you or I spend our time thinking about the Atom Bomb. This, however, does not mean that wizardry is not important in Shona society nor the Atom Bomb in ours. The ordinary Shona man will keep his windows closed at night because he fears the *zwidoma*; but being a matter of habit he will scarcely give a moment's thought to the reason for his actions. As a prudent family man he will ensure that his house is protected against wizardry as well as medicines can protect it. He or his wife will obtain such charms as are necessary to protect his children. He need not place any very great faith in these protective measures; but obviously a prudent householder does not take unnecessary risks. He will, no doubt, conform to the social norms of his community; but whether or not he will do so because he fears an allegation of wizardry may be arguable and is, in any event, dependent on his personality. For the rest he will give wizardry hardly a thought until and unless circumstances arise which render it relevant. If a child dies, as a prudent family man, he may conceive it his duty to discover the cause of its death so as to prevent further deaths; and, if wizardry is divined, will no doubt take appropriate action including, if necessary, action against the wizard—particularly if he becomes emotionally involved as is likely in a situation such as this. If his wives quarrel and their conflict is expressed in terms of wizardry he must obviously take remedial action although here, no doubt, his efforts will be directed mainly to settling the dispute. If he comes into political or other conflict with an equal there is, of course, the possibility that one of the parties to the dispute will attempt to appeal to public opinion in terms of the idiom of witchcraft, or of sorcery. The ordinary man, however, on the whole manages to avoid such conflicts.

Conclusion

It is easy, then, to overestimate the importance of wizardry beliefs in Shona society. After all, the number of cases which come before the courts and which arise from allegations of wizardry is not very great. On the other hand it may be recalled that the Prime Minister of an African state not far from Rhodesia recently accused a leading opponent of his régime of sorcery. The truth of the allegation need not concern us; but that the accusation was an effective weapon to use against a political enemy and potential rival there can be no doubt. Wizardry beliefs may seldom be of any great relevance in the life of the ordinary Shona; but when the context arises in which they are relevant they become of great significance. Wizardry beliefs are particularly relevant when dealing with the most important of all matters, a person's birth, health and death and, indeed, wizardry beliefs are first and foremost concerned with, and derive their emotional content from, the eternal enigma of death, especially the death of the young and of the healthy.

Turning now from the subject matter of this study to the methods used by me. These methods differ from the conventional methods of social anthropology in their heavy reliance on written sources instead of on personal observation in the field. This was forced upon me as I was, when I obtained the material, a civil servant employed in Salisbury with little opportunity of going elsewhere for any length of time. Informants were readily obtainable, but obviously it was not possible to live as a member of an African community. I think, however, that although the use of written sources supplemented by the use of informants has its draw-backs, it also demonstrates the enormous value of a study of written records to the social anthropologist. I would suggest that a comparison of written material obtained from Governmental and other sources with material obtained in the field is, at least on occasion, a more fruitful approach than relying on one or other of these sources exclusively. Written records, for example, can assist in the assessment of the relative importance to the community of events which are observed in the field as they indicate the sort of matter which has become the concern of the

Government, either by reason of the action of the community in appealing to the Government, or because the conduct of persons in the community was such that the Government has had to take an interest in the matter. An illustration of the manner in which Government records (in this case, again, court records) can be used as the starting point of an anthropological study is the Jones report on medicinal murder in Basutoland, which led to the pinpointing of malaise in the structure of the chieftaincy. Here an anthropologist was actually retained by the Government.

Cases where the Government takes an interest are unlikely to be selected at random but will be selected for a particular reason —in the case of Shona wizardry allegations often on the basis of the consequences to the person named as a wizard. The various processes of selection whereby a case is brought to the notice of the Government are of interest and may afford some guide to the quality and nature of the observed behaviour patterns. No doubt where an observed social phenomenon is of everyday occurrence the observer in the field is in a good position to assess its significance; but if it is of some rarity obviously no aid to interpretation should be ignored, as is also the case where the very presence of the observer has the effect of modifying normal behaviour patterns. In a study such as the present, for example, it is unlikely that a European observer would normally be permitted to observe conduct which amounts to a serious offence against the Witchcraft Suppression Act. However greatly he may gain the confidence of a community some circumspection in this regard is inevitable. If cases may be subject to a process of selection before being brought to the attention of the Government they are also, from another point of view, unselected in that they do not reflect the bias of a particular observer. It is easy when studying a society to take a special interest in a particular aspect of the society and, as a result, to ignore other aspects. An example of this is to be found in Gelfand's writings where detailed descriptions are to be found of doctor-diviners at work. Gelfand in his descriptions hardly mentions the Pentecostal Churches and one could be pardoned for assuming that the Shona diviner is exclusively a diviner

Conclusion

of traditional type. A random selection of half a dozen cases brought under the Witchcraft Suppression Act will immediately show that this is not so. Even if a social study relies entirely on field observations the examination of written sources will at least provide, in suitable cases, a useful corrective against this sort of unconscious bias in the observer.

A problem of general interest to both the social anthropologist and the historian is the extent to which the sort of material ordinarily found in the archives of a Government can be used to throw light upon the state of contemporary society. When dealing with the societies of the past this sort of material is often the only source of information available. There is a clear and obvious need for the study of such sources in relation to a living society so that the processes whereby material is recorded in writing or not so recorded are fully understood and the uses of this sort of literature exploited to the full. I hope, even if this book serves no other purpose, it will lead to a greater appreciation of the usefulness of written sources and, in particular, of court records, in the study of an African society.

APPENDIX II

WITCHCRAFT SUPPRESSION
CHAPTER 50

To suppress the practice of pretended witchcraft [18th August, 1899.]   *Ord. 14, 1899*

1. This Act may be cited as the Witchcraft Suppression Act (*Chapter* 50).   Short title.

2. In this Act 'witchcraft' includes the 'throwing of bones,' the use of charms and any other means or devices adopted in the practice of sorcery.   Interpretation of term.

3. Whoever imputes to any other person the use of non-natural means in causing any disease in any person or animal or in causing any injury to any person or property, that is to say, whoever names or indicates any other person as being a wizard or witch shall be guilty of an offence and liable to a fine not exceeding one hundred pounds or to imprisonment for a period not exceeding three years, or to corporal punishment not exceeding twenty lashes or to any two or more of such punishments.   Punishment for imputation of witchcraft.

4. Whoever, having so named and indicated any person as a wizard or witch, is proved at his trial under section three to be by habit and repute a witch doctor or witch finder shall be liable, on conviction, in lieu of the punishment provided by section three to a fine not exceeding two hundred and fifty pounds or to imprisonment for a period not exceeding seven years or to corporal punishment not exceeding thirty-six lashes or to any two or more of such punishments.   Punishment for imputation of witchcraft by habitual or reputed witch doctor or witch finder.

5. Whoever employs or solicits any other person—   Punishment for employing witch doctor or witch finder.

    (a) to name or indicate any other person as a wizard or witch; or

Appendix II

(b) to name or indicate by means of witchcraft or by the application of any of the tests mentioned in paragraph (b) of section *eight* or by the use of any non-natural means any person as the perpetrator of any alleged crime or other act complained of; or

(c) to advise him or any other person how by means of witchcraft or by any non-natural means whatsoever the perpetrator of any alleged crime or other act complained of may be discovered;

shall be guilty of an offence and liable to a fine not exceeding twenty-five pounds, or in default of payment to imprisonment for a period not exceeding six months.

Punishment for witch doctor or witch finder practising witchcraft or supplying witchcraft materials.

6. Whoever, professing a knowledge of so-called witchcraft or of the use of charms, either as a witch doctor or witch finder, advises or undertakes to advise any person applying to him how to bewitch or injure any other person or any property, including animals, and any person who supplies any other person with the pretended means of witchcraft, shall be guilty of an offence and liable to the punishments provided by section *four*.

Punishment for applying means or processes of witchcraft for the injury of persons or property.

7. Whoever, on the advice of a witch doctor or witch finder or any person pretending to the knowledge of witchcraft or the use of charms, or in the exercise of any pretended knowledge of witchcraft or of the use of charms, uses or causes to be put into operation such means or processes as he may have been advised or may believe to be calculated to injure any other person or any property, including animals, shall be guilty of an offence and liable to the punishments provided by section *four*.

Punishment for the naming or indicating of thieves, etc., by witchcraft, charms, etc.

8. Whoever—

(a) by the exercise of any witchcraft, conjuration, use of charms or of any other unnatural means pretends to discover where or in what manner any property supposed or alleged to have been stolen or lost may be found or to name or indi-

Appendix II

cate any person as a thief or perpetrator of any crime or any other act complained of; or

(b) in the pretence of discovering whether or not any other person has committed any crime or any other act complained of, applies or advises the application or causes to be applied to such person the 'boiling water test' (that is to say the dipping by such other person of any of his limbs or portion of his body into boiling water), whether such dipping is voluntary or compelled, or administers or advises or causes the administration of, to such other person, with or without his consent, any emetic or purgative;

shall be guilty of an offence and liable to the punishments provided by section *four*.

9. Any money, animal or other thing received by any person by way of payment or reward for or in respect of any exercise or pretended exercise of so-called witchcraft or of the use of charms, or for or in respect of advising any person as to any mode or method of bewitching or injuring, by non-natural means, any other person or property, including animals, or for or in respect of indicating any person who by non-natural means is supposed to have bewitched or injured any other person or any property, including animals, or for or in respect of the performance of any of the acts mentioned in section *eight*, shall be deemed to have been obtained by fraud, and the person so receiving such money, animal or other thing shall be liable to be prosecuted for fraud and to suffer such punishment as is by law provided for such offence.

<small>Money, etc., received as payment or received for practice of witchcraft, etc., shall be deemed to have been received by fraud, and punishment for such fraud.</small>

APPENDIX III

AFRICAN NGANGA ASSOCIATION OF SOUTHERN RHODESIA CONSTITUTION

1. *NAME*: This Association shall henceforth be known as the 'Nganga Association of Southern Rhodesia.'
2. The African Nganga Association shall have Regional (Branch) Associations throughout Southern Rhodesia. The branches so formed shall affiliate to the mother body, the Southern Rhodesia African Nganga Association.
3. Each Branch of the Association shall have its own Executive comprising: the Chairman, Vice Chairman, Secretary, Vice Secretary, Treasurer and four Committee members.

AIMS AND OBJECTS
4. (a) The Association shall endeavour to follow the most up-to-date methods in the CARE and TREATMENT of patients.
   (b) It shall also see to it that everyone who practises as a Nganga must be a member approved by the Association.
   (c) Every Nganga must keep a record of all cases that come under his treatment. He must also keep a record of the medicine and treatment he gave.

JOINING AND SUBSCRIPTION FEES
5. (a) Every Nganga shall pay a joining fee of (£1) to the association to become a registered member.
   (b) Every member of the Association shall pay a subscription fee of (10s.) every six months. Every member who fails to pay his subscription within six months shall cease to be a member of the Nganga Association.

THE EXECUTIVE OF THE NGANGA ASSOCIATION
6. The executive of the Nganga Association shall consist of the following office bearers:
   (a) The President and his Vice.
   (b) The Chairman and his Vice.
   (c) The General Secretary and his Vice.
   (d) The General Treasurer.
   (e) Four Members of the Committee.

Appendix III

FUNCTIONS OF THE EXECUTIVE

7. (a) The executive shall endeavour to make known the Association to all Ngangas with a view to encourage them to join the Association as well as to inform them of important events taking place within and without the Association which are of interest to Ngangas.
   (b) The Executive shall seek powers in future to punish any person who may practise as a Nganga having not joined the Association.
   (c) Any Nganga who intentionally fails to discharge his work well or who despises other Ngangas shall be brought under disciplinary measures by the Executive.
   (d) The Executive shall also seek to know that everyone practising as a Nganga has inherited this practice from his ancestors or may have been trained by a hereditary Nganga for a period of not less than two years.
   (e) The Executive shall publish a journal every three months showing the work of the Association and the methods followed by Ngangas in the treatment of patients. The journal shall be styled;

'MUKAFRIKA'

   (f) In the long run the Executive shall, if possible, form a bigger and wider Association of all the Ngangas in the Federation.

DISCIPLINARY MEASURES

8. (a) Any person who uses the name of the Association, deceiving people that he is a Nganga, shall be brought under trial and shall pay a fine of not less than £100.
   (b) No Nganga shall charge exorbitant sums of money for minor treatment. The treatment charges should be reasonable.

MONEYS OF THE ASSOCIATION

9. (a) All moneys of the Association shall be banked and a careful and thorough record shall be kept by the treasurer.
   (b) For banking and withdrawals, at least two signatories must be attached to the form either of banking or withdrawal.
   (c) No money must be drawn without the approval of the full Executive sitting together, and the purpose for such withdrawal must be explained.
   (d) The Treasurer shall present a full and audited financial statement at the annual general meeting.
   (e) The books of the Association shall be audited by a firm of commercial auditors each year.

Appendix III

OFFICIAL RECOGNITION

10. No member shall be admitted into the Healing Profession unless having previously administered a good amount of LOYALTY to the chief of his village, who shall in all cases recommend such a Nganga to the District Commissioner (N.O.) or other Authorities.

BIBLIOGRAPHY

ANONYMOUS. 1935. 'Muchape'. *Nada*, XIII, 17.

ANONYMOUS. 1935. 'The African Explains Witchcraft'. *Africa*, VIII, 4, 504-559.

ASHTON, H. 1952. *The Basuto*. London: Oxford University Press.

BELL, E. M. 1961. *Polygons*. Salisbury: Univ. College of Rhod. and Nyasaland. *Occ. Pap.* No. 2.

BRUWER, F. P. 1963. *Die Bantoe van Suid-Africa*. Johannesburg: Afrikaanse Pers-Boekhandel.

BULLOCK, C. 1928. *The Mashona*. Cape Town: Juta.

1950. *The Mashona and the Matebele*. Cape Town: Juta.

CARNEGIE, D. 1894. *Among the Matebele*. London: The Religious Tract Society.

CENTRAL STATISTICAL OFFICE. *Final Report of the April/May 1962 Census of Africans in Southern Rhodesia*. Salisbury.

CRAWFORD, J. R. 1963. 'Marriage to the Ngozi and the Mainini Custom.' *Nada*, XI, 27-8.

DAVIES, C. S. 1931 'Chikwambo and Chitsina.' *Nada*, IX, 41-4.

DOKE, C. M. 1931. *Report on the Unification of the Shona Dialects*. Hereford: Stephen Austin for the S. R. Government.

FIELD, M. J. 1960. *Search for Security*. London: Faber.

FORTUNE, G. 1959. *Bantu Languages of the Federation*. Lusaka. Rhodes Livingstone Communication No. 14.

EVANS-PRITCHARD, E. E. 1935. 'Witchcraft.' *Africa* VIII, 4, 417-422.

1937, *Witchcraft, Oracles and Magic among the Azande*. Oxford: Clarendon Press.

GARBUTT, H. W. 1910. 'Native Witchcraft and Superstition in South Africa'. *Proc. Rhod. Sci Ass.* IX. 40-48.

GELFAND, M. 1956. *Medicine and Magic of the Mashona*. Cape Town etc.: Juta.

1959. *Shona Ritual*. Cape Town etc.: Juta.

1962. *Shona Religion*. Cape Town etc.: Juta.

1964. *Witch Doctor*. London: Harvill Press.

GLUCKMAN, M. 1955. *Custom and Conflict in Africa*. Oxford: Blackwell.

HANNAN, M. 1959. *Standard Shona Dictionary*. London: Macmillan.

HOGBIN, I. 1958. *Social Change*. London: Watts.

HOLLEMAN, J. F. 1952. *Shona Customary Law*. Cape Town: O.U.P.

1958. *African Interlude*. Cape Town etc.: Nasionale Boekhandel.

Howman, R. 1935. 'Mteu—The Supreme Court of the Mashona'. *Nada*, XIII, 23-5.

Hughes, A. J. B. 1955. 'Uzimu: some Preliminary Notes on Vengeance Magic amongst the Rhodesian Ndebele.' *Human Problems*, XIX, 27-43.

—— 1956. *Kin, Caste and Nation among the Rhodesian Ndebele*. Manchester University Press for the Rhodes-Livingstone Institute.

Hunt, N. A. 1950. 'Some Notes on the Witchdoctor's Bones.' *Nada*, XXVII, 40-46.

—— 1954. 'Some Notes on the Witchdoctor's Bones.' *Nada*, XXXI, 16-23.

—— 1962. 'More Notes on the Witchdoctor's Bones.' *Nada*, XXXIX, 14-16.

Hunter, M. 1961. *Reaction to Conquest*. 2nd ed. London: Oxford University Press, for International African Institute.

Jones, G. I. 1951. *Basutoland Medicine Murder*. H.M.S.O. (Cmd. 8209).

Junod, H. A. 1913. *The Life of a South African Tribe*. Neuchatel: Attinger Frères.

'Kandamakumbo' 1938. 'Ordeals.' *Nada* XV, 70-1.

Kingsley Garbett, G. 1960. *Growth and Change in a Shona Ward*. Salisbury: Univ. College of Rhod. and Nyasaland. *Occ.Pap.* No. 1.

Krige, E. J. & J. D. 1943. *The Realm of a Rain Queen*. London: Oxford University Press for International African Institute.

Kuper, H., Hughes, A. J. B. & Van Velsen, J. 1955. *The Shona and Ndebele of Southern Rhodesia*. London: International African Institute.

Marwick, M. G. 1950. 'Another Modern Anti-Witchcraft Movement in East Central Africa.' *Africa*, XX, 2, 100-12.

—— 1952. 'The Social Content of Cewa Witch Beliefs.' *Africa*, XXII, 2, 120-35; 3, 215-33.

—— 1963, 'The Sociology of Sorcery in a Central African Tribe.' *African Studies*, XXII, 1.

Melland, F. H. 1923. *In Witchbound Africa*. London: Seeley, Service and Co.

—— 1935. 'Ethical and Political Aspects of Witchcraft.' *Africa*, VIII, 4, 495-503.

Middleton, J. & Winter, E. H. (Eds.) 1963 *Witchcraft and Sorcery in East Africa*. London: Routledge and Kegan Paul.

Mitchell, J. C. 1956. *The Yao Village*. Manchester Univ. Press for Rhodes-Livingstone Institute.

Nadel, S. F. 1935. 'Witchcraft and Anti-Witchcraft in Nupe Society.' *Africa*, VIII, 4, 423-447.

O.Neil, J. 1906. 'Superstitions of the Amakalanga of the Mangwe District.' *Zambesi Mission Record*, III, 146-49 & 185-88.

PAUW, B. A. 1960. *Religion in a Tswana Chiefdom*. London : Oxford University Press for International African Institute.
PARRINDER, G. 1958. *Witchcraft*. Pelican Books.
POSSELT, F. W. T. 1935. *Fact and Fiction*. Bulawayo.
RADCLIFFE-BROWN, A. R. 1952. *Structure and Function in Primitive Society*. London : Cohen and West.
RICHARDS, A. I. 'A Modern Movement of Witchfinders.' *Africa*, VIII, 4, 448-61.
SCHAPERA, I. (Ed.) 1937. *The Bantu Speaking Tribes of South Africa*. Cape Town : Maskew Miller.
SELOUS, F. G. 1893. *Travel and Adventure in South East Africa*. London : Rowland Ward.
SMARTT, C. F. 1964. 'Short-term Treatment of the African Psychotic.' *Central. Afr. Jnl. Med.* X, 9; Suppl. Sept 1964.
SMITH, E. W. 1935. 'Inzuikizi.' *Africa*, VIII, 4, 473-480.
SOUTHERN RHODESIA. (annual). *Report of the Secretary for Internal Affairs*. Salisbury : Government Printer.
SOUTHERN RHODESIA. (annual). *Report of the Secretary for Justice*. Salisbury : Government Printer.
STEAD, W. H. 1946. 'The Clan Organization and Kinship System of some Shona Tribes.' *African Studies*, V, 1, 1-20.
SUNDKLER, B. G. M. 1961. *Bantu Prophets in South Africa*. 2nd. ed. London : Oxford University Press, for International African Institute.
TRACEY, H. 1934. 'The Bones.' *Nada*, XII, 23-6.
 1963. 'The Hakata of Southern Rhodesia.' *Nada*, XL, 105-7.
TURNER, V. W. 1961. *Ndembu Divination*. Rhodes-Livingstone Paper No. 31. Manchester University Press for the Rhodes-Livingstone Institute.
VAUGHAN-WILLIAMS, H. 1946. *A Visit to Lobengula in 1889*. London : Shuter and Shooter.
WERBNER, R. B. 1964. 'Atonement Ritual and Guardian Spirit Possession among the Kalanga.' *Africa*, XXXIV, 3, 206-23.
WHITE, C. M. N. 1947. *Witchcraft, Divination and Magic*. Lusaka : Government Printer.
 1961. *Elements in Luvale Beliefs and Rituals*. Rhodes-Livingstone paper No. 32. Manchester University Press for Rhodes-Livingstone Inst.
WHITFIELD, G. M. B. 1948. *South African Native Law*. 2nd ed. Cape Town : Juta.
WILSON, J. D. W. 1944. *Life in Shakespeare's England*. Pelican Books.

INDEX

Accusations of wizardry, pattern of, 130–61
accused, consequences for, 291
African Appeal Court, 25, 39
African councils, 21
African Councils Act, 21
African Land Husbandry Act, 20, 23, 27
African Marriages Act, 31, 34
African Purchase Areas, 18–19
Africans (Urban Areas) Accommodation and Registration Act, 18
Ambo cannibalism, 285–6
ancestral spirits, see *vadzimu*
animal spirits, see *mashave*
ant-bears, and suicide, 116–17
ant-bears, killing of, 117–18
anti-sorcery cults, 282–3
Apprenticeship Act, 10
arson, against witches, 249
Ashton, 121, 238
assault
    of witches, 248–9
    leading to death of wizard, 253–5
attempted murder, 49–56

Bantu-speaking tribes, 10–11
baptism and spirit possession, 231–3
    divination during, 230–3
Beattie, 160
Bell, E. M., 17
bone-throwing, 187–9
    see also *hakata*
bridewealth, 150
British South Africa Company, 9
British South Africa Police, 21
Bruwer, 189
Bullock, 119, 161, 218, 258, 260

cannibalism, 112–15
Carnegie, 119, 252
cases
    Joshua v Taruwodzera, 231–3

Marufu v Ehraim, 258
Quegele v Nawu, 258
R v Aaron and Siliva Matshuma, 96–7, 252–3, 263
R v Aaron Hodza, 206–7
R v Aaron Ndhlovu, 125, 276
R v Abner Phiri and Others, 170–2
R v Bhuja Amos, 268
R v Brown, 95, 128–9
R v Chemere alias Mahondoro, 95, 113, 205–6, 268
R v Chemwe, 164–5
R v Chiangwa, 6
R v Dawu, 43, 45–9, 111, 113, 116, 121
R v Dumbu, 121
R v Elias, 117
R v Elias alias Elijah, 112, 276
R v Ester Mancube, 125, 248
R v Garayi, 43, 210–12
R v Gwatipedza and Amos, 193–4
R v Gombwe, 270–1
R v Gwayi, 184, 256
R v Hunda, 219
R v Jackson William Maseko, 127–8
R v James, 262
R v Jeka, 256
R v Joshua Taruwodzera, 112
R v Kani, 42–3, 118–19, 166–8, 209
R v Kateya, 95, 180, 270
R v Kiwanyana, 228–30
R v Kufa, 113, 242
R v Kufa and R v Chingono, 173–5
R v Kukubula, 132, 181, 244, 246, 273–6
R v Kukubula alias Bernard, 197–202
R v Kwame, 123–4
R v Macheka, 163–4
R v Machuchu, 122, 196–7
R v Mack alias Chowa, 112, 172–3
R v Madubeko, 116, 227

Index

cases—*cont.*
R v Magwenzi, 87–8
R v Mahloro, 248
R v Makina, 95
R v Mandebele, 116, 185
R v Mangisi, 267
R v Mangwari, 261–2
R v Manyepa, 216
R v Mapfumo, 236–7
R v Mapfumo Mufonganyedza, 113, 125, 237–8
R v Maria, 125
R v Maria Mdhlawuzo, 189
R v Mateyo, 163–4
R v Mathias and Kariba, 89, 151, 253
R v Matiyo, 235–6
R v Mazwita, 59, 111, 118, 267
R v Mazwita and others, 49–56, 116, 121, 266
R v Mison and others, 105–6, 125, 126, 177–9
R v Modas, 84–5, 113
R v Moses, 116
R v Mpabanga, 204–5
R v Mubiwa, 86, 209, 258
R v Mudzingwa and Tanda, 151
R v Muramwiwa and others, 216–17
R v Mutambo Sayikondi and Musokwe, 240–2
R v Muteto, 115
R v Ndomene James, 168, 248–9
R v Njini, 269–70
R v Nyadzino, 242–3
R v Paradza, 113, 180
R v Pargwavuya, 195
R v Peter alias Lelizwe, 116, 125
R v Pfacha, 230
R v Rori alias Vincent, 165–6
R v Rosi, 57–9, 111, 256
R v Ruka, 112, 275
R v Sandonda, 218, 219–20
R v Sengani, 130, 162–3
R v Shango and Mudzingwa, 108–9
R v Shonayi Chipembere Juwere, 120
R v Sihwanda, 122, 163
R v Sineki, 203

R v Sineki alias Nicholas, 220–1
R v Sophie, 79
R v Tachinson, 79, 209–10
R v William, 43
R v Zaba, 263
R v Zalepi, 59, 114–15
R v Zindoga alias Nice, 84, 113
R v Zwavanjanya, 249
R v Zwichayira, 165
causation and witchcraft, 66–70
census, Rhodesian, 1962, 12–13
Cewa
 marriage, 155
 patterns of witchcraft allegation, 145–7
Chaminuka legend, 227–8
charms, 127
Chaza, Mai, 225, 228
chieftaincies, 22–7
 succession to, 23–5
chikwambo, 260–1
child mortality
 and wizardry allegations, 156
 and witchcraft, 72
child murder, 45–9
chipotswa, 97–8, 101, 126
chitsinga, 97–9, 101, 126
chitukwani, 118
Christianity
 and divination, 204–5
 among Shona, 90–2
confessions
 and malnutrition, 65
 corroboration of, 64
 of witchcraft, 44–65
 readiness of, 59
 reasons for
  age, 60–1
  status, 61–3
cosmology, Shona, 284–5
Council of Chiefs, 26
Courts
 criminal, 2–3
 magistrates', 2–3
 tribal, 2
Crawford, 88
criminal cases, and wizardry beliefs, 42–4
cure of witch, 271–5
cure of wizard's victims

Index

by calling in doctor, 268–71
by removal from area of wizard's activities, 265–7
by withdrawal of wizardry, 267–8
Customary Law, 256–7

Dare, 25–6, 28
defamation, 258–9
disease and witchcraft belief, 69–70
District Commissioner, 21, 25
divination,
   among Shona, 190–7
   and Christianity, 204–5
   as a trial, 194–6
   casual, 181
   during a service for the sick, 236–8
   during baptism, 230–3
   general, 179–83
   in the Pentecostal churches, 221–43
   methods, 183–208
   Ndebele and Kalanga, 183–90
   on request, 238–43
   outside traditional norms, 206–8
   psychic, 179–80
   psychological, 180–1
   with medicine, 239–43
diviners, 41–2, 59–60, 74, 94
   fees, 203
   foreign, 197–202
   traditional, 183–208
      and modern social conditions, 202–8
divorce and witchcraft, 144–5
Doke, 12
Douglas, 282
dreams, 208–10

education
   and witchcraft, 173–7
   Shona, 16–17
emotional reaction to witchcraft, 70
employment, Shona, 14–15
Europeans, in Rhodesia, 9–10
Evans-Pritchard, 73, 107, 192, 209, 265
execution of wizards, 251–5

familiars, 56, 115–22
Field, 65
Fortune, 12

franchise, 10

Garbutt, 119
Gelfand, 77, 78, 84, 89, 104, 106, 107, 109, 113, 124, 125, 182, 190, 228, 260, 268, 294
Gluckman, 139, 140–1, 153
Guta re Jehova, 225, 228

hakata, 190, 191–2
   throwing by suspects, 196–7
Hannan, 266
High Court, 3, 4, 25
   trial records, 4–5
Hogbin, 130
Holleman, 23, 27, 28, 29, 33, 35, 63, 90, 106, 155, 195, 256, 257, 259
house property complex, 143–5
housing, Shona, 15–16
Howman, 73, 215, 217
Hughes, 119, 153, 243, 259
human flesh, use in witchcraft, 112–15
Hunt, 190
Hunter, Monica, 139, 156, 180
husband, attitude to witch, 255–6

Industrial Conciliation Act, 10, 14
informants, 7–8
inheritance of witchcraft, 142–3
inyanga, 187–9
isangoma, 184–8
   similarity to Pentecostal prophet, 226–7

Junod, 89, 270

kakumarara, 274
Kalanga
   divination among, 183–90
   wizardry allegations tabulated, 135–6
Kingsley Garbett, 13, 14, 28, 137, 141, 267
kinship structures, 138–57
Krige, 132, 138, 140, 153–4
Kuper, 38
Kuper *et al.,* 119

Land Apportionment Act, 10

Index

lightning, 123–4
lineage
  and chiefs, 22–3
  and witchcraft allegations, 143–7
  division, 148–9
  segmentation, 29
  structure and *vadzimu*, 81–2
  structure, Shona, 28–37
  typical, Zezuru, 30–1
lion spirits, see *mhondoro*
Lovedu, position of wife in household, 153–4

malice and witchcraft, 68
mangoromera, 106
marriage, 31–7
  among Cewa, 155
  among Yao, 155
  and lineage links, 34–7
  payments, see *rovoro*
Marriage Act, 31, 34
Marwick, 132, 138, 145–6, 147, 154, 283
Mashave, 82–6
medical taboos, 101
medicines, 103–6
  witch's, 125–6
medicine horns, 126
mhondoro, 24–5, 26, 86–8
Middleton and Winter, 74, 75, 143, 160, 282, 285
migrant workers, 17
mirror gazing, 205
Mitchell, 147, 155
misfortune and witchcraft, 93–107
muchapi movement, 283
mudzimu, 78–80, 205–6
  and misfortune, 94
music and *shave* ritual, 86

Nada, 220
names, Shona, 212–13
nationalism, 90–1, 19–20
Native Commissioner, 9–10
Native Department, 9
Native Law and Courts Regulations, 27
natural forces, control of by witches, 122–4

natural phenomena, and witchcraft beliefs, 68–9
Navaho, witchcraft allegations among, 145
Ndebele
  and Shona, divinations, numerical differences between, 250
  divination among, 183–90
  groups, 37–9
  position of wife in household, 152–3
  wizardry allegations tabulated, 135–6
nganga, 74, 191–4
Nganga Association of Southern Rhodesia, 300–2
ngozi, 88–90, 94–5, 201–11, 260
  sending of by witch, 124–5
Nkomo, Joshua, 19, 20
nocturnal travels of witches, 121–2
non-lineage members, and wizardry allegations, 139–40

old age, and wizardry allegations, 156–7
O'Neil, 262
ordeal, 214–21
  boiling water, 218–20
  muchapi, 220–1
  poison, 215–18, 282–3

Parrinder, 72, 113, 157
patrilineal society, and wizardry allegations, 139–41
Pauw, 222, 225, 230, 231
Pentecostal churches, 83, 95–6, 278
  and divination, 204–5
  and spirit possession, 228–30
  as anti-sorcery movements, 283–4
  beliefs of, 222–3
  divination in, 221–43
  hierarchy, 225–6
  origin, 224
personification of evil, 71–2
perverted conduct, 285–6
physical force, and witchcraft, 64–5
Pondo
  society, 156
  witchcraft, sexual aspects, 158
Posselt, 192, 194

Index

preparatory examination, 2–4
preparatory examination records, 3–4
Prophet at the Gate of Heaven, The, 234–6
Prophet on the Mountain of God, The, 233–4
prosecutions, statistics, 6
protection against wizardry, 127–9
public opinion, manipulation by wizardry beliefs, 280–1, 290
purification rites, 229–30

Radcliffe-Brown, 71
rainmakers, 187–8
rattle divination, 202
religion and witchcraft, 73–93
religious beliefs, Shona, 77–93
Rhodesian society, structure of, 8–39
Richards, 198, 220, 283
ropa, 25
rovoro, 31–3
runhare, 260–1

sacrifice, 79
sadunhu, 27
Sampson, Agnes, 59
samusha, 28
scepticism, 67
Schapera, 119
Secretary for Internal Affairs, 21, 23
Secretary for Justice and Internal Affairs, reports, 6
Selous, 228
Services Levy Act, 18
sex taboos, 99–100
sexual antagonism and witchcraft, 157–8
sexual intercourse
  with familiars, 120
  as cure for wizardry, 270
shadow taking, 211–12
shave and misfortune, 94
Shona
  and Ndebele divinations, numerical differences between, 250
  cosmology, 284–5
  divination among, 190–7
  Eastern, wizardry allegations tabulated, 133–4
  education, 16–17
  employment, 14–25
  housing, 15–16
  'moral community', 286–7
  names, 212–13
  population, 11–14
  position of wife in household, 151–2
  religious beliefs, 77–93
Sithole, Ndabaningi, 19
Smartt, 65
social conditions and the traditional diviner, 202–8
social conflict as source of wizardry allegations, 288–9
social functions of taboos, 101–2
social norms, breach of, 278–80
social relevance of witchcraft, 71–2
sorcery
  and misfortune, 95
  and witchcraft, distinction between, 40–1, 73–4, 141–2, 287–8
sources of information, 1–8, 293–5
spirit possession, 108–10
  and Pentecostal churches, 228–30
subuku, 28
suicide
  and ant-bears, 116–17
  and witchcraft allegations, 245–7
Sundkler, 222, 224, 225, 226, 228, 230, 231, 236

taboos, 99–103
  in Pentecostal churches, 230
ticket labour, 208
tokens, 195
Tracey, 190
Tribal Trust Land, 13–14, 17, 19
  political structure, 20–8
Turner, 202

Uganda, witchcraft in, 75–6
urbanization, and witchcraft allegations, 159–60
urbanization and witchcraft beliefs, 168–9
uzimu, 262–4

vadzimu, 29–30, 71, 77–82, 90–1
  and lineage structure, 81–2
vampires, 79
Vaughan-Williams, 187–8

vengeance, magical, 259-65
vengeance spirits, see *ngozi*
village heads, see *samusha* and *subuku*
village, social structure of, 27-8, 139

ward courts, see *dare*
ward heads, see *sadunhu*
way of life, and witchcraft, 277
wealth, and witchcraft allegations, 159
Werbner, 82-3, 136, 141
White, 275
Whitfield, 38
wife
  position in Lovedu household, 153-4
  position in Ndebele household, 152-3
  position in Shona household, 151-2
Wilson, Monica, 158
Winter, see Middleton and
witch
  attitudes of husband to, 255-6
  control of natural forces, 122-4
  cure of, 271-5
  defined in Witchcraft Suppression Act, 8
  making of
    by another witch, 111
    by spirit possession, 108-10
  medicines, 125-6
  nocturnal travels, 121-2
  sending *ngozi*, 124-5
witchcraft
  and child mortality, 72
  and education, 133-7
  and divorce, 144-5
  and misfortune, 94
  and religion, 73-93
  and physical force, 64-5
  and sorcery, distinctions between, 40-1, 73-4, 141-2, 287-8
  and way of life, 277
  as personification of evil, 71-2
  allegations
    and urbanization, 159-60
    and wealth, 159
    attitudes towards accused's, 248-55
  confession, 44-65
  inheritance of, 142-3
  manifestations, beliefs in, 111-26
  social relevance of, 71-2
Witchcraft Regulations, 1895, 5
Witchcraft Suppression Act, 5, 7, 42, 297-9
wizard
  attitude of, 244-8
  death of, caused by assault, 253-5
  execution of, 251-5
  supernatural indication of, 208-12
  treatment of, 250
wizardry
  allegations
    against non-lineage members, 139-40
    analysis of figures, 136-8
    analysis in percentages, 140
    and child death, 156
    and old age, 156-7
    and patrilineal society, 139-41
    Eastern Shona, tabulated, 133-4
    Ndebele and Kalanga, tabulated, 135-6
    no diviner present, 161-79
    pattern of, 130-61
    reasons for, 130-1
  and criminal cases, 42-4
  beliefs
    and public opinion, 280-1, 290 290
    basis of, 66-73
    effect on behaviour, 292-3
    in urban areas, 168-9
  cases, decline in numbers, 278
  evidence of, 40-2
  protection against, 127-9

Yao
  marriage, 155
  patterns of witchcraft allegation, 147

zwidoma, 56